F. & M. J. ⟨ **W9-BCN-872**

About the Writers

Irving Hexham is professor of religious studies at the University of Calgary, Alberta, Canada. He obtained his Ph.D. in history from the University of Bristol and is the author of seven books, including two written with his wife, Karla Poewe.

Mark Konnert is associate professor of history at the University of Calgary, Alberta, Canada. He received his Ph.D. from the University of Southern California.

Peter and Carine Barrs met in France, where Carine received her M.A. in French Literature. In 1998 they moved to Missouri, where Peter received his M.A. Peter teaches upper school French at Mary Institute and St. Louis Country Day School.

---

http://www.christian-travelers-guides.com

Visit our Web site for even more information. You'll find:

- Links to many of the cities and sites listed in our guidebooks
- Information about Christian hotels and bed and breakfasts
- Lists of English-speaking churches so you can plan where to worship
- Information about evangelical organizations in each country
- Diagrams comparing different architectural styles
- Examples of Christian art
- Brief essays on topics of interest to Christian scholars and travelers
- Readings from key historical texts
- Suggested readings for daily devotions as you travel around Europe

Plan your next trip with
http://www.christian-travelers-guides.com

"In an era that often overlooks the significance of the past as such, and certainly the Christian past, Professor Hexham's well-crafted guides for heritage tourists truly fill a gap. Don't leave home without one!"

J. I. Packer
professor, Regent College, Vancouver
author of _Knowing God_

"Using vacations to discover the riches of the Christian tradition is a great idea that's long overdue."

Bruce Waltke,
professor, Regent College, Reformed Theological Seminary
and a member of the _NIV_ translation team

"At last! A guidebook which treats churches as windows onto the living faith of Christianity and not just as museums or graveyards. These books bring church history alive."

David V. Day
principal, St. John's College, University of Durham
and frequent broadcaster on the BBC

"Excellent...we can all learn from these books."

Terry Muck
professor, former editor-in-chief of _Christianity Today_

THE
CHRISTIAN
TRAVELERS GUIDE TO

FRANCE

IRVING HEXHAM, GENERAL EDITOR

written by **MARK KONNERT, PETER BARRS, AND CARINE BARRS**

ZondervanPublishingHouse
Grand Rapids, Michigan

A Division of HarperCollins*Publishers*

This series of books is an unintended consequence of serious academic research financed by both the University of Calgary and the Social Sciences and Humanities Research Council of Canada. Both institutions need to be thanked for the support they gave to the original academic research that allowed some of the authors to visit many of the places discussed in these books.

The Christian Travelers Guide to France
Copyright © 2001 by Mark Konnert, Peter Barrs, and Carine Barrs

Requests for information should be addressed to:

ZondervanPublishingHouse
Grand Rapids, Michigan 49530

Library of Congress Cataloging-in-Publication Data
Konnert, Mark W., 1957-.
    The Christian travelers guide to France / Irving Hexham, general editor; Mark Konnert, Peter Barrs, and Carine Barrs.
        p. cm.
   ISBN: 0-310-22588-4
    1. France—Guidebooks. 2. Christians—Travel—France—Guidebooks.
I. Barrs, Peter. II. Barrs, Carine. III. Hexham, Irving. IV. Title
DC16.K66 2001
914.404'84—dc21
                                            00-047715
                                            CIP

All Scripture quotations, unless otherwise indicated, are taken from the *Holy Bible: New International Version*®. NIV®. Copyright © 1973, 1978, 1984 by International Bible Society. Used by permission of Zondervan Publishing House. All rights reserved.

All rights reserved. No part of this publication may be reproduced, stored in a retrieval system, or transmitted in any form or by any means—electronic, mechanical, photocopy, recording, or any other—except for brief quotations in printed reviews, without the prior permission of the publisher.

Interior design by Todd Sprague

Printed in the United States of America

01 02 03 04 05 /❖ DC/ 10 9 8 7 6 5 4 3 2 1

Contents

Glossary of Religious Terms 221

PREFACE

Remember how the LORD your God led you.

Deuteronomy 8:2

The task of history . . . is to establish the truth of this world.
Karl Marx (1955:42)

Memories of paintings, sculptures, museums, and churches last a lifetime.
Edith Schaeffer—*The Tapestry*

O ur series of books is designed to awaken an awareness of Europe's Christian heritage among evangelical Christians, although we hope all Christians and others who are simply interested in Christianity will also find them helpful. Anyone visiting a large bookstore will quickly discover that it is possible to buy travel guides with titles like *Pagan Europe, Occult France, Magical Britain,* and *The Traveler's Guide to Jewish Germany,* alongside more traditional travel guides which attempt to take in everything worth seeing. Yet even books like the *Frommer's, Fodor's,* and *Rough* guides, although they mention Christian places and events, tend to underplay the Christian contribution to Western Civilization through neglect or a negative tone. Therefore, our guides have been written

to correct what we see as a major oversight in existing works.

Our series is concerned with people and events of historical significance through their association with particular places. Thus we attempt to locate the development of ideas which have changed the world through their relationship with people and places. Consequently, we suggest visits to particular places, because by visiting them you can gain a better understanding of the times when important events took place.

The central theme of these books is the contribution of Christianity to Europe and the world. But not everyone discussed in these books was Christian. Indeed, many of the people we mention were strongly anti-Christian. Such people are included because it is impossible to understand our own times without appreciating the destructive forces that have attempted to replace Christianity by secularism and neopagan religions.

HISTORY AND MEMORY

Christianity is rooted in history. The New Testament begins with a genealogical table that most modern readers find almost incomprehensible (Matthew 1:1–17). The purpose of this genealogy is to locate the birth of Jesus in space and time according to the standards of Jewish history. The appeal to the first eye-witnesses, in the prologue to the gospel of Luke, is also clearly intended to engage the skepticism of Greco-Roman readers by providing specific historical data against which ancient readers could weigh the writer's claims (Luke 3:1–2). The Gospels contain many references to historical data and specific geographic locations. So important is historical truth that its denial becomes a mark of heresy for New Testament authors (1 Corinthians 15:1–8; 1 John 4:1–3).

Clearly, the Bible is steeped in history and the remembrance of history. Both the Old and New Testaments constantly reminded their readers about particular historical events (cf. Deuteronomy 4:9–14; Acts 7). Thus, parents are commanded to teach their children the significance of history (Deuteronomy 6:4–25) both by retelling the story and through commemorations which enact the central acts of salvation (Exodus 13:3–16; 1 Corinthians 11:23–26). Further, an appeal is frequently made to visible memorials that remind people of God's wonderful deeds (Acts 2:29–36). We also find both Jews and early Christians visiting historic sites as acts of devotion (Luke 2:21–41; Acts 21:17–27).

The importance of history, and the way in which we remember past events, is recognized by many influential opponents of Christianity. Karl Marx, for example, argued that the ability to control history, or rather the interpretation of history, was an essential step in the abolition of religion. Almost a century later, Adolf Hitler made a similar appeal to history and historical necessity. Both Marx and Hitler, following in the footsteps of Enlightenment skeptics like Tom Paine, sought to establish the truth of their revolutions by denying the validity of Christian history.

Our books are, we hope, a small contribution to the reestablishment of a sense of history and cultural pride among Christians. Following the biblical model, we believe that visiting places and seeing where great events took place help people remember and understand the present as well as the past (Joshua 4:1–7). It is our hope that these books will bring history alive, and with a sense of history a growing awareness of the realities of faith in our world. As Francis Schaeffer loved to point out, there is a flow to history because Christian faith is rooted in space and time. To forget our history is the first step to the abandonment of our faith, the triumph of secularism, the ascendancy of New

Age spirituality, and the rebirth of paganism.

SEEKING SPIRITUAL ROOTS

The great truth of the New Testament is that Christians are children of God by adoption. Today many people have forgotten that the New Testament preaches the revolutionary doctrine that our relationship to God is not through physical descent, but by adoption (Romans 8:23, Galatians 4:5; Ephesians 1:5).

The implications of this doctrine are profound. All Christians are united by bonds of faith and love, not physical relationships (Ephesians 2). Thus, Christianity is not a tribal religion rooted in local communities bound by kinship bonds. Rather, it is a world faith that unites all believers.

Repeatedly, both the Old and New Testaments point to examples of faith which we are encouraged to follow and remember (Joshua 4; Luke 11:29–32; Acts 7; Hebrews 12). Remembering acts of courage and obedience to God strengthens our own faith. This fact was long recognized by the leaders of the church. Throughout history, Christians have told and retold stories of courage and faith. Yet today these stories are all but forgotten. Lives of the saints which were once standard texts for every educated person and pious believer are now rarely read, and books like *Foxe's Book of Martyrs* (1554) are left unopened.

Today, Christians are quickly forgetting their rich spiritual heritage as Christian biographies are replaced in popular culture by secular gossip. Popular magazines, radio, and television are full of "lives." But they are the lives of pop singers, film stars, television personalities, and secular politicians. Instead of teaching spiritual lessons, they repeat trivia and revel in scandal. Something has been lost. And it is this something that can be recaptured by Christians who begin to search for their spiritual roots.

Visiting France to learn about great acts of faith can be a rewarding experience, and it is something all Christians, regardless of race or nationality, can find profitable. This spiritual quest helps us see our own lives in perspective and understand our times against a much greater backdrop than tonight's television news. That is the quest this book encourages you to begin.

Part I

FRENCH HISTORY

EARLY HISTORY

Other than Italy and Greece, France is perhaps the European country with the longest continuous Christian history. From the very early days of the church down to the 20th century, France has been at or near the center of almost every important development in Christianity.

The country now known as France has been home to human beings for many thousands of years. Occupied by 1000 B.C. by groups of ethnically related Celtic peoples, France formed part of an early European civilization with its characteristic religious beliefs known as Druidism. Druidism remains very shadowy, since there were no written texts, but seems to have been similar to the religions of other primitive peoples, with an emphasis on the ubiquity of spirits (animism) which require sacrifice and appeasing. Throughout France numerous sites have been unearthed which demonstrate that Celtic religion practiced human sacrifice and

dismemberment, such as those at La Cloche at Pennes-Mirabeau, a small hilltop fort near Marseille, or the site at Glanum, at St. Remy, near the mouth of the Rhône river, or at Ribemont-sur-Ancre in Picardy.

The Celtic tribes had spread across Europe from Turkey to Spain and northern Italy to Ireland in the millennia before the birth of Christ. Fierce and warlike, they threatened other peoples and civilizations, including the infant republic at Rome, which they invaded in 325 B.C. In addition to the "Celts" (or "Gauls" as the Romans were to call them), several Greek cities were established along the Mediterranean coast as these people sought to escape the poverty and overpopulation of their homeland. Most notable among these Greek cities was Massilia, or Marseille.

THE ROMAN EMPIRE

Roman expansion throughout Italy and Greece, and northward into the area of modern-day Italy occupied by Celtic peoples (Cisalpine Gaul), brought renewed conflict. In 121 B.C., the Romans established a colony in southern France, known to them simply as "The Province" (Latin: *Provincia*), the origin of the name *Provence*. From their base along the Mediterranean, the Romans came to realize the wealth of the territory to the north. After decades of struggle, the Gauls were finally defeated in 52 B.C. when the Celtic chieftain Vercingetorix fell to the Roman armies of Julius Caesar at Alesia.

Brought under the rule of the Roman Empire, the province of Gaul formed an important part of the Roman Empire for more than 200 years, and its inhabitants developed a hybrid Gallo-Roman culture, which included religion. Indeed, Celtic residents of southern Gaul had already absorbed elements of Greco-Roman religion before the conquest, through their commercial and cultural contacts with the Greek settlements of the south and with Italy. But conquest brought the Roman influence to a new level, demonstrating the syncretic nature of both Celtic and Roman religion. Roman religion, at least in its public manifestations, was primarily a state religion, based on the satisfaction of the Olympian gods through the correct performance of public rituals and sacrifice. As the Roman Empire expanded, and the Romans came into contact with different cultures and religions, they absorbed many of the gods and practices of the conquered peoples into the Roman pantheon, while imposing the Roman state religion. In southern Gaul, over time, the Celtic religion died out, completely replaced by Roman religion, as evidenced by the construction of Roman temples at Nîmes and Vienne, which still stand, and at Orange and Narbonne, of which only vestiges remain. Further north, the Celtic residents developed more of a hybrid religion, still venerating their own gods, but combining their attributes with those of the Roman pantheon. In addition, under Roman influence and pressure, the practice of human sacrifice (which the Romans detested) was abandoned.

Christianity expanded outwards from Palestine, aided by the missionary journeys of Paul and the widespread dispersion of Jewish communities throughout the Roman Empire. The new religion soon expanded its influence beyond the Jews to the Gentiles, largely through the influence of Paul. That is, Christianity became fully separate from Judaism, no longer a sect or heresy of Judaism, but a religion in its own right, with universal appeal, as Paul wrote in Galatians 3:28: "There is neither Jew nor Greek, slave nor free, male nor female, for you are all one in Christ Jesus." Contrary to much popular belief, the Roman authorities were not immediately nor irrevocably opposed to the new religion. Whenever possible, the Romans preferred to let subject peoples regulate their own affairs, including religion, as long as these did not pose a threat to Roman control, and as long as the formalities of official Roman religion were observed, thereby assuring continued Roman power and prosperity. In other words, there was no logical reason, at least from the Roman perspective, why Christianity should not take on elements of Roman religion, and why Christ should not be absorbed into the Roman pantheon. Christians, of course, rejected such eventualities out of hand, refusing to venerate the emperor as a god, and refusing to take part in the rituals of Roman religion. Nevertheless, Christians were not persecuted as a matter of official Roman policy, except at certain periods, such as under the Emperor Nero (ruled A.D. 54–68), who blamed Christians for the fire which virtually destroyed Rome, and under the Emperor Decius in A.D. 250, prompted by fears for the Empire's future and by resentment of Christian attitudes towards the celebration of Rome's millennium in A.D. 248. The most savage persecution was launched by the Emperor Diocletian (A.D. 284–306) in A.D. 303 due to fears of Christian penetration into the higher ranks of the army and the civil service. As this suggests, Christianity had continued to expand despite, and perhaps because of, these episodes of persecution. The steadfastness and courage of Christian martyrs impressed many pagan Roman observers, and inspired them to inquire more closely into Christian beliefs. As the early writer and Church

father Tertullian wrote (c. A.D. 160–230): "The blood of the martyrs is the seed of the church." Quite apart from official persecution, Christians were often singled out for unofficial discrimination and persecution by ordinary people. It was widely believed (based on misunderstanding of the language of the Lord's Supper) that Christians practiced cannibalism and incest, and that their nocturnal gatherings were in fact nothing more than sexual orgies. So Christians often found themselves victims of mob violence, or of the actions of local officials acting on their own authority.

The earliest concrete evidence of Christian activity in Gaul displays precisely this. Around A.D. 177, a small group of Christians was persecuted and martyred in Lyon. Among them was Blandina, a slave woman, whose courage and fortitude earned her canonization. Christians had been subject to mob violence, and eventually the governor imprisoned a group of Christians, ordering them to recant or be thrown to the beasts. They refused, and the sentence was carried out. Although she was tied to a post, the beasts refused to touch Blandina. Eventually, the sentence was carried out, and Blandina died along with 47 others.

The situation of Christians within the Roman Empire (including Gaul) changed dramatically in the early 4th century with the accession of the Emperor Constantine (306–37). For most of the 3rd century, the Roman Empire had drifted aimlessly and declined precipitously. Emperor replaced emperor in revolving-door coups; the key to political power was armed might.

This situation changed with the accession of the Emperor Diocletian (284–305), who defeated all his rivals for power, and reestablished imperial power on a new footing. The revived Roman Empire of Diocletian was very different from what it had been. Diocletian recognized that the Empire was too large to be governed by one man, so he established a coalition of four emperors known as the Tetrarchy. The imperial government became more intimately involved in all areas of local life, including those which, like religion, had previously been left to local discretion. As mentioned above, in 303 Diocletian launched the most savage persecution of Christians thus far, ironically, not because he was an especially evil man, but rather because he believed that Christians, by refusing to honor the old gods, threatened the security and prosperity of the empire he had worked so hard to revive. Upon his retirement in 305, however (Diocletian being one of the very few emperors to leave office alive), his putative successors fought among themselves. One of them, Constantine, emerged victorious, having defeated his last remaining rival at the Battle of the Milvian Bridge outside Rome in 312. Immediately prior to the battle, he apparently dreamed a dream or had a vision (the accounts vary on this point) in which he saw a flaming cross with the caption, "In this sign, conquer."

Once in power, Constantine established toleration of Christianity and generally favored it over other religions, which were still permitted. Constantine also became intimately involved in Church affairs, settling disputes and enforcing orthodoxy. Among his many other accomplishments, he built a new capital for the Empire at Constantinople (now Istanbul), to bring the center of political power closer to the demographic and economic centers of the Empire in the Middle East. Among other things, this made the bishop of Rome the most important official in the city, and this may be seen as the beginnings of papal power over the Church. From Constantine on, all the Roman emperors, except one, were Christians. Finally, Emperor Theodosius I (378–95) banned all other religions, making Christianity the official state religion of the Roman Empire.

During the waning days of the Roman Empire in the west, Christianity continued to expand, now as the official religion, rather than as a persecuted and disreputable sect. Important cities became the seats of bishops, who exercised significant power, not necessarily because they were power hungry, but often because there was no one else to do it, and because they were looked to for leadership by the community. In Gaul, there were a number of important places, people, and events which deserve mention in this period. Saint Geneviève (423–512) became the patron saint of Paris through her exploits. When the city was threatened with attack by the Huns of Attila in 451, she persuaded the inhabitants not to flee, but to stay and pray for deliverance. Attila was defeated and Paris was saved. Caesarius, bishop of Arles (469–542), elaborated the doctrine of purgatory, which was later formally endorsed by Pope Gregory the Great (590–604). St. Hilary, bishop of Poitiers (d. 367), combatted Arianism and introduced to Gaul the traditions of monasticism which he had observed in the Middle East. Similarly, St. Martin of Tours (d. 397), though born in Hungary, had come to Gaul in his service with the Roman army. Having become a Christian and demonstrated his piety through acts of charity, he established a monastery at Marmoutiers, on the banks of the Loire river. In 372, he was persuaded to become bishop of Tours, a position he held until his death in 397. During this period, Tours became one of the leading centers of Christianity in Gaul, and after his death, St. Martin's tomb became an important pilgrimage site and was credited with a number of miracles. Indeed, it is not too much to say that, after Christ himself, St. Martin was the most important figure in early medieval Christianity in Gaul.

THE MIDDLE AGES

As the Roman Empire was weakened by agricultural depression, population decline, and strategic overextension, the various Germanic or "Gothic" tribes began to press in on its boundaries, with Roman authorities able to do little to stop them. Among the most important tribes who invaded were the Visigoths, Vandals, Burgundians, and Franks. "Barbarian" mainly in the sense of being less advanced than the Romans, many of these tribes had already been converted to Christianity by the time they invaded Roman territory, albeit to Arian Christianity, whereas the Gallo-Romans followed the form of Christianity established in Rome. Thus, they found themselves at odds with the Gallo-Roman populations they conquered not only in terms of ethnicity and culture, but also in religion. The Germanic tribe known as the Franks (ultimately to give their name to the country) invaded somewhat later, in the 5th century A.D., from their homeland in northwestern Germany and the Low Countries. Unlike many other invading tribes, such as the Visigoths, the Franks were still pagan at the time they invaded. Under their warrior chieftain Clovis, they conquered much of northern and central Gaul. Clovis was married to a Burgundian princess named Clotilde, who had been converted to the Roman form of Christianity. His queen persuaded Clovis to convert to Christianity on the eve of a battle with the archenemy Arian Visigoths. After his victory, Clovis was baptized by St. Remigius (Fr: St. Rémi), the bishop of Reims in the cathedral at Reims, where according to legend, either a dove or angel descended carrying a vial containing the holy oil with which the bishop anointed the king. This vial (the Sainte Ampoule) was used at the coronation of subsequent French kings. Again, according to legend, the holy oil or chrism it contained either never diminished or was miraculously replenished for each coronation. Clovis and his successors of the Merovingian dynasty fought viciously among themselves over the next several centuries, and the kingdom established by Clovis was weakened and fragmented, although it remained at least nominally Christian.

It is doubtful, though, how much ordinary people, or even Clovis himself and his successors, understood of their religion. There is a good deal of evidence to suggest that pagan practices survived alongside Christianity, and that most people, apart from the clergy and the remnants of the educated Gallo-Roman elite, viewed the Christian God as simply a more powerful god who might influence their worldly affairs and whose worship would guarantee access to an afterlife in paradise. These pagan survivals are evident in the legends whose heroes and local holy men were simply Christianized as saints by the religious authorities, or indeed by simple popular acclaim.

Under the Merovingian kings, the Frankish kingdom fragmented and the kings became nearly powerless when compared to local warlords. The 6th and 7th centuries really were the Dark Ages, both because conditions were terrible, and also because not much is known

about the period. For the history of Christianity, both in general and within France, there were several important developments. One was the incursion from the south by Arab Muslims, or Moors, from Spain, most of which they had conquered by the early 8th century. In 732 the Moorish advance into France was halted by the Frankish commander Charles Martel (Charles the Hammer) near Poitiers, thus marking the furthest westward extent of Islamic expansion. The other was the revivification of Frankish Christianity by monks and missionaries from Celtic Ireland and Anglo-Saxon England. Due to unsettled political conditions and the general misery of the times, Christianity (and civilization as a whole) came dangerously close to disappearing entirely from France. During the Anglo-Saxon invasions of England (c. 4th–5th centuries A.D.), refugees from Christian Roman civilization in Britain had taken refuge in Ireland, where they established a unique and flourishing Celtic Christian civilization. During the 6th and 7th centuries, Irish missionary monks evangelized among the pagan Anglo-Saxons, and in the 7th and 8th centuries, both Irish and English missionaries worked in what are now France and Germany, establishing monasteries (the most important being at Corbie and Luxeuil), training priests, converting the pagan, and teaching the essentials of Christianity to those who were nominally or officially "Christian." It was largely due to these monasteries, and the monks who lived in them, that ancient literature, both pagan and Christian, survived these troubled times.

Meanwhile, the power of the Frankish kings continued to decline. By the 8th century, real power had come to reside with an official called the mayor of the palace, which itself had become hereditary in one family, that of Charles Martel (known subsequently as the Carolingians, after their greatest king Charles the Great, or Charlemagne). The royal descendants of Clovis, known as the "do-nothing kings" *(les rois fais-néants),* were largely ceremonial figureheads. Finally, in 751, Pepin the Short, son of Charles Martel, received permission from the pope to have himself crowned king of the Franks. The last Merovingian king was imprisoned in a monastery.

Pepin's son, Charles the Great, or Charlemagne, expanded the Frankish kingdom to its furthest extent. Besides his military conquests, Charlemagne took seriously his duties as a Christian ruler. Drawing largely on the expertise of non-Frankish clergy such as the Englishman Alcuin of York, the Visigoth Theodulph of Orléans, and the Italian Paul the Deacon, Charlemagne sought to improve and standardize the religious life of his subjects. He sent to Italy and elsewhere for the most authentic copies of the Vulgate and the Benedictine Rule. He ordered each bishop in his kingdom to establish a school for the training of priests, the better to serve

their flocks. Charlemagne and the papacy cooperated very closely, each having an interest in peace, prosperity, and the religious education of ordinary people. On Christmas Day 800, while visiting Rome, Pope Leo III crowned Charlemagne Roman Emperor, reviving (on paper at any rate) the Christian Roman Empire of Constantine and Theodosius.

Following Charlemagne's death in 814, his empire too began to fall apart due to feuding among his successors and invasions from the pagan Norsemen (or Vikings) and Magyars (or Hungarians), and Muslim Saracens. By the 10th century, Charlemagne's single kingdom had split into two: the kingdom of the West Franks, or West Francia (later to evolve into France) and the kingdom of the East Franks or East Francia (the Holy Roman Empire of the Middle Ages, and the precursor of modern Germany). Within these kingdoms, however, the power of the kings was very limited. Necessities of security and defense meant that each local area was largely governed by a local strongman or warlord, who acknowledged the theoretical authority of the king in an arrangement known as feudalism. The last Carolingian king of West Francia died in 987 and was replaced by Hugh Capet, who founded the Capetian dynasty.

The Christian Church as a whole also fell prey to the disorders and violence of the times. Although unified in theory under the leadership of the pope, there was a good deal of local variation in practice and belief. The Church too needed protection (indeed, churches and monasteries were the Vikings' preferred targets) and so became enmeshed in feudalism and the power politics of the day. As a result, many clergymen lost sight of their spiritual roles and were more devoted to the wealth and power that their positions brought. Powerful positions such as bishop and abbot often became hereditary in noble families. As would happen repeatedly in the history of Christianity, voices of reform arose from within the Church.

During the 10th and 11th centuries, the chief source of reform was the Benedictine monastery of Cluny in Burgundy in eastern France. Eventually, Cluny became the mother house of a network of reform-minded monasteries, which sought to remedy the complacency and worldliness of much of contemporary monasticism. In time, however, the Cluniac order too became worldly and complacent. By the 12th century, new voices of reform had arisen from within the monastic world. Most austere were the Carthusians, who arose in eastern France in the late 11th century. More important were the Cistercians, who were begun in 1098 when a small group of Benedictine dissenters established a monastery at Cîteaux at a remote site in eastern France. The Cistercians emphasized the poverty in the traditional monastic vows of poverty, chastity, and obedience, unlike the Cluniacs who emphasized

richness of worship. The Cistercians also produced perhaps the most influential person of the high Middle Ages (ca. 1000–1300) in St. Bernard of Clairvaux (1090–1153), an influential preacher, theologian, writer, and Church reformer.

France was also at or near the center of several other important developments in Christianity during the Middle Ages. After about 1000, conditions in Europe as a whole began to improve: the economy picked up, trade (which had virtually disappeared since the end of the Roman Empire) revived, population began to grow, old cities grew larger, and new cities were founded. In short, European civilization of the high Middle Ages (ca. 1000–1300) was a dynamic, confident, and vibrant civilization, in large part unified by its allegiance to a single faith and a single church, the Roman Church. With improved conditions, however, came challenges, not least for the Church. Growth in cities perplexed an organization which had adapted itself to a rural environment over a period of centuries. At the same time, newly prosperous merchants, craftsmen, and professionals began to seek a deeper and more profound faith, rather than the ritualistic and rather simplified Christianity which had been provided for peasants in earlier eras. As a result, reform movements arose, most notably the Mendicant (that is, begging) orders of the Dominicans (founded by the Spaniard St. Dominic in 1216) and the Franciscans (founded by the Italian

St. Francis of Assisi in 1210). Less happily, many people's spiritual needs were not being met within the official Church; as a result, several heretical groups sprang up. Within France, the two most notable were the Waldensians and the Cathars, or Albigensians.

The Waldensians, or Poor of Lyon, were founded by Peter Waldo (or Valdez), a merchant in the city of Lyon, who, much as St. Francis would later do, sold all his possessions, lived by begging, and began to preach in towns. Denied permission to preach by the Church, Waldo and his followers defied the Church authorities and continued to preach. The Waldensians' characteristic beliefs were their opposition to the wealth and corruption of the Church, and their insistence that religious practices be based on Scripture alone, thereby eliminating much of current Catholic practice. In many ways, they anticipated the positions of the Reformers of the 16th century. Condemned as heretics in 1184 and sporadically persecuted, the Waldensians survived primarily in the remote Alpine valleys of southeastern France and northwestern Italy until the time of the Reformation in the 16th century, when they were incorporated into various Protestant churches.

More serious than the Waldensians was the threat posed by the Cathars or Albigensians, so called because they were particularly strong in the southwestern French town of Albi. Like the Waldensians and other heretical groups, the Cathars protested against the wealth and corruption of the Church (anti-clericalism). Unlike other groups, however, the Cathars adopted a completely non-Christian belief known as Manicheanism, ultimately derived from ancient Persia. According to this belief, there were two gods: one, the god of evil—with whom they identified the God of the Old Testament—ruled the world of physical matter; the other, the god of good—with whom they identified Christ—ruled the world of the spirit. They believed in reincarnation, and their goal was to escape the cycle of rebirth. The elite among the Cathars (the *perfecti*) denied themselves material pleasures, including wealth, material possessions, and physical appetites, including sex and sometimes food and drink to the point of starving themselves to death. Ordinary Cathars did not go to these extremes, but supported the *perfecti*. Alarmed by their explosive growth in southwestern France, Pope Innocent III tried every means at his disposal to combat what was seen as a vile and dangerous heresy. (Indeed, the Dominicans were founded in part to combat the Cathar threat through preaching.) Ultimately, peaceful means having failed, in 1208 he proclaimed a crusade against them. After two decades of bloody warfare, Catharism was defeated and suppressed, leaving only small pockets of believers in remote alpine areas.

France and French people were also instrumental in the Crusades, a series of military expeditions to recover the Holy Land first from the Muslim Arabs, and later from the Muslim Turks. The First Crusade was proclaimed in 1095 by Pope Urban II (1088–99) at Clermont-Ferrand in south-central France. Participation from the French rulers and nobility was notable and enthusiastic, especially in the Sixth and Seventh Crusades (in 1248 and 1270 respectively), which were led by the pious King Louis IX (St. Louis; 1226–70). Over a period of three centuries there were at least eight such expeditions, some of which managed some initial success. Ultimately, however, the Crusaders could not establish lasting control of the Holy Land. Acting as both religious wars and plundering expeditions for European rulers and nobles, the Crusades have left at best a mixed legacy. While they are evidence of religious zeal and of a dynamic civilization, they left a trail of violence in both Europe and the Middle East. On their way to the Holy Land, Crusader armies often massacred Jewish communities, and once in the Holy Land often massacred the Muslims they conquered, most notably after the First Crusade's conquest of Jerusalem in 1099. At least partly as a result of the Crusades, Christian-Muslim relations have been largely hostile right down to the present day.

Throughout the Middle Ages, culture, literature, and intellectual life were almost completely dominated by the Church, largely because during the Dark Ages, the Church was the only institution with the interest in and ability to preserve what came down to them of ancient pagan and Christian writings. As a result, all serious literature was written in Latin (which remained the language of the Church and of government) and education remained the monopoly of the Church. Up until about 1000, schools were intended primarily to educate priests and monks, and were attached to cathedrals or monasteries. After about 1000, this situation began to change because of several different developments. Economic revival and the growth of cities produced a class of laypeople—merchants, craftsmen, professionals, and the like—who needed a basic education to pursue their occupation. Secondly, previously unknown ancient manuscripts, including but not limited to those of Aristotle, began to be known again in western Europe after a period of many centuries. These discoveries excited many people, and the cathedral and monastic schools expanded their mandate into what we would call philosophy or the liberal arts. Among the cathedral schools, those of northern France were preeminent, including those in Laon, Chartres, Reims, and elsewhere. Eventually, the cathedral school of Paris became the best known, and by 1200 or so, there was a University of Paris in operation, an evolution of the earlier cathedral school. The University of Paris was among the earliest universities in Europe. For the rest of the Middle Ages, the University of Paris was the leading educational and intellectual institution in Europe. Its Faculty of Theology was preeminent, and its undergraduate component, the Faculty of Arts, was also first-rate. It counted among its teachers some of the leading minds of the period, including Albert the Great, Thomas Aquinas, St. Bonaventure, William of Ockham, and many others. Within the University, the college known as the Sorbonne became the most prestigious, but was far from the only one.

It was among the scholars at the University of Paris that the newly discovered literature of ancient Rome and Greece, especially that of Aristotle, was harmonized with and reconciled with Christianity into a coherent worldview. This was primarily the achievement of Thomas Aquinas, who emphasized that divine revelation and human reason could not conflict, that they were ultimately compatible through the use of logic. While this was a great intellectual achievement, it had the unfortunate side effect of locking the Church into one particular view of how the universe worked. The Aristotelian/Thomist synthesis was so persuasive and seemingly so consonant with Christian theology that it reigned supreme until challenged by new scientific discoveries in the 16th and 17th centuries. By then, religious authorities were so invested in the model of the universe it presented that any challenge to it (such as those of Nicolas Copernicus and Galileo Galilei)

were treated as heresy, not because they challenged biblical truths (indeed both were devout Christians, and Copernicus was a priest), but because they challenged the Aristotelian/Thomist synthesis, which had been adopted as truth by the Church.

This was also the great age of cathedral construction, leaving for us today some of the sublime monuments built by the hand of man to glorify God. Many people look askance at these structures, wondering if perhaps there was not a better way to use the resources which they absorbed, for example in feeding the poor. This, however, is a specious argument. This was an age without the technical ability to transport bulky items, such as food, from one place to another; "feeding the poor" was therefore for the most part impossible. These great churches also served as "Bibles in stone and glass" in an age when the vast majority of people were illiterate peasants, eking out a precarious living on the soil. Moreover, each great civilization leaves its mark in monumental architecture: ancient Egypt had its pyramids, Greece its temples, Rome its roads and aqueducts. In our own day, we seem drawn to mammoth shopping malls and sports stadiums. Who are we to criticize medieval Christians, who sought to glorify God with the very best their society had to offer?

At the same time, the Church emerged as the most powerful institution in medieval Europe. Cooperation with Charlemagne and his successors brought increased political influence, even after the Carolingian empire fragmented. Moral reform, largely engendered by the Cluniac and Cistercian movements, brought to power within the Church a succession of men who were determined to use the wealth and power of the Church to construct a more Christian society. Popes such as Gregory VII (1073–85) and Innocent III (1198–1216) brought the power and prestige of the Church to its zenith during the Middle Ages. Although motivated by laudable goals, they inevitably involved the Church in political power struggles with the rulers of the time, especially the Holy Roman Emperors, the successors of Charlemagne, and rulers of Germany and northern Italy. The political struggles became an end in themselves, and methods of politics came to prevail within the Church. Popes of the high Middle Ages were driven by these struggles to claim extreme powers for themselves, including that the Church was superior to secular authority, that popes were able to depose kings and emperors who ruled on the pope's behalf and with his permission, and that "submission to the pope was altogether necessary for salvation." The struggle with the emperors was largely over by the mid-13th century, but the Church's authority was not to remain unchallenged for long.

The history of Christianity and of the Church in the later Middle Ages is largely a story of decay and decline. While the popes and emperors had been locked in their bitter struggles, other rulers continued to grow more powerful. Foremost among these were the kings of France. From very modest beginnings, controlling just the area around Paris around the year 1000, the kings of the Capetian dynasty had expanded their power and territory at the expense of their own vassals and others, like the king of England (who was also duke of Normandy, and ruled other "French" territories as well). A clash between the powerful king of France and a Church which claimed supreme spiritual and political power was inevitable. This struggle began when King Philip IV (the Fair; 1285–1314) clashed with Pope Boniface VIII (1294–1303) over taxation. Philip was involved in a war with Edward I of England and wanted to tax the wealth of the Church. Pope Boniface felt that such taxation would subordinate the Church to the king and forbade it in his bull (a papal decree is known as a bull) *Unam Sanctam,* which stated the supremacy of the Church in its most extreme form. Philip responded by sending a group of armed thugs to make the pope an offer he couldn't refuse. Boniface died shortly thereafter, and a long papal vacancy ensued. Finally in 1307, a French clergyman was elected Pope Clement V and settled down in Avignon. Avignon, on the banks of the River Rhône, was not yet part of France, but it offered easier communications with France, and better relations with France was Clement's top priority. In addition, Rome was at that point torn by vicious feuding between the noble clans who ran the city; Avignon therefore offered the additional benefit of physical security. Although intended as a purely temporary exile from Rome, the popes resided in Avignon for a period of 70 years, known as the Avignon Papacy, or "the Babylonian captivity of the Church," after the 70 years the children of Israel spent in exile in Babylon. During this period, a succession of seven popes reigned, all of them French. These popes in turn appointed a majority of French cardinals. It thus appeared to many that the papacy had become a puppet of the kings of France. This was not necessarily the case, but perceptions were as important as reality. Moreover, these popes did cooperate with the French kings in several important matters, most notably the suppression of the Order of the Temple, whose wealth the king coveted. Tried on trumped up charges of Satanism, homosexuality, and sorcery, the Templars were abolished in 1312.

While the popes were resident in Avignon, the Church increasingly strayed from its spiritual mission. The Avignon popes built themselves an enormous palace and encouraged the cardinals to do likewise. They concentrated more on the fiscal and administrative machinery of the Church than on shepherding the flock of the faithful. Though not necessarily evil, or even noticeably corrupt (though some of these popes were both), they simply saw the Church as an organization to be administered rather than as the body of Christ. Although it is easy to criticize from a distance of a number of centuries, one must keep in mind that this unfortunate state of affairs was deeply rooted in the past. The popes and clergymen of the Middle Ages were not content to preach from the sidelines. They were concerned about real moral reform, and in order to accomplish this, they joined in the fray with kings and emperors. Inevitably and tragically, the means of this reform (a strong and well-governed Church) became confused with the original end.

The seventh and last of the Avignon popes, Gregory IX, returned the papacy to Rome in 1377 but died shortly thereafter. The new pope, Urban XI, was an Italian and quickly alienated the French majority in the college of cardinals. They left Rome, declared Urban's election invalid, and elected one of their number as Pope Clement VII. Clement then returned to Avignon. For almost 40 years, Christendom was split in its allegiance between two popes—one in Rome and another in Avignon. France and its allies followed the Avignon pope, while England and its allies followed the Roman pope. Germany and Italy were split in their allegiance. In 1406, a Church council met in Pisa to attempt to end this Great Schism, deposing the popes in Rome and Avignon, and electing a new one. Unfortunately, they only added to the confusion, for now there were three popes, a situation which would not be remedied until the Council of Constance (1414–17).

Throughout the 15th century, the Church as a whole continued its drift and decline. Popes fought with Church councils over who had ultimate authority, the upper hierarchy of the Church was more concerned with its worldly power and material wealth than with its spiritual mission, and the popes were more concerned with their role as rulers of part of Italy than they were with their spiritual responsibilities. Secular rulers, always seeking to enhance their power over their territories and subjects, were quick to take advantage of this situation. In particular, the kings of France were able to increase their control over the Church within their kingdom. Two documents especially, the Pragmatic Sanction of Bourges (1438) and the Concordat of Bologna (1516), allowed the kings to dominate the Catholic Church within France. This state of affairs is known as Gallicanism—the conception that the French Church was semiautonomous within the larger Roman Catholic Church. For purposes of personnel and administration, the king was in charge, while in matters of theology and doctrine, the French Church was subject to the pope and Rome.

RENAISSANCE, REFORMATION, AND RELIGIOUS WAR

Meanwhile, the movement of the Renaissance produced a group of thinkers and writers who increasingly questioned both the theology and practices of the Roman Church. Known as humanists, they were international and cosmopolitan in outlook. Foremost among them was Erasmus of Rotterdam (1465/6–1536). In his many writings, he advocated a return to what he termed "The Philosophy of Christ": a deemphasis on formal theology and ceremonies, and a corresponding return to the simple practices of the early church and on the importance of inner belief rather than outer observance. Inherent in this "Philosophy of Christ" was the idea that Christianity consisted not of a set of doctrines to which one assented, but that the essence of Christianity was living as Christ lived. Erasmus was the most prominent of these thinkers, but these ideas found many disciples all over Europe including, in France, men such as Jacques Lefèvre d'Etaples and others, who found a home in Meaux, where Bishop Guillaume Briçonnet was very interested in reform. Together, the humanists furnished a penetrating critique of the Church; however, none of them intended to break apart the unity of Christendom. They all insisted that they intended to reform the Church, not fragment it.

Meanwhile, a religious revolution had broken out in Germany, where an Augustinian friar named Martin Luther had challenged the authority of the Church on the issue of indulgences. Luther, through his reading of the Gospels and Romans, had arrived at the position that no part of salvation was within man's power; it was entirely due to God's grace. Human effort availed nothing for salvation. If this were so, many of the beliefs and practices of the Church were untenable, most notably the sacrament of confession and the indulgences which were closely allied to it. Luther's writings were condemned by the University of Paris, but the advent of the printing press made control of information impossible. Luther's ideas found an audience in France, but mostly among humanists and intellectuals; they lacked the broad social appeal that they had in Germany. Among those who were convinced by Luther's writings was a young Catholic law student from Noyon in Picardy, named Jean Cauvin (or John Calvin, as he is better known to us).

The royal government's attitude toward Lutheran ideas was ambiguous. King Francis I (1515–47) was involved in a life-and-death struggle with Holy Roman Emperor Charles V, a staunch Catholic and sworn enemy of Luther. Thus, Francis found natural allies among German Lutheran princes, which influenced his religious policy at home. He was also concerned to protect the Galli-can Church from Roman interference, which made him reluctant to follow the pope in condemning Luther and his ideas. Moreover, his sister, Marguerite of Angoulême, was very involved in religious reform, and many of Luther's disciples in France were close to her. The net result was that without systematic government persecution, Protestantism (as non-Catholic Christianity now became known) gained a toehold in France. The Protestant movement in France, however, remained inchoate and unorganized.

This was to change due to the impact of John Calvin (1509–64). Born a Catholic in Noyon, he was a law student in Paris when he underwent a religious conversion experience sometime in the early 1530s (the exact date is unclear). In 1534, the appearance of Protestant posters or placards in several cities throughout France prompted King Francis to undertake a brief but severe campaign against the "Lutherans" (all non-Catholic Christians were called "Lutherans" regardless of their specific beliefs). As a result, Calvin found it prudent to leave France. In 1536, he was on his way to Strasbourg (then a German Protestant city) when he was forced to make a detour through the Swiss city of Geneva. A fellow French Protestant named Guillaume Farel, who had lived in Geneva for several years, convinced Calvin to stay and help him reform the church in Geneva. From 1536 until 1538, Calvin and Farel worked together in Geneva before falling afoul of the city government. Expelled, Calvin spent two years in Strasbourg before returning to Geneva in 1540, where he would spend the rest of his life.

A man of great logical insight, formidable moral authority, and great organizational genius, John Calvin was especially concerned with the conversion of his homeland. He established an Academy for the training of pastors and missionaries. Geneva became a magnet for religious refugees, not just from France, but from all over Europe. After about 1555, therefore, a previously inchoate and amorphous French Protestant movement was remade in a Calvinist mode. Calvinism in France appealed especially to certain social groups: the nobility (by the early 1560s about half of the French nobility was Protestant), and the urban middle and working classes. It made few inroads among the peasants. Put another way, Calvinism appealed disproportionately to the literate and to those who had access to the world beyond their village. Consequently, it was concentrated in the cities. This Huguenot movement (French Calvinists became known as Huguenots) reached its high water mark in the early 1560s, when approximately ten percent of France's 16–18 million people belonged to the new faith.

Calvinism, however, was not unopposed by the forces of the Catholic Church. King Henry II (1547–59) was harsher toward the Protestants than his father Francis I had been, resulting in more severe persecution and several prominent executions. As the Huguenot movement grew in numbers, they became bolder and more confident, provoking greater fear and resentment among zealous Catholics. In the early 1560s, religious passions reached a fever pitch, with numerous armed confrontations and riots between the supporters of the two creeds.

This religious tension was complicated by political considerations. As mentioned above, Calvinism had attracted numerous noble converts. Among these were members of two of the most prominent noble clans in France: the Montmorency and Bourbon families. On the other hand, the other great noble faction, that of the Guise family, remained zealously Catholic. In 1559, Henry II died prematurely in a jousting accident. He was succeeded by his eldest son, Francis II (1559–60), a sickly and dim-witted teenager. He was married to a Guise princess, Mary Stuart (better known as Mary Queen of Scots). Thus the Guises, led by the duke of Guise and his brother the cardinal of Lorraine, took over the government, alienating the other noble factions. Moreover, the Guises used their newfound power to crack down even harder on the Huguenots. In March of 1560, a group of Huguenot noblemen plotted to kidnap the king, or as they thought of it, to "rescue" him from his "evil advisors." The royal court was then in residence at Amboise. This conspiracy or "tumult" of Amboise failed, and the leading conspirators were executed. Francis II died in December 1560 and was succeeded by his younger brother Charles IX (1560–74), then an under-age minor. His mother, the Italian princess Catherine de Medici, was named regent for the period of her son's minority. Catherine, hoping to preserve royal power against the noble factions, tried to calm things down. She relaxed the persecution of the Huguenots and sponsored a conference where she hoped representatives of the two creeds could work out some sort of compromise. Ultimately, these hopes proved vain. No matter how much practical toleration she was willing to extend to the Huguenots, it was never enough for them, but it was always too much for the zealous Catholics. Moreover, any edict of toleration was completely unenforceable: the Huguenots ignored its restrictions, while the Catholics ignored the protection granted the "heretics."

In March of 1562, the massacre of Wassy (Vassy) began the period of 35 years of civil and religious war known as the Wars of Religion. The Huguenots, under their noble leaders, took up arms to defend themselves, seizing a number of important cities, including Lyon, Rouen, and Orléans. This was the first of a series of eight civil wars (known as the Wars of Religion) which were to tear France apart over the next 37 years, until 1598. Each war would end with an "Edict of Pacification" setting out the freedoms which the Huguenots were to enjoy (but never extending to complete religious liberty). None were effective or enduring—it was always less than the Huguenots wanted and more than zealous Catholics wanted to give.

The most famous (or infamous) event of the wars occurred in 1572 with the St. Bartholomew's Massacre. Catherine de Medici, still trying to reconcile the religious factions, had decided to marry her daughter Marguerite to the prominent young Huguenot nobleman Henry of Navarre, a prince of the Bourbon family and the future King Henry IV (1589–1610). The wedding took place in Paris in August 1572. Virtually every prominent Huguenot was present for this event, including Gaspard de Coligny, the Huguenots' military leader and member of the Montmorency family. On August 23, Coligny was shot and wounded as he walked through the streets of Paris. Faced with Huguenot suspicion and mistrust and the possibility of renewed war, Catherine and the king decided, urged on by the duke of Guise, to seize the opportunity to eliminate the Huguenot leadership in one fell swoop. What was intended as a surgical strike against the Huguenot leadership soon became a widespread massacre, as the Catholic mobs of Paris, in some cases urged on by radical priests and militant civic officials, attacked and killed anyone suspected of heresy. Many simply seized the opportunity to settle old scores, religious or not. The massacre in Paris went on for a period of almost a week, claiming perhaps 3000 lives. The massacres also spread to perhaps a dozen other cities, including Rouen, Lyon, Troyes, Orléans, and Meaux, claiming perhaps another 10,000 victims.

The wars continued, with neither side able to prevail. By the mid-1580s, the situation had changed somewhat. Zealous Catholics, alarmed by what they saw as an increasing Protestant presence, formed the Catholic League under the leadership of the duke of Guise, to protect and promote the Catholic cause in France. Moreover, in 1584, King Henry III's (1574–89) younger brother died. (He was the youngest of the four sons of Henry II, three of whom would reign as king—Francis II, Charles IX, and now, Henry III.) This meant that, according to the laws of succession, the heir-presumptive to the throne was young Henry of Navarre, a Huguenot, should Henry III die without a legitimate male heir, as appeared increasingly likely. The Catholic League and the duke of Guise attempted to dictate royal policy to the king, in order to crack down on the Huguenots, and to exclude Navarre from the succession. In December of 1588, in a desperate attempt to free himself from the duke of Guise and the Catholic League, during a meeting of the Estates-General at Blois, Henry ordered Guise's murder, as well as that of his brother, a cardinal of the Catholic Church. Rather than crippling the Catholic League, however, the king's actions only roused further opposition. Declared a tyrant by the University of Paris, excommunicated by the pope, his subjects released from their vows of obedience, Henry III was himself assassinated by a Dominican monk in 1589.

The Huguenot Henry of Navarre now became King Henry IV of France (1589–1610). However, the majority of his subjects did not acknowledge him as king because of his religion. By carefully timing his conversion to the Catholic Church in 1593, Henry IV was able to win over all but the most fanatical Catholics. He was able to enter Paris in 1594, and by 1598, the last opposition to his rule was overcome.

By now, however, his Huguenot supporters had become suspicious of him. In order to allay their fears, in 1598 he issued the Edict of Nantes. The Edict of Nantes guaranteed the Huguenots full civil rights, as well as the right to worship wherever they were already worshiping at the time of the Edict. That is, they were not to suffer any legal obstacles because of their religion. Moreover, in order to guarantee these rights, the Huguenots were granted as security some 150 fortified towns, and were allowed to maintain their own army, to be paid for out of the royal treasury. Though not yet our current conception of religious liberty or toleration, the Edict of Nantes at least provided for limited freedom of worship and gave the Huguenots some security for the future.

PEACE, COUNTER-REFORMATION, AND LOUIS XIV

Once peace was restored, French Catholicism began a period of ferment and rapid reform. It was as if the energies which for the previous 35 years had been directed towards eliminating heresy were now redirected inward toward renewing the vitality of Catholicism. Many charitable orders were founded, such as the Daughters of Charity, founded by St. Vincent de Paul. This was also the golden age of organizations of pious laypeople, such as the Company of the Holy Sacrament, which sought to reinvigorate the religious lives of the Catholic laity. There were missions undertaken in remote parts of the country to educate people in the basics of their faith. Schools were founded for the same purposes. In short, in the early 17th century, the Counter-Reformation came to France.

This golden age, however, did not last for much more than several generations before it foundered on the rocks of Jansenism. Based on the writings of the Dutch Catholic theologian, Cornelius Jansen (1585–1638), published posthumously in 1640, the Jansenists sought to restore what they perceived to be a proper balance to the Church's teachings on salvation. In their view, the official view of the Church, upheld largely by the Jesuits, came dangerously close to Pelagianism—the view that man can save himself through his own efforts. They put a greater emphasis on the total unworthiness of man and the absolute necessity of God's grace. Based in the abbey of Port-Royal-des-Champs, near Versailles, Jansenism became popular among magistrates at the upper levels of the judicial system. They also attracted a brilliant young scientist named Blaise Pascal, who in his *Provincial Letters* countered the attacks of the Jesuits, condemning them for their overly optimistic view of human nature and their moral casuistry. Jansenists were also notable for their strict morality and austerity, leading one historian to characterize the movement as "perdition for the unfortunate many and ascetic gloom for the fortunate few." The quarrels over Jansenism would last into the 18th century, and had the unfortunate effect of rupturing the unity of French Catholicism and ending a half-century of remarkable religious vitality.

Meanwhile, the Huguenots were increasingly on the defensive. Stunned and demoralized by several high-level defections, they became more strident and aggressive in defense of their liberties, rebelling against King Louis XIII (1610–43) several times during the 1620s. In 1628, their great stronghold, the Atlantic seaport of La Rochelle, succumbed to the royal army after a year-long siege. The following year, having been decisively defeated, Louis imposed upon the Huguenots the Grace of Alais, which allowed the Huguenots to keep their right to worship, but stripped from them their fortified towns and army. To their credit, the king and his chief minister Cardinal Richelieu resisted pressure to abolish their right to worship, recognizing that belief cannot be forced, and that any attempt to abolish Protestantism would likely lead to renewed civil war. Nevertheless, having lost the capacity to defend themselves, the Huguenots now endured a precarious existence, their only security the willingness of the king to abide by his commitments.

The long reign of King Louis XIV (1643–1715) was notable for several developments in the realm of Christianity. Although a devout Catholic, Louis's personal religion could best be described as conventional and superficial. Nevertheless, he took his religious duties seriously. He disliked the Jansenists intensely. Not only did they stick out as dissenters in an age where religious uniformity was actively sought, their austere lifestyle was an implicit rebuke to the lavish court life best exemplified in the construction of a new palace at Versailles. Moreover, many Jansenists had been actively involved in the revolt called the Fronde during Louis's childhood. In the king's mind, therefore, Jansenism was associated with dissent, rebellion, and disloyalty, if not outright treason. Over the course of his reign, Louis actively persecuted the Jansenists, securing the condemnation of the pope in the bull *Unigenitus* in 1713. The con-

vent of Port-Royal was razed to the ground, and the central tenets of Jansenism declared heretical.

Louis's relations with the pope and Rome were complicated. On the one hand, Louis was styled "The Most Christian King," an honorary title granted to all French kings. On the other hand, France had a long tradition of Gallicanism, autonomy from the administrative authority of Rome. Louis was therefore reluctant to appear to be subservient to the pope, while still striving to maintain his reputation as a loyal son of the Church. Moreover, Gallicanism was strong among the Jansenists. In order to secure their condemnation by the pope, Louis was forced into the difficult situation of cooperating with the pope and the ultramontanists (those who upheld the power of the pope over the Church in France; primarily the Jesuits) against those who would otherwise have been the strongest proponents of royal control over the Church.

At the same time, Louis found himself in conflict with the pope and Rome over matters of finance and administration. There was a bitter confrontation with Pope Innocent XI (1676–89), when for a time it appeared that France might actually break away from the Roman Catholic Church.

It was in this context that in 1685, Louis XIV revoked the Edict of Nantes, which had guaranteed the Huguenots' right to worship since 1598, although their political and military might had been eliminated in the 1620s. Unlike the Jansenists, Louis bore the Huguenots no personal grudge; indeed, they had been the only major group in France to remain completely loyal during the Fronde. Nevertheless, Louis disliked dissent, and as he grew older and more pious, he began to feel acutely that their existence detracted from his power and glory as king. From the time he took power in 1661 on, he began to enforce a stricter interpretation of the Edict of Nantes, for example limiting the Huguenots' access to Protestant education, and forbidding further conversions to Protestantism. A slush fund was established to reward those who converted to Catholicism, and violent soldiers were billeted on those who refused. Many Huguenots converted to escape these consequences. By the 1680s Louis and his advisors were convinced that there were so few Huguenots left that the Edict of Nantes was unnecessary. This was also at the height of Louis's conflict with the pope. Therefore, partly in order to demonstrate his Catholicism, on October 17, 1685, Louis XIV revoked the Edict of Nantes, making it illegal to be a Protestant in France. Protestant worship was outlawed, Huguenot churches were destroyed, pastors were expelled from France, and all remaining Huguenots were simply declared to be Catholics.

At the time, the revocation was considered to be the most glorious achievement of the reign. Nevertheless, it proved costly to France. Of the one million Huguenots remaining in France, about 200,000 chose exile over conversion. France thus lost a wealthy, well-educated, and hard-working minority. The exiles went to the Dutch Republic and its African colony in the Cape of Good Hope, England and its American colonies (notably Charleston, South Carolina), and German Protestant territories, notably Brandenburg/Prussia. Although the loss of these people was not a severe economic blow to France, they did help enrich their new homelands. More importantly, the revocation spread abroad a group of anti-Louis, anti-French activists, many of whom quickly attained places of influence in their new countries. The revocation thus played a large role in binding together the alliances which fought France in the War of the League of Augsburg (1689–97) and the War of Spanish Succession (1702–14).

Nor was the revocation successful within France. Although many Huguenots did convert, some continued to illegally practice their former faith, while still others steadfastly refused conversion at all. There was thus an underground Huguenot church. From 1701–10 there was a Huguenot revolt against royal policies in the Cévennes, a remote and mountainous region of south-central France. Known as the revolt of the Camisards, its bloody and difficult repression required an army which could otherwise have been used against France's foreign enemies. Until Protestant worship was again legally recognized shortly before the Revolution, Huguenot worship was outlawed, but not eliminated. The failure of the revocation of the Edict of Nantes serves as yet another reminder (if any more are needed) of the futility of coercion in matters of belief.

ENLIGHTENMENT AND REVOLUTION

In the course of the 17th and 18th centuries, assumptions about the way the universe was constructed and operated which had been universally accepted for centuries, were profoundly challenged. The scientific views of the ancient Greeks which had reigned supreme throughout antiquity and the Middle Ages were shown to be dramatically flawed during the course of the scientific revolution of the 16th and 17th centuries. According to the new view of the universe which emerged by the end of the 17th century, the universe, although still divinely created, was a rational and harmonious machine, which left little room for the traditional God of Christianity who had sent his Son to redeem humankind. The old views had been closely integrated with Christian theology, so that when traditional scientific views were challenged, religious authorities—both Catholic and Protestant—took them as challenges to their power and theology. Church leaders often ignored scientists' protestations that they were devout Christians seeking only to better understand God's creation. Thus, largely because of the religious authorities' own attitudes, modern science developed in a largely secular, even anti-Christian atmosphere. Although both Protestant and Catholic churches were hostile to the new science, the fragmentation of religious and political authority in Protestant Europe allowed these views to be expressed more freely than in Catholic areas. As a result, and somewhat unfairly, the Catholic Church came to be regarded as the enemy of truth and progress.

In the 18th century, the methods and concerns of the new science came to dominate intellectual life as a whole. In other words, if human minds were capable of discerning the immutable laws which governed the physical universe, was it not natural to expect that they could also discover the natural laws which governed human affairs? This movement is known as the Enlightenment, and its leading lights as *philosophes*. Reason and nature became the yardsticks by which human institutions were to be measured. Was an institution rational? Was it natural? Could it be justified on the basis of the "natural laws" which governed human society? If not, it could be safely discarded. Tradition and divine revelation were excluded as sources of authority. Although the Enlightenment was a European movement, it was centered in France. Many of the most important *philosophes* were French—Voltaire, Montesquieu, Diderot, and Rousseau—and those who weren't spent long periods in France and tended to write in French. The Enlightenment had a corrosive effect on the Christian dominance of European society. Although there were atheists in the Enlightenment, its most characteristic religious belief was Deism: there is a God who created the universe, but he no longer intervenes in his creation or in human affairs. The analogy is often made to a clockmaker who makes the clock and winds it up, but whose presence is not necessary for its continued functioning. Religion then, for the *philosophes,* consisted of honoring the Supreme Being in a rational way, rather than in organized churches with their hierarchies, "superstitions," intolerance, and dogmas. The Christian God, and traditional Christianity, were regarded as myths and superstition, used by the powerful to dominate the ignorant. Organized religion came to be seen as the enemy of reason and progress, and since France was a Catholic country, and since the Catholic Church was an international and powerful organization, it came in for particular enmity. Indeed, Voltaire, the most famous of the *philosophes*, adopted as his motto, "Ecrasez l'infâme," or "Crush the infamous thing," by which he meant superstition and organized religion in general, and the Catholic Church in particular.

The views of the Enlightenment largely won the day among the educated elite in France and in western Europe as a whole. What had once been radical and dangerous ideas were, by the later 18th century, accepted as common sense and became a kind of new orthodoxy, and began to have an effect on society at large. Thus, in 1787, on the eve of the French Revolution, French Protestants were granted full civil rights, in effect undoing the revocation of the Edict of Nantes a century earlier.

The connection between these new ideas and the political upheavals of the French Revolution have been the subject of much debate among historians and others. Although it is difficult to draw direct cause-and-effect conclusions, and although the direct causes of the French Revolution lay elsewhere, it does seem probable that the views of the Enlightenment with their irreverence and skepticism toward traditional institutions played a role. In other words, although the Revolution was caused by largely political factors, once it was underway the ideas of the Enlightenment came to the fore as people struggled with how to replace the old institutions.

The immediate causes of the French Revolution lay in the bankruptcy of the royal government, royal ineptitude, and a patently unfair taxation system in which the nobility and the wealthy middle class paid almost nothing, while the bulk of the tax burden fell on the vast majority who were poor peasants, in other words, those least able to pay. Faced with the failure of reform plan after reform plan, the royal government finally decided to call a meeting of the Estates-General, a kind of national representative assembly, to deal with its fiscal problems. The Estates-General had not met since 1615. The assembly opened in May of 1789, and events quickly spun out of control. Within four years, the monarchy would be abolished, France declared a republic, and the king and queen beheaded for treason. In short, traditional institutions were completely overthrown. Although religion cannot really be numbered among the causes of the Revolution, the Revolution would have a profound impact on Christianity in France. Even in the Revolution's early moderate phase, the Catholic Church was dramatically affected. In 1790, the Church's "feudal" privileges were abolished. These included the tithes which were normally paid on agricultural production and all sorts of fees and privileges. That same year, the Church's lands were expropriated by the revolutionary government. That these were accomplished with little opposition probably reflects the public's widespread perception of the need for radical reform. In 1791, however, this consensus broke down. The occasion was the Civil Constitution of the Clergy which came into effect on August 24, 1791. In essence, this converted the Catholic Church into a government department and the clergy into civil servants. It also provided for the election of clergy and bishops, and expressly forbade French citizens to have any contact with any foreign bishop or his agents (i.e., the pope). At the same time, however, the pope's general authority over matters of doctrine was preserved, even while he was excluded from all administration of the Catholic Church within France. The Civil Constitution's most divisive feature, however, was the oath which it required all clergy to swear to the new revolutionary constitution. All but seven of about 180 bishops refused. In total, only 54 percent of the French clergy swore the oath. The result was a schism within the Catholic Church in France. The constitutional Church was made up of the juring clergy (those who swore the oath), who had the legal sanction of the government. Meanwhile, the refractory clergy (those who refused) led their flocks underground. More than anything else, this divided the French people, and ultimately led to a long and bloody civil war known as the Vendée. This region in the west of France, in the area around Rennes, south of the Loire river, was distinguished for the religious zeal of its peasants, their devotion to the king, and for its countryside of *bocage* (hedges and ditches) which made quick transit difficult. In this region more than 90 percent of the clergy rejected the constitutional oath. After the execution of Louis XVI in January 1793, and renewed military conscription, the area rose in rebellion against the revolutionary government, amassing a rebel army of up to 45,000 men which would hold off government forces for a decade. It was a revolt inspired by loyalty to the Catholic Church and the monarchy.

The most radical phase of the Revolution began in 1793 with the triumph in the National Convention of Maximilien Robespierre and the Jacobin party. Although chronologically only a small part of the French Revolution, this is the phase most associated with the Revolution in most people's minds. Not only was there a Reign of Terror to suppress political dissent, Robespierre and the Jacobins also sought to remake French society. Part of this effort was the attempt to install a "Cult of Reason," that is a system of religious belief that conformed to "reason" and "nature" as outlined in the Enlightenment. All reference to Christianity was to be purged; a campaign of "dechristianization" was begun. Thus, in October 1793, a new republican calendar was declared, which did away with the religious connotations of the old calendar. Years were not to be counted from the birth of Christ, but from the birth of the Republic (September 22, 1792). The seven-day week was replaced with a ten-day week; religious observances normally held on Sunday could henceforth only be held when Sunday corresponded with the secular day of rest, the *décadi,* which occurred once in every ten-day week. That same

month in Reims, at a public ceremony, Sainte Ampoule—which held the sacred oil of Clovis used in the coronation ceremony—was smashed. The royal tombs at St. Denis were removed and desecrated and the images of kings removed from Notre-Dame in Paris. All over France churches were invaded, vandalized, and despoiled, including the great abbey church of St. Germain-des-Prés in Paris. Priests were intimidated and forced to renounce their status, and many were slaughtered. On November 10, at Notre-Dame de Paris, now converted into a "Temple of Reason," there was a "festival of liberty" in which an actress representing liberty emerged from a "temple of philosophy," where the high altar had formerly stood, attended by phalanxes of patriotic virgins clad in white. On November 22, the municipal government of Paris closed all the city's churches. Nevertheless, despite the anti-Christian violence of some, many, including Robespierre, believed that the process had gotten out of hand and that dechristianization threatened to destabilize the government through popular opposition.

In July of 1794, Robespierre and the Jacobins fell from power, and a law passed in February of 1795 decreed that religion was a purely private matter, and declared the freedom of all creeds to worship as they liked. These anti-Christian measures, which reached their height in 1793, were to tarnish the

Revolution in the eyes of devout Catholics, leading to severe problems in Church-State relations for the next century.

Protestants suffered less severely from the Revolution, in large part because unlike the Catholic Church, they were in no way part of the power structure. Indeed, Protestants were among the Revolution's earliest and most avid supporters, especially during its early moderate phase. So much so, in fact, that in the minds of many Catholics, the Revolution was to be explained as a Protestant plot. Protestant churches held no treasures to be looted, nor was Protestantism intimately connected with the cult of monarchy, as was the Catholic Church. In fact, just the opposite was true.

After his seizure of power in 1799, Napoleon Bonaparte, ever the opportunistic and realistic politician, realized that some sort of accommodation would have to be reached with the Catholic Church in order to pacify the long and bloody revolt of the Vendée. Accordingly, in 1801 the French government reached an agreement or Concordat with Pope Pius VII, which ended the cycle of bare toleration and persecution that had begun in 1792, and reintegrated the Roman Catholic Church into French society. The government recognized that Catholicism was the religion of a majority of the French people. The split between the constitutional church and the refractory church was repaired by having all bishops resign. Henceforth,

bishops were to be appointed by the government and consecrated by the pope, a situation similar to what had pertained before the Revolution. Priests were to be paid by the government. The revolutionary land settlement was kept—the confiscated lands and property were not returned. The government retained the right to police public worship. Indeed, Napoleon hoped to use the national Church to propagate obedience: under the Empire, the clergy were asked to teach an imperial catechism which would "bind the consciences of the young to the august person of the Emperor." Napoleon also halted the campaign to enforce the republican calendar, which was abolished in 1806. In an ironic twist, in the regime established under the Concordat, the pope's authority in France was greater than in the pre-revolutionary Gallican era. As historian William Doyle said, "The authority of the Papacy had received far more fulsome recognition from the heirs of a Godless revolution than ever it had won from the Most Christian Kings of the old regime."

Nevertheless, the ambiguous status of the Catholic Church in France was to cause significant tension throughout the rest of the 19th century. Yet, despite the interference by the state in religious matters, the religious climate under Napoleon as compared to that of the revolutionary years was like coming out of a dreadful storm into bright sunshine. Although the Catholic Church was given a privileged position within France, freedom of conscience and religion were maintained. Protestants gained considerably under a state that was no longer openly hostile to religious belief. One million Calvinists were organized into "consistories," and their pastors were paid by the state.

Having conquered much of Europe, Napoleon provoked an anti-French coalition of Britain, Austria, Prussia, and Russia, which ultimately undid the Emperor's conquests. Napoleon abdicated at Fontainebleau and went into exile on the Italian island of Elba. The Bourbon dynasty was restored to the throne in the person of Louis XVIII, a younger brother of the executed Louis XVI. Napoleon, however, taking advantage of the political squabbling that followed his abdication, slipped back into France and marched on Paris, rallying troops still faithful to the emperor on the way. Between March and June 1815 in a period known as the Hundred Days, Napoleon ruled France again, but his return to power was to be short-lived: the Allies managed to rally again and defeat Napoleon once and for all at the Battle of Waterloo. The Bourbons, in the person of Louis XVIII, were restored to the throne for the second time in less than two years!

FRANCE IN THE 19TH AND 20TH CENTURIES

The French political scene in the 19th and 20th centuries is characterized by a bewildering number of changes, revolts, and reversals of fortune. Between the empires, the monarchical restorations, the five republics, the various revolutions (not to be confused with the Revolution!), and the added confusion of such things as citizen kings and despotic republicans, it really is quite a task to keep the history of post-revolutionary France straight in one's head. Yet, despite the incredible instability, there is a common thread that runs through the last 200 years of history: the consolidation of an extremely centralized nation-state in which the state is not only a political system but the ultimate and final reference point for all that defines an individual's life, right down to esthetic and moral judgements. Ask most any French man, woman, or child today about where values come from and they will tell you that values are republican notions of virtue: in other words, France today believes that absolute values come from the state and date back about 150–200 years. In the same way that the historical existence of Jesus Christ and his death on the cross defines history for the Christian, the Revolution and republicanism define history for the French. The overwhelming majority of French children today are growing up with no notion that religion has anything to do with right and wrong, let alone anything to do with everyday modern life.

The history of 19th- and 20th-century France is thus, in some respects, the history of the rise of the state. Yet, as Alexis de Tocqueville points out in *The Ancient Regime and the French Revolu-*

tion, France's consolidation as a centralized nation-state was not simply the work of the Revolution but rather had already been begun in the 18th century. The Revolution and then Napoleon and those who followed simply built on the existing centralization.

THE RESTORATION

In the aftermath of Waterloo, there were two factions that strove for power in France: the royalists who were determined to resurrect an absolute monarchy, and the liberal "republicans" who saw the revolutionary changes as irreversible. Louis XVIII was shrewd enough to realize that a return to a monarchy of divine right was impossible, and he therefore carefully chose moderate ministers. However, in 1820, the assassination by a fanatical Bonapartist of the duke of Berry, the last Bourbon still young enough to produce a male heir, put an end to the period of moderate rule and returned the ultra-royalists to power. When Louis XVIII died in 1824, the throne went to his younger brother, Charles X, who was the very embodiment of ultra-royalism. In 1830, having lost seats in the government to moderates, Charles dissolved the Chamber, narrowed suffrage, and ended the liberty of the press. These ordinances led almost immediately to an uprising in Paris: during *Les Trois Glorieuses* (July 27–29), army units began to fraternize with the insurgents, and by the time the king, who was off in the country hunting, returned, Paris was in the hands of the rebels. Among the rebels were republicans, led by the Marquis de Lafayette, and constitutional monarchists, who offered Louis-Philippe of the House of Orléans as their candidate. The monarchists won out as Lafayette decided a constitutional monarchy would be safer and more stable than Jacobin rule. In what is known as the July Monarchy, Louis-Philippe was declared king. The Tricolore—the revolutionary red, white, and blue flag—was restored, and Louis-Philippe, the "Citizen King," pursued a moderately conservative policy with the help of the gifted minister and historian François Guizot. Guizot believed that the constitutional monarchy was the perfect culmination of French political history: a compromise between the monarchy and the reforms of the Revolution. However, many republicans had not forgiven Louis-Philippe for "confiscating" their revolution of 1830, and the 1840s saw the rise of radical socialist theories expounded by such men as Charles Fourier, Pierre-Joseph Proudhon, and Barthélemy-Prosper Enfantin. When, in 1846–47, crop failures led to economic crisis, republican leaders took advantage of the discontent and restless mood to organize opposition in a series of "banquets," as political meetings were illegal. On February 22, 1848, one of these "banquets" was stopped and protestors began to clash with the police: the protestors wanted Guizot to be replaced, and the king, who did not want to call in the army and thus cause large-scale bloodshed, decided to appease them. Yet, as often seems to be the case in history, the king's concession came too late: protestors who had gathered outside Guizot's residence clashed with guards, and 40 were gunned down. The king was held responsible, and when angry crowds gathered at the palace, Louis-Philippe abdicated.

SECOND REPUBLIC AND SECOND EMPIRE

The protestors demanded a republic, and a provisional government, largely dominated by radical socialists, was set up. In an unprecedented reform, universal manhood suffrage was proclaimed, taking in one day the electorate from 200,000 to 9,000,000. A right-to-work declaration was issued, obliging the state to find work for all citizens; national workshops were established to provide jobs. In desperate need of money to fund its workshops, the government imposed a surcharge on each franc of property tax, a measure which hurt above all the peasantry. Elections were called, and the republicans and constitutional monarchists beat the radicals dramatically. The workshops were closed, which resulted in huge riots in Paris: chaos had struck again after less than a year. Feeling they needed a strong leader, the republicans and monarchists proposed Louis-Napoleon, nephew of Napoleon, mainly because his name conveyed an aura of glory and public order; he was elected by universal suffrage in a landslide victory. In principle,

the government which was set up seemed the most democratic in Europe: the president was elected for four years by universal suffrage and the assembly for three years by the same method. However, what was not clear was the exact relationship between the president and the legislative, and what would happen in a deadlock. The deadlock came soon: socialist in his leaning and wishing more power, Louis-Napoleon found himself at odds with the conservative legislature, and in 1851, he staged a coup d'état, arresting 70 members of the assembly and proclaiming himself president for ten years. Soon after, Louis-Napoleon proclaimed himself emperor by means of a plebiscite. The Second Empire lasted from 1852–1870. It was a time of relative stability and was marked by economic growth especially in industry, where the French finally started to catch up with the British. It was also marked by a number of liberal reforms such as secondary education for girls, the right for workers to form unions and strike, and further freedom of the press. However, in 1870, just as the regime was moving toward a more solid parliamentry system, war with Bismarck's Prussia struck. Bismarck was looking for an excuse to attack and had it when the French blocked the ascension of a Hohenzollern prince in Spain. French troops were ill-prepared: they suffered a number of quick defeats, and Louis-Napoleon himself was taken prisoner at Sedan. Hearing the news, Parisians converged on the Imperial assembly and demanded a new republic. A provisional government was set up, and the Second Empire was over.

THIRD REPUBLIC

The first task of the government was organizing the defense against Bismarck's forces. Leon Gambetta, one of the most forceful members of the radical republicans, was given the role of leading the French defense and was lifted out of besieged Paris by a hot-air balloon. Despite his efforts and a few victories, the French were overpowered, and in 1871, the provisional government decided to capitulate. Yet no sooner had peace been made with the Germans than the new government was faced with a civil war known as the Paris Commune. Outraged by what they saw as a dishonorable peace and then further angered by the ending of the wartime moratorium on debts and rents, Parisians were in a restless mood. Sensing the unrest, Adolphe Thiers, leader of the new assembly, decided to confiscate the National Guard cannon on the Montmartre hill. However, a bloody struggle took place when the government troops found the cannon defended by National Guard soldiers who were joined by a local crowd. Thiers withdrew his forces and the protestors improvised a municipal self-government they called the Commune. It was only after the terrible fighting of "Bloody Week" that Thiers and the assembly's forces finally took

control, and when it was over, they executed 20,000 Communards on the spot.

In 1875, the provisional government established a new constitution which ushered in the Third Republic (1875–1945) and gave France many of the political forms it still has today: a two-house legislature with an indirectly legislated senate, and a president elected for seven years.

The first years of the Third Republic were marked by rivalry between monarchists, Bonapartists, and radical republicans. In the late 1870s, it looked like France might well return to a constitutional monarchy. However, two ugly events, the Panama scandal and the Dreyfus affair, led to the radical republicans taking firm control of the Republic in the early 1890s. The Panama scandal involved a large number of deputies and senators taking bribes to cover up the failure of the Panama Canal Company, and gave fuel to the rising socialist movement which saw the scandal as proof of the corruption of the ruling class. The Dreyfus affair was not only a political crisis but also a moral and spiritual crisis that involved the whole nation. In 1894, Alfred Dreyfus, a career army officer of Jewish origin, was charged with selling military secrets to the Germans. He was tried and convicted by a court-martial and sentenced to life imprisonment. However, secrets continued to leak, and rumors began to circulate, suggesting that another officer, not Dreyfus, was guilty of the original offense. A retrial was called for, but the army refused. By 1898, the affair had become a violently divisive issue, with intellectuals of the left leading the fight for Dreyfus while right-wing politicians and the Catholic journals defended the honor of the army. When the army's documents condemning Dreyfus were discovered to be forgeries, the right and the moderates who had tried to stay aloof of the struggle were discredited and the radicals, thenceforth called the Radical-Socialist Party, took control of political life. The Church was hurt terribly by its stance and by the rise of the radical left: a wave of anticlericalism followed, and nearly all religious orders were dissolved and exiled. The Church and State were definitively separated.

WORLD WAR I

On June 28, 1914, Austrian Archduke Francis Ferdinand was assassinated: it was the international maneuvering following the assassination that led to the outbreak of World War I. French statesmen had long seen the possibility of general war and suspected the German government desired such a war. Therefore, believing it imperative to keep their allies, they supported the Russians and the Serbs, a stance which led to Germany's declaration of war against France just weeks later. As both sides dug into defensive positions, the "trench warfare" became increasingly awful. Morale was low and there were serious mutinies. Despite General Pétain's heroic defense

and recapture of Verdun in 1916–17, there was much talk of defeatism in 1917. However, the energetic and dogged Georges Clemenceau who was committed to a fight to the finish was given the position of premier in the government, and he managed to infuse a new will into the country. When the Germans launched a last major offensive in March 1918, Clemenceau replaced the cautious Pétain with the attack-minded General Foch and persuaded the Allies to accept Foch as supreme commander. The German drive was checked, and on November 11, an armistice was signed. The war lasted for four long years and was won at terrible cost to the French: 1.3 million dead and over 1 million crippled. Large parts of northern industrial and agricultural France were completely devastated. It was no doubt on account of these losses and from the feeling that France could not again endure such a strain that the Treaty of Versailles was so harsh on the Germans. Tragically, Hitler's rise to power in the early 1930s was created by the economic hardship that Versailles inflicted on the Germans.

WORLD WAR II

Having attempted a policy of appeasement even after the invasion of Czechoslovakia, the French and the British reluctantly declared war on Germany when Hitler invaded Poland in September 1939. The attack on France came just months later, and when President Roosevelt refused open intervention, the

French cabinet decided to capitulate despite the desperate efforts of Churchill to keep the French in the war. A collaboration government, headed by Pétain, was set up at Vichy (thereafter known as the Vichy government), though Hitler only tolerated Vichy as it was a useful device to help police the country and collect the occupation costs levied by the Germans. Though some representatives of the Vichy government did all they could not to enforce the deportation and outright killing of Jews and refugees, on the whole, the collaboration government was Hitler's right arm in France. Yet, within weeks of the 1940 collapse, groups of Frenchmen had begun to resist, hiding refugees and harassing German troops through guerrilla warfare. Charles de Gaulle, under-secretary of war, had flown to London just before the declaration of Vichy, setting up an organization called Free France which spoke for French resisters everywhere. He boldly claimed the status of a legal government-in-exile, insisting on his right to speak for France in the councils of the Allies. When Paris was liberated in August 1944, de Gaulle headed a triumphal parade down the Champs Elysées and established a provisional government which was formally recognized by the Allies in October 1944.

POST-WAR FRANCE

Once the heritage of the Vichy regime had been dealt with (over 100,000 citizens were either sent to prison or lost their civil rights and 800 were executed), there was a clear consensus that a reform of the Third Republic was needed. De Gaulle favored a strong presidency, while the Communists, Socialists, and Christian Democrats wanted a one-house legislature subject to grass-roots control by the voters. Believing he had the support of the people, de Gaulle employed a ploy whereby he suddenly resigned as head of the provisional government; he imagined the public would insist he return, which would give him the necessary support to impose his constitutional ideas. However, the public was simply stunned and confused and failed to react. A new constitution was drafted which in reality differed very little from the Third Republic: power remained concentrated in the lower house of parliament, and shaky coalition cabinets succeeded one another at brief intervals.

The Fourth Republic was marked by crisis in the French colonies. First there was Indochina: Ho Chi Minh's Vietnamese nationalist movement took over northern Indochina in 1946, and when French negotiations failed, a bloody eight-year war ensued, which ended in defeat for the French and the creation of independent North and South Vietnam. In late 1954, just six months after the fighting in Indochina ended, Algerian nationalists started a rebellion which proved the end of the Fourth Republic. Unable to negotiate a settlement and unwilling to give up Algeria because of the 1 million European settlers there, the government found itself in deep trouble when the possibility of an army coup in Algiers became apparent in 1958. De Gaulle took advantage of the situation by announcing directly to the French people that he was prepared to take power if called on to do so. With the situation so out of hand in Algiers, the National Assembly promptly voted de Gaulle full powers for six months, thus putting an end to the Fourth Republic.

A new constitution embodying de Gaulle's conception of government was drafted: the president was now to be elected by local electorate rather than by the Parliament, and he would select the premier who would be less subject to the whims of the National Assembly. Despite protests from pro-colonialists, in 1962, de Gaulle secured a settlement with the Algerians whereby Algeria gained its independence in exchange for guarantees of safety for French colonialists and their property. The 1960s were the golden years of the Gaullist era: France had a strong economy boosted by immigrant labor, and de Gaulle was able to play a role in European and international policy making. However, beneath the surface, basic discontents persisted, and these erupted in the riots and violence of May 1968. When police came to break up a radical student rally in Paris that had turned violent, a struggle ensued, and the incident quickly became a major confrontation: barricades went up, and workers joined the students in protest by staging massive strikes. When negotiations failed with the labor leaders, a number of factions announced their intent to carry out a true revolution and end the Fifth Republic. In a dramatic radio address, de Gaulle then appealed to the French people, presenting himself as the last barrier to anarchy or Communist rule. Middle-class citizens rallied around him, and when the Communist leaders refused to join the other radicals in a resort to force if necessary, the confrontation moved to the polls, where the Gaullist Union won a landslide victory. Yet de Gaulle had been shaken by the events, and when, in 1969, two of his proposed amendments were rejected, he silently abandoned his office, feeling he had lost the confidence of the French people.

Since de Gaulle, the government of France has been shared fairly equally by right-wing and left-wing presidents and governments, though the trend has been toward a socialist state: social security is comprehensive for all citizens, both in terms of health care and retirement. Indeed, in American terms, the French right is best compared to the Democrats. The only serious challenge that the Fifth Republic has faced has been the "cohabitation" of a president and an assembly of opposing political sway. This happened first under the socialist President Francois Mitterand, and is taking place again now under the right-wing President Jacques Chirac. For the moment, the outcome of such cohabitation has been a happy one as the president has been able to conserve popularity by remaining somewhat aloof from difficult policy decisions, appearing rather as a stabilizing figurehead of the nation, and the opposition have enjoyed having an important role to play. Yet, as the French have shown time and time again, they are quick to anger and to mobilize themselves, so one can never be sure if another revolution is not around the corner.

CHRISTIANITY IN FRANCE SINCE 1800

France is one of the great nations in the history of Christianity: one of the first provinces to be evangelized under the Roman Empire, founder of some of the most important monastical orders, birthplace of a central figure of the Reformation, John Calvin, the heritage of France's role in Christian history for 2000 years is evident in the churches one finds in almost every village in the country. Despite France's long history at or near the center of Christianity, in France today, less than ten percent of the population are nominally Christian, and perhaps less than three percent are evangelical believers. Indeed, were it not for the visible testimony of the churches and religious art, one might think that France had only very recently been exposed to the gospel. The majority of people are ignorant of Christianity's fundamental doctrines of sin and grace.

Neither publicly nor in private is any connection made between morality and religion, and in that respect, 20th-century France can best be compared to pagan Greece at the time of Christ: France is indeed a modern pagan society.

When and how did such a dramatic dechristianization occur in France? The immediate answer is the French Revolution of 1789 and the persecution of the Church that followed. Yet, while the Revolution was no doubt a critical event in the dechristianization of France, it is not alone a sufficient explanation. Neither England nor Germany experienced a radical revolution like the French, and these nations are in much the same state of dechristianization today as France. The French people did not turn against the Church overnight: rather, the systematic rejection of Christianity that we see today in France is the result of a gradual process that started in the 18th century. It is the process that Francis Schaeffer describes, whereby philosophical ideas are gradually taken up by art, theology, politics, popular culture, and finally by the common man himself: the average citizen in France today is where French Enlightenment philosophy was about 200 years ago: staunchly anti-Christian and somewhere between the materialistic determinist Diderot and the New Age humanist Rousseau.

The Revolution was a critical event because it put into practice the persecution of the Church that Voltaire advocated, and went as far as to replace

Christianity with the vaguely deist natural religion of Rousseau. The radically anti-Christian nature of the French Revolution could not have occurred had not both the men who came to power, and those common citizens who participated in so much persecution, already rejected the Christian faith. The history of the Church in the 19th and 20th centuries is, sadly, the continuation of that rejection.

THE CATHOLIC CHURCH IN FRANCE: 1800–PRESENT

The history of Christianity in 19th- and 20th-century France is overwhelmingly the history of the Catholic Church. Following the revocation of the Edict of Nantes in 1685, Protestants were systematically persecuted so that since the late 18th century, Protestants have never made up even two percent of the population, and evangelical Protestants considerably less than one percent.

Napoleon's rise to power ended the persecution of the Church and brought back the majority of the clergy who had refused to sign an oath of allegiance to the revolutionary government. He signed a Concordat with Rome in 1802 which recognized Catholicism as the major religion in France but maintained state control of Church lands and nominations. Protestants were granted official recognition by the state, and for the first time, Protestant pastors, like Catholic priests, were salaried by the state. Though some urged the creation of a French Catholic church separate from the Vatican, the Church remained overwhelmingly committed to Rome. The energy of the Church went mainly into restoring the ecclesiastical organization which had been completely broken down by the Revolution.

The inauguration of the Third Republic in 1870 saw the renewal at the political level of anti-clericalism. Many republican politicians like Jules Ferry were radically anti-Christian and were committed to bringing about a secular state. With reason, they saw education as the most important means of accomplishing this secular state: almost all primary and secondary school teaching was carried out by the Church and various monastic orders, and thus most children were receiving a religious education. With a series of bills in the late 1890s, the Third Republic first banished almost all the religious orders from education, which forced many schools to close, and second, established obligatory secular education. The village priest and the primary school teacher were now opposed to each other, and, closer to the state and with more practical knowledge, the teacher or *instituteur* replaced the priest as the figure of authority in the village.

Then, in 1894, just as men like Ferry were preaching rational positivism and denouncing the negative influence of the Church on France's young, the Dreyfus affair exploded. While many republicans led the defense of the falsely accused Dreyfus, the Church on the whole sided with Dreyfus's accusers, even when it became more and more obvious that Dreyfus was indeed completely innocent. The Church's authoritarian, in some cases anti-Semitic (Dreyfus was a Jew) stance gave the anti-Christian legislators just the evidence they needed to show the Church's anti-republicanism. In 1905, the state separated itself definitively from the Church. This meant that the state no longer paid the salaries of the priests, and this led to a huge drop-off in the number of recruits to the priesthood. However, it also meant that the Church was no longer subject to the control of lay associations. Despite the financial hardship, the separation law was on the whole beneficial to the Church: it had the effect of greatly reducing the intensity of the republicans' anti-Christian campaign, as they had much less reason to suspect and denounce a disestablished Church.

World War I saw the participation and mobilization of a great number of Catholics and Protestants alike, and this helped to further ease relations between the Church and the state. World War II was less positive for the Church, as some of its members actively supported the Vichy regime; nevertheless, a great many Catholics and Protestants were at the forefront of the resistance. The latter part of this century has witnessed the further lessening of active hostility towards the Church on the part of the republicans, both because of the continuing separation of Church and state, and because of the general decline in the Church's influence in society. Most people's attitude today is one of skeptical amusement rather than fanatical criticism.

THEOLOGY AND SPIRITUALITY IN FRANCE: 1800–PRESENT

The facility and precipitation with which the majority of the French people embraced the profanation and persecution of Christianity during the Revolution revealed a strong undercurrent of latent dechristianization: already in 1789, the majority of Frenchmen were Christians simply by custom and not by faith. Apart from a few exceptions, the 19th and 20th centuries have seen the progression of that dechristianization.

If the majority of the intellectual elite, the bourgeoisie, and city dwellers had accepted the glorification of man and vague deism of the Enlightenment by the time of the Revolution, many Catholic and Protestant theologians had been equally influenced by these Enlightenment notions. In an 1801 sermon, the Protestant pastor P. H. Marron defines Christianity in these terms: "the profound sentiment of the grandeur and goodness of God, the conviction of his presence, and the legitimate anticipation of the riches of eternity." Christ, original sin, and grace have been lost, to be replaced by a sufficiently vague notion of divine providence and a guilt-free humanity.

The 19th century in France saw the rise, in both Protestant and Catholic circles, of an often bitter struggle between historic Christianity and the new liberal theology. Conservative theology won out among the Catholics as the majority were committed to loyalty to the Vatican. Yet, with the proclamation by Pius IX in 1855 of the doctrine of the Immaculate Conception and the confirmation by the Vatican of a number of visions of the Virgin Mary (notably at Lourdes and La Salette), Catholicism in France became more and more centered around the cult of Mary. Indeed, in France today, it is not an exaggeration to say that Catholicism and the cult of Mary are one and the same. Among the Protestants too, orthodox theology won out on the whole. This was due in a large part to a *Reveil* or "Awakening" that took place between 1818 and 1840. Inspired by the Wesleyan revival in England, the Reveil was engineered by both foreign evangelists, mostly from Britain and Switzerland, and by Frenchmen such as the Monod brothers (Adolph and Frédéric) and Antoine Vermeil. The center of the Reveil was the Seminary in Montauban which trained pastors in the historic theology of Calvin, Luther, and the first Reformers.

With the rise of socialist thought in the latter part of the 19th century, Christian socialist movements were started by both Catholics and Protestants. Pastors like Jean-Frédéric Oberlin and Tommy Fallot insisted that Christian regeneration was possible only through trying to bring earth a little closer to heaven. In the end, this Christian socialism moved away from the doctrine of grace by suggesting that salvation could come only through social action.

The 20th century in France, like most everywhere else, has seen the continuation of the struggle between liberal and historic Christianity, and unfortunately, some progression by the liberals. The liberal Swiss theologian Karl Barth with his distant mystical God and denial of Christ's finished work on the cross had a large influence in France, as did the prominent liberal figure Albert Schweitzer.

Despite the victory of evangelical theology in both Catholic and Protestant circles in the 19th century, neither church was able to bring about a return to Christianity among the people: rather, more and more people were turning away. There were a number of factors involved in the continuing dechristianization. First, the radical anticlericalism of the Revolution had taken Christianity out of people's lives; it was no longer necessary to be a Christian even by custom. Certainly, it had taken it out of their hearts as well: how much harder to reaccept what one has consciously rejected, both in thought and in action. Indeed, missionaries even today will tell you that in some respects, France is a much harder missionary terrain than Africa and many parts of Asia because in the latter, the people have not said no to Christianity once before. Second, the acceptance by writers, artists, and politicians of Auguste Comte's rational positivism (a direct heritage of Enlightenment thought) led people to put their faith in science and reason as the path to inevitable progress. Third, neither the Catholic nor the Protestant churches adapted their ministry to the changing face of society. With industrialization, huge numbers of people moved to the cities, creating new working class suburbs. Both Catholic and Protestant churches were organized almost exclusively around rural parishes, and they failed to plant new churches in the growing suburbs. In 1927, a priest sent to the new suburb of Bobigny in Paris found just a dozen believers among the 40,000 workers.

The 1960s and 1970s saw the widespread acceptance by popular culture of the Enlightenment ideals of individualism, sexual freedom, and faith in humankind. France was a culture of Voltaires, Diderots, and Rousseaus, where historical Christianity had no place whatsoever in the lives of the majority of the people. There were faithful Christians, both Catholics and Protestants, as there have been throughout the last two centuries, but they were a neglected and scorned minority.

What is the state of Christianity in France today? Though on the outside France may seem as secular as ever, there is reason for hope. As postmodernism is rejecting the emptiness and irrationality of rational positivism, so people are recognizing their spiritual needs. The *Journées Mondiales de Jeunesse* (World Youth Week) organized by the Catholic Church in 1997 brought hundreds of thousands of young people from France, Europe, and all over the world to Paris to celebrate and profess their faith: indeed, France was somewhat taken aback by the fervor of the meetings. New churches, especially the Pentecostal church, are having success in bringing the gospel to the new suburbs. However, a return to spirituality does not automatically mean a return to Christianity: the last decade or so has seen a huge increase in the popularity of psychics and New Age gurus as people who have rejected Christianity turn to something new. The challenge facing the Church is to reach out effectively to a spiritually starved population.

Part 2

FRENCH LITERATURE, ART, AND ARCHITECTURE

FRENCH LITERATURE

Properly speaking, there was no such thing as French literature before the Middle Ages. Until that time, what we know as France was part of a larger Roman civilization whose literary language was Latin, and whose people spoke a variety of local dialects, many derived from the literary Latin of classical Rome; hence the term "Romance languages" as applied to Italian, Spanish, and French. There were important writers who lived and worked in France in Roman times (or Gaul, as the Romans called it).

French would not emerge as a literary language on its own until well into the Middle Ages. Most literature in French was in the form of poetry and written for lay audiences, while serious scholarly and religious writing were continued in Latin prose. One of the earliest literary expressions of the French language was the *Song of Roland (Chanson de Roland)*. Written around 1080 and based on earlier oral poems, this epic describes a military action during Charlemagne's retreat from Spain. Greatly embellishing the historical record, the writer transforms a minor skirmish into a mighty battle where Count Roland, the emperor's nephew, saves the Christian army from the perfidy of the Muslim horde, but at the cost of his own life. The *Song of Roland* is the premier example of a literary genre which would remain tremendously popular throughout the Middle Ages and beyond. This is the *chanson de geste*, or epic poem concerning great deeds on the battlefield and among the nobility (think King Arthur and the knights of the Round Table).

Another popular genre in the medieval period was the literature of courtly love. This celebrated the romantic and erotic love of the knight for his lady and was subject to strict conventions: the love was always outside marriage (remember that among the nobility most marriages were arranged); it is often unrequited—the lady rejects the lover's advances, but consumed by his passion, the knight persists; sometimes, however, the knight wins the favor of the lady (think Lancelot and Guinevere). The premier example of the literature of courtly love in French is the *Romance of the Rose*, an extended allegory which describes the quest of a knight for his lady's favor. It was extremely popular throughout the Middle Ages, though to modern readers it is long, boring, arcane, and obtuse.

Other popular forms of literature in the Middle Ages included the *aubade* or dawn song, the *fabliaux*, humorous and often crude stories in verse, and lives of the saints, intended to inspire devotion to the saint in question and emulation of his or her virtues. Among the most notable authors of the late Middle Ages was the sometime vagabond and criminal François Villon (b. 1431), whose lyrical poems evoke a sense of world-weariness and sad nostalgia.

During the 16th century, the French language emerged as a serious literary language, suitable for weighty and serious matters. This corresponded with the flowering of the Renaissance in France

and is most clearly seen in the efforts of a group of seven poets known as the *Pléiade*, whose leading lights were Pierre de Ronsard (1524–85) and Joachim du Bellay (1522–60). Their manifesto was *La défense et illustration de la langue française (The Defense and Illustration of the French Language)*, which promoted French as a serious literary language. Also notable in the 16th century was the physician François Rabelais (1494–1553), who in his tales of the giant Gargantua and his son Pantagruel, poked merciless fun at the pretension, absurdity, and hypocrisy he saw around him. Rabelais deliberately tried to shock his readers, and his books are often crude and raunchy, delighting in the pleasures of the flesh, though always with a serious moral purpose.

In a different vein entirely are the essays of Michel de Montaigne (1533–92), a nobleman and judge from Bordeaux. Though a Catholic, he was distressed by the violence of the Wars of Religion and retired to his country estate to ponder the ways of the world. His *Essais* are a plea for tolerance and compassion. Since we can be absolutely sure of very little, we ought not to persecute others for holding contrary beliefs. In Montaigne's words, "I shall leave here ignorant of everything except my ignorance."

For Christians, especially Protestant Christians, the 16th century was also a notable period in French literature. First and foremost comes John Calvin (1509–

64), who wrote copiously in both Latin and French. Most notable among a wide variety of works—sermons, biblical commentaries, polemical works, and books of devotion—was his *Institutes of the Christian Religion* (fourth and final edition, 1559), a magisterial work of systematic theology. Less well-known is Clément Marot (1496–1544). As a court poet, he wrote numerous secular poems, but his most important legacy was his versification of the Psalms. Marot himself flirted with Protestantism, dying in exile in Italy, but his Psalms lived on among the Huguenots, who adopted them as an expression of their Reformed faith.

It was in the 17th century that French literature, like French political and military power, reached a position of European dominance most visibly symbolized in the château at Versailles. Key to this development was the standardization of style instituted by the Acadamie Française (founded 1635), which dictated language and styles of literature. Among the most notable figures of 17th-century literature are the tragic playwrights Pierre Corneille (1606–84) and Jean Racine (1639–99). In contrast to the noble world portrayed by these tragedians, a world in which the protagonists sought to fulfill ideas of honor, courage, and fidelity in the midst of a hostile and capricious world, stand the comedies of Jean-Baptiste Molière (1622–73). His plays, such as *Tartuffe* and *Le Bourgeois Gentilhomme (The Bour-*

geois Gentleman), poked merciless fun at the pretensions and foibles of everyday life. His particular targets were hypocrites, social climbers, and con-men and their gullible victims.

René Descartes (1596–1650) was an influential and important scientist, mathematician, and philosopher. His best-known work is *Discours de la méthode (Discourse on Method),* which established the primacy of human rationality in the perception of reality. Blaise Pascal (1623–62) was likewise a brilliant mathematician before leaving science for the Jansenist movement. His *Pensées (Thoughts)* and *Lettres provinciales (Provincial Letters)* reveal him as a man of deep piety and keen insight into the human condition and its relationship to God.

The 18th century was the era of the Enlightenment, when human rationality became uppermost in literature and philosophy. Most of the giants of the Enlightenment were French. François Marie Arouet, better known as Voltaire (1694–1778), was far and away the leading figure of the Enlightenment. He wrote literature in almost every genre: drama, fiction (his best-known story is *Candide*), philosophy, history, politics, social criticism, etc. Throughout, his main goal was to purge society of "ignorance," "superstition," "fanaticism," and "irrationality." The main target of his attacks was the Catholic Church, especially in the Calas affair, though Voltaire himself maintained a belief in a Supreme Being who created the world but no longer intervenes in it—"If God did not exist, it would be necessary to invent him." Other important figures of the Enlightenment were Montesquieu (1689–1755), whose *Esprit des lois (Spirit of the Laws)* provided much inspiration for the U.S. Constitution, and Denis Diderot (1713–1784), editor and moving spirit of the *Encyclopedia*, an ambitious and controversial attempt to catalogue all knowledge according to Enlightenment principles for the betterment of humanity. The *philosophes* emphasized the possibility of progress and reform through education and the application of reason to human affairs. In an effort to reach and educate the broadest possible audience, they emphasized a simple but elegant style.

Jean-Jacques Rousseau (1712–78) started out as a figure of the Enlightenment, but became dissatisfied with the movement's extreme emphasis on reason. Rousseau came to believe that society corrupted humans, and that the key to a happy and productive life was to live in harmony with nature and one's emotions. Among his most influential works were *Le contrat social (The Social Contract)*, which described his ideal government, the novel *Emile*, which explored issues of how to rear and educate children without corrupting them, and *Julie*, which emphasized the primacy of emotion over reason, and of spontaneity over calculated will. Rousseau was the most important precursor of the Romantic movement in France.

The major effect of the French Revolution on literature was to remove government censorship of the publishing industry. Thus, although there were some important political works, much Revolutionary literature is characterized by its libelous, scandalous, and often pornographic nature.

When the turmoil of the Revolutionary and Napoleonic eras had subsided, the Romantic movement in literature emerged onto center stage. Unlike many German Romantics who emphasized the pagan past as their model, French Romantics tended to draw their inspiration from an idealized vision of the Catholic medieval past. We see this especially in the works of François-René de Châteaubriand (1768–1848), who extolled the simpler times and noble passions of a nostalgically remembered past, much like Sir Walter Scott in English literature. This literary fascination with the Middle Ages touched on architecture when the novelist Prosper Mérimée (1803–70), in his capacity as inspector of historical monuments, collaborated with the architect Viollet-le-Duc in the restoration and reconstruction of many medieval sites, including the fortifications of Carcassonne and the Abbey at Vézélay. Among other celebrated Romantic figures were the poets Alfred de Musset (1810–57) and Alphonse de Lamartine (1790–1869). Without question, however, the towering giant of the Romantic era was the poet, playwright, and novelist Victor

Hugo (1802–85), the most significant literary figure in post-Revolutionary France. His *Notre-Dame de Paris* (or *The Hunchback of Notre-Dame*, as it is colloquially known in English), did much to save and restore the Notre Dame Cathedral in Paris. His best-known work, however, is *Les Miserables*, a sprawling epic of poverty, injustice, love, and redemption. The moving tale of Jean Valjean and his pursuer Inspector Javert has been filmed many times and of course made into a hit musical.

The 19th century was also the golden age of the novel, in France as in England. Besides the masterpieces of Hugo, there were the many novels of Honoré de Balzac (1799–1850). In his novels, such as *Père Goriot (Father Goriot)* and *La Cousine Bette (Cousin Bette)*, Balzac, in reaction against the sentimentality of the Romantics, incisively and often unsparingly gives an unrelenting picture of French society. The novels of Stendhal (Marie-Henri Beyle, 1783–1842), such as *The Red and the Black* and the *Charterhouse of Parma*, introduce a new and modern type of hero—the psychologically isolated outsider at odds with the prevailing norms of society. George Sand (the masculine pseudonym of Amandine Aurore Lucile Dupin, 1804–76) was as notorious for her romantic liaisons—with Fréderic Chopin and the poet Alfred de Musset among others—as for her novels with their socialist and feminist ideals. Gustave Flaubert (1821–80) was one of the first and finest realist novelists. *Madame Bovary* was his first and best-known novel, with its pathetic heroine and her adulterous love affair ending in suicide, and its meticulous and harsh criticism of the pretensions of provincial bourgeois life. Emile Zola (1840–1902) was, after Hugo, perhaps the greatest novelist of the 19th century. His novels, such as *Germinal*, are called "naturalist"; that is, he believed that human conduct and ideas were directly linked to heredity and environment. He also played a central role in the Dreyfus affair with his open letter *J'accuse (I accuse)* condemning the conduct of the government, the church, and the army. Among other important naturalist writers of the later 19th century were Guy de Maupassant (1850–93) and Anatole France (1844–1924).

In poetry, the reaction against Romanticism took shape in the Parnassian school, which retreated from the intense personalism of the Romantics, emphasizing beauty of form. There were also the Symbolists, who maintained that imagination was the real interpreter of reality, and who expressed their ideas indirectly, through symbols, rather than directly, as with the realists. They also encouraged experimentation in form, in contrast to the strict formalism of the Parnassians.

Charles de Baudelaire (1821–67) was the first and most prominent Symbolist. His *Fleurs du mal (Flowers of Evil)* depicts all of human experience, including the most sordid, which led to his prosecution for obscenity. His life was as decadent as much of his poetry, and he died prematurely at age 46. Among his Symbolist successors were Stéphan Mallarmé, Paul Verlaine (1844–96), and Verlaine's homosexual lover Arthur Rimbaud (1854–91). Verlaine shot and wounded Rimbaud in a lovers' quarrel and was jailed for two years. While in jail, Verlaine returned to the Catholicism of his youth and wrote a volume of devotional poetry.

As elsewhere in the Western world, French literature in the 20th century is difficult to categorize, subject as it was to the flux of war, despair, and moral relativism. Marcel Proust (1871–1922), a chronic invalid who seldom left his room, wrote the massive 16 volume *A la recherche du temps perdu (Remembrance of Things Past),* the most intricate and detailed psychological novel of all time, especially the first novel in the collection *Du côté de chez Swann (Swann's Way).* André Gide (1869–1951) was born into a strict Protestant family and most of his works, such as *Les cahiers d'Andre Walter (The Notebooks of Andre Walter)* and *L'immoraliste (The Immoralist),* deal with conflict between individual freedom and responsibility. Another important tendency in 20th century French literature is existentialism: man is alone in a meaningless universe; only human activity can create its own meaning— existence precedes essence. Foremost among French existentialists have been the philosopher and writer Jean-Paul Sartre (1905–80) and his lifelong companion, Simone de Beauvoir (1908–86). The Algerian-born novelist Albert Camus (1913–60), though not an existentialist himself, struggled in his novels such as *L'Etranger (The Stranger)* and *La peste (The Plague)* with issues of the apparent absurdity of life in a meaningless universe. Ultimately, for Camus, the way out lay in a kind of liberal humanism, in which people act with compassion and dignity despite the absurdity of life.

There were however, a number of important Christian writers who stand out in contrast against this background of gloom, despair, and anxiety. Charles Péguy (1873–1914), a Catholic poet and essayist, wrote deeply felt devotional poetry. Likewise, Paul Claudel (1868–1955), a career diplomat, wrote poetry, plays, religious works, and literary criticism. Throughout, his Catholic faith asserts itself, especially in his most important poem, *Cinq grandes odes (Five Great Odes).* François Mauriac (1885–1970)—like Anatole France, Sartre, Camus, and Gide a Nobel laureate— was a profoundly devout Catholic who was concerned in his novels with basic moral conflicts. Deeply aware of humanity's sinful nature, he shows how the desires of the flesh offer no real satisfaction and are in diametric opposition to the spiritual path, which alone offers hope and redemption.

FRENCH ART

France is home to some of humankind's earliest artistic efforts, including the cave paintings at les Eyzies-de-Tayac and Lascaux. Throughout the Celtic and Roman periods and into the Middle Ages, France was part of a larger empire or civilization, and there was little that was unique to art or artistic styles in the region. Since the late Middle Ages, however, not only have French artists developed distinctive styles, but they have also set trends which have been influential elsewhere.

During the Middle Ages, such art as survives was overwhelmingly religious in subject matter. This was due to several factors: it was an age dominated by religious values, and the church and its clergy were practically the only people with the wherewithal and interest to patronize artists. With the economic revival of the high Middle Ages beginning in about A.D. 1000, there were increasing resources available to be devoted to artistic endeavors. Correspondingly, we see an elaboration in artistic styles which parallels the shift in architecture from Romanesque to Gothic. In Romanesque style, typically the statuary which adorned churches, the human figure is highly idealized, following late Roman and Byzantine models: large hands, large and expressive eyes, and minimal attention paid to the anatomy of the human form. In short, these are not representations of

real people, but of highly idealized types, designed to elicit a certain feeling in the viewer. With the shift to Gothic, human figures become much more realistic: a sense of proportion is introduced, greater attention is paid to anatomy, and one gets the sense that the figure is meant to portray a real person, rather than an ideal type or virtue, as for example, in the smiling angel in Reims. In addition, Gothic statues stand out further from the structure of the building itself, adding to the sense of reality.

Little painting survives from before about the 14th century, and again it is overwhelmingly religious in subject matter. Favorite subjects included Mary with the infant Jesus, the Adoration of the Magi, the Virgin with the Christ Child, scenes from the lives of the saints, and of course, the Crucifixion. By the late Gothic period (14th–15th centuries), painters had achieved a realism similar to that in sculpture. One interesting thing to note is that with a few exceptions, the names of these artists are unknown to us. Painting and sculpture were considered crafts, much like goldsmithing or woodcarving. Especially skilled crafts, to be sure, but crafts nonetheless. The idea of the artist as an inspired and sometimes tortured genius was largely a creation of the Renaissance. French artists, like those in the neighboring Netherlands, excelled primarily in the painting of miniatures, especially those in illuminated manuscripts like the *Très riches heures du duc de Berry*. The most important French painter of this period was Jean Fouquet (ca. 1420–81).

By the late 15th and early 16th centuries, the art of the Italian Renaissance was beginning to have an impact in France. This influence included even greater realism, especially in matters of perspective and anatomy, greater attention to the natural world, and—though most art continued to portray religious subjects—an expansion in the themes treated, including especially scenes from classical antiquity and mythology. The wars in Italy (beginning in 1494) hastened and expanded this influence in France. King Francis I (1515–47) was especially taken with Italian artistic styles, and brought them back to France. Most notably, perhaps, he induced the great Leonardo da Vinci to settle in France, where he died in 1519. This Italian Renaissance influence is also seen in the châteaux built by the king and the great nobles, including Fontainebleau, Chambord, and part of the Louvre. Francis continued to patronize Italian artists, but this revival of interest in art also produced French artists, including the father and son pair of Jean (1485–1541) and François Clouet (1510–72), both court painters of Francis I.

The Wars of Religion (1562–98) understandably interrupted artistic development. When peace was finally restored under Henry IV (1589–1610), a more restrained classicism was the order of the day. It was almost as if

people believed that harmony and order could be restored to a chaotic and violent world simply by portraying it as such on canvas. This classicism was entrenched in 1648 with the foundation of the Royal Academy of Painting and Sculpture, which dictated artistic styles much as the Academie Française dictated literary styles. The most important French painters of the period were Simon Vouet (1590–1649), Nicolas Poussin (1594–1665), Philippe de Champaigne (1602–74), Georges de la Tour (1593–1652), and the Le Nain brothers, Antoine (ca. 1588–1648) and Louis (ca. 1593–1648). Their works are characterized by harmony and balance, so unlike the flamboyant and often excessive Baroque style then in vogue in Italy, Germany, and Spain.

This trend towards classicism was only accelerated in the reign of Louis XIV (1643–1715), as artists were heavily employed in royal construction projects, especially the palace at Versailles. Following the Sun King's death in 1715, a reaction set in, not only against his style of rule, but also against his taste in art: heavily classical, bombastic, and highly allegorical, with numerous references to classical mythology intended to glorify the person of the king and the institution of the monarchy.

In interior decoration, the predominant style of the early 18th century is known as rococo. This is a highly ornamented style, incorporating a rock and shell motif, usually in white and gold, and often covering the entire room. In painting, aristocratic taste now took over from royal patronage, emphasizing pastoral scenes, often with classical overtones, still lifes to ornament the houses of the elite, and of course portraits of aristocrats and their families. Leading painters included Antoine Watteau (1684–1721) and Jean-Honoré Fragonard (1732–1806).

The mid-18th century once again brought a reaction to this previous style, now considered too busy and frivolous, largely as a result of the cultural literary movement known as the Enlightenment. Classical models were once again in vogue, but not the heavily allegorical and mythological classicism of Louis XIV. This neoclassicism tended to emphasize classical history and civic heroism. This is seen especially in the works of the preeminent painter of the period, Jacques-Louis David (1748–1825). David was caught up in Revolutionary politics, and painted a famous picture of the death of the radical Revolutionary martyr Marat. He was a favorite of Napoleon Bonaparte and painted a huge picture of Napoleon's coronation as emperor, now in the Louvre.

Until the mid-19th century, a certain eclecticism reigned in French art. The quasi-official neoclassical style dictated by the Academy was represented in the painting of Alexandre Cabanel (1823–83) and Jacques-Auguste-Dominique Ingres (1780–1867). At the same time, Gustave Courbet (1819–77), Honoré Daumier (1808–79), and Jean-François Millet (1814–75) represented an avant-garde that fostered realism, with subjects drawn from everyday urban and rural life. The Romantic movement is represented in France by Théodore Géricault (1791–1824) and Eugène Delacroix (1798–1863).

In 1874, a group of young painters led by Claude Monet (1840–1926) and Pierre-Auguste Renoir (1841–1919) held an exhibition separate from the annual Salon of the French Academy, which had previously rejected their work. Their style came to be known as Impressionism, after the title of one of Monet's pictures: *Impression—Sunrise*. Their goal was not primarily to portray the world as it was, but rather as it was filtered through the artist's imagination. They were especially intrigued by the play of light which as it changes alters our perception of reality. Other impressionists included Camille Pissaro (1830–1903), and for a time Edouard Manet (1832–83) and Edgar Dégas (1834–1917). The new style was condemned at first, but by 1880 it had triumphed, and by 1886 it had been superseded.

Georges Seurat (1859–91) employed a pointillist technique in which the paintings consist of tiny dots of pure color which are mixed in the eye of the viewer. Vincent van Gogh (1853–90) settled in France in 1886, bringing with him his bold use of colors and swirling brushstrokes to create an expression of emotion rather than an impression of the external world. Paul Cézanne (1839–1906) was heavily influenced by the Impressionists, but soon struck out on his own in his use of color and form, arriving at a more expressionistic style. Paul Gauguin (1848–1903), whose paintings emphasized lush color and two-dimensional forms, was heavily influenced by Japanese art and by native styles, especially those of Polynesia, where he settled in French Tahiti in 1891. The giant figure in 19th- century sculpture is Auguste Rodin (1840–1917), who dispensed with academic conventions in favor of the representation of inner truths, often through tormented, twisted forms and rough textures.

In the early 20th century, French artists (or artists working in France) continued at the forefront of modern art. One of the avant-garde movements was Fauvism, led by Henri Matisse (1869–1954). (*Fauve* is French for "wild beast.") The Fauvists were distinguished for their bold and arbitrary use of primary colors. Matisse spent the last years of his life in Nice, designing the Chapelle du Rosaire in nearby Vence. Other important Fauvists include Maurice de Vlaminck (1876–1958) and for a time, Georges Braque (1882–1961). Braque subsequently became interested in Cézanne's treatment of shapes, and along with Pablo Picasso (1881–1973) was instrumental in forming the Cubist school. Cubists broke the objects of their paintings into geometric shapes (planes, spheres, cylinders), which were depicted in a limited range of colors. Dadaism

grew out of the despair and hopelessness incurred by the First World War, and was the negation of all accepted social and artistic ideas. Dadaists deliberately sought to shock and bewilder. Surrealism was an artistic movement of the 20s and 30s which portrayed an irrational dream-like fantasy universe, prompted by the artist's subconscious. Important surrealists include Marcel Duchamp (1887–1968), Francis Picabia (1879–1953), and René Magritte (1989–1967).

Since the Second World War, France has continued to be at the forefront of the artistic avant-garde. Abstract art (art with no reference to external world or the objects in it) in all its various manifestations, has coexisted with the modernist movements discussed above, and indeed with older approaches to art as well. Just about all that one can say in summing up is that no one school or approach is dominant. The current artistic scene in France, as elsewhere, is best characterized by a wide-ranging eclecticism, subject only to the whims of the artist and the marketplace.

ARCHITECTURE, CHURCHES, AND ARTISTIC STYLES

Inevitably, many of the sites which a Christian visitor to France will want to see will be churches. Indeed, France is home to many of humankind's most noble efforts to glorify God in stone and glass. It is not unusual, however, for tourists to become confused, both as to the structure of churches (very different from what contemporary North American Christians, especially evangelical Protestants, are accustomed to), and as to artistic style: whether a given church is Romanesque, Gothic, Renaissance, Baroque, or neoclassical. This section is intended to provide a brief description of these elements, in order to increase the enjoyment and understanding of your visit. It is not intended as a technical introduction to architecture, as there are many fine books which provide greater depth and detail than is possible here.

Large churches in France (indeed in Europe as a whole) are generally cruciform in shape; that is, they are shaped like a cross. The longer, or vertical portion of the cross, comprising the nave, is almost always oriented on an east-west axis, with the altar towards the eastern end. Thus, the main entrance to the church is almost always through the western end; as a result, the "front" of most churches is its western facade. The shorter or horizontal portion of the cross is known as the transept.

ROMANESQUE CHURCHES

At first Christians met in private homes, or in structures built for other purposes. In the 4th century when Christianity became the official religion of the Roman Empire, they began to build structures specifically as churches. It was natural for them to adopt the basic Roman style of public building, or basilica, essentially a long, narrow building with rounded-arch windows and round barrel-vaulting. As the Roman Empire in western Europe declined and faded away, this style of building was continued and further elaborated, and is known to us as Romanesque, or "Roman-like." This was the dominant style of churches in France until well after 1000. This includes the Carolingian period (after the Emperor Charlemagne, or Charles the

St. Etienne Cathedral, Nevers (Nièvre)

Interior of a Romanesque Church

Great, c. 800). There are few remaining Carolingian churches in France, such as that at Germigny-des-Prés. Romanesque churches, however, abound.

The picture on page 59 shows a good example of a typical Romanesque church. Note the rounded arches and small windows, few in number. The walls needed to be thick to support the weight of the church, and great height was not possible. The picture on the right shows a typical interior of a Romanesque church. Again, note the rounded arches. The interiors of Romanesque churches tend to be solemn and dark, often invoking a sense of mystery.

GOTHIC

After about the year 1000, European society underwent a significant economic, cultural, and technological transformation. Better materials and more settled conditions allowed builders and architects to experiment with new plans and techniques. Out of this experimentation emerged the style known to us as Gothic. Builders came to understand how to better distribute and support weight through the use of pointed arches, ribbed vaulting, flying buttresses, and other such innovations. As a result, the height of churches was raised, and with better engineering, less weight came to bear on the walls, which meant that windows could be enlarged, allowing magnificent achievements in stained glass (Fr: *vitrail*). France was the home-

land of Gothic architecture, and contains many of the finest examples: St-Denis was the first church to be so constructed, followed in short order by Notre-Dame de Paris, Sens, Chartres, Amiens, and

Interior of a Gothic Church

many others. The picture above shows the nave of a Gothic cathedral.

Compared to a Romanesque nave, a Gothic nave is of much greater height, with its fluted pillars, ribbed vaults, and pointed arches bearing the weight of the structure. As a result, it is much lighter than a Romanesque interior. The general feeling one gets from a Gothic church is of being drawn upwards. There are few more awesome experiences than standing in the midst of a great cathedral, your vision drawn inexorably upwards, bathed in the colored light of stained-glass windows, knowing that for centuries Christians have stood on the same spot and experienced the same sensations while worshiping God.

The picture below shows the facade of a Gothic cathedral in Reims, France. Note the great towers reaching up to heaven, the great rose window, the pointed arches.

The Gothic style predominated for over four centuries, and as one might expect, it underwent some evolution and development. There were also regional variations, such as Norman Gothic and Burgundian Gothic. In general, the major changes came about as builders discovered how to construct churches so that less weight would rest on the walls, and therefore more space could be given to sculpture, carvings, and windows. In Early Gothic churches such as St. Denis, Notre-Dame de Paris, and Sens, the major distinction from Romanesque architecture is the greater height of the nave, made possible by ribbed vaulting and pointed arches. This was elaborated in the 13th century in cathedrals such as those at Chartres, Reims, and Amiens, whose style is often called Lanceolate Gothic, because the windows of the nave were divided vertically into two "lancets" topped by a round opening. In high Gothic style, such as St. Urban's Basilica in Troyes or the Sainte Chapelle in Paris, the supporting function of the walls was reduced further, so that the walls appear to be made of stained glass rather than stone. In the 15th century, the technical developments came to a halt, but churches became ever more elaborately decorated. This is known as Flamboyant Gothic, because much of the ornamentation resembled flames.

RENAISSANCE

In the late 15th and early 16th centuries, Italian Renaissance styles began to creep into France. These represented a move away from the soaring spaces and elaborate ornamentation of Flamboyant Gothic. (In fact, it was the people of

Reims Cathedral

the Renaissance who coined the term "Gothic" to describe this style of art and architecture, because it was the worst word they could think of for a style they found hideously ugly.) Nevertheless, Renaissance style had little impact on church architecture in France, for it overlapped with the last stages of the Gothic. Renaissance style, with its restraint and regularity reflecting the classical influence of Greece and Rome, was important in secular buildings, such as palaces and the townhouses of aristocrats. Francis I (1515–47) rebuilt the Louvre in Renaissance style, as well as the country château of Chambord. There is really nothing in France to compare with the great Renaissance churches of Italy, such as the cathedral or *duomo* in Florence.

BAROQUE AND FRENCH CLASSICISM

In the late 16th and early 17th centuries, a style known as Baroque came to dominate much of European art and architecture, especially in Catholic areas. It is characterized by great drama, emotion, color, and theatricality. It attempts to overawe the senses with grandeur. In part, at least as far as church architecture goes, it was an attempt to appeal to people's sense of drama and emotion, emphasizing the power and grandeur of God, climaxing at the moment when Christ is resacrificed in the Mass. On the exterior, Baroque churches are characterized by great and elaborate ornamentation, often including great domes. Inside, they feature elaborate and colorful decoration, often highly colored in blue, white, or gold, often with twisting columns reaching skyward. If Romanesque churches invoke a sense of mystery, and Gothic churches a sense of airiness and lightness, then Baroque churches invoke a sense of grandeur, drama, and majesty. One only need think of St. Peter's in Rome, the largest and most grandiose Baroque church of all. There are, however, few such Baroque churches in France, when compared to Germany, Austria, Spain, or other Catholic areas of Europe, and these are mostly in Paris. There are several reasons for this. One has to do with France's tradition of Gallicanism, or autonomy in church affairs. In other words, whatever style was popular in Rome would almost by definition be unpopular in France. Moreover, in France, beginning in the 17th century, there was a tradition of centralized artistic control, embodied in different academies, which pronounced on "approved" styles, not only in architecture, but also in painting, sculpture, music, and literature as well. In addition, Baroque was the style adopted by France's great enemies of the day, the rulers of the Habsburg dynasty in Spain and Austria, with whom France was embroiled in bitter warfare for the first half of the 17th century. As a result, French architecture in the 17th century was generally more restrained and classical than many of the frothy Baroque creations evident in Italy, Germany, Austria, or Spain. Elaborate Baroque decoration, however, is evident in many interiors, such as in the royal chapel at Versailles.

ENLIGHTENMENT NEOCLASSICISM

With the movement called the Enlightenment in the 18th century, architectural styles changed once again. With its emphasis on reason and nature, the Enlightenment rejected the excesses of the Baroque, and sought a purer and simpler style, which they found in neoclassicism, or the revival of ancient Greek and Roman styles. This, they believed, was more fitting to a calmly rational age than the exuberance of the Baroque, or the superstitious awe (as they saw it) of the Gothic. This too shows up in church architecture in France, notably in Paris in the church of the Madeleine (St. Mary Magdalene) and of Ste. Geneviève, now known as the Panthéon, both resembling classical pagan temples more than any traditional Christian church. This style was especially attractive to the revolutionaries, who saw themselves as heirs to the virtues of classical Greece and republican Rome.

THE 19TH CENTURY

No single style dominated the 19th century the way that Gothic dominated the High Middle Ages. There was a significant Gothic revival, inspired in great part by the Romantic movement. This was a reaction against the restrained and cold rationality of the Enlightenment, which sought to emphasize feeling and emotion. Unlike Germany, where many Romantics turned to their pagan Teutonic origins (exemplified in the music of Wagner, for example), in France, many Romantics sought a return to the Catholic Middle Ages. Hence the interest in and revival of Gothic art and architecture. It was at this time that many of the great medieval churches, which had been allowed to decay, were saved from destruction and completed and/or restored. The most important figure in this architectural romanticism was Viollet-le-Duc, responsible in great part for the restoration of Notre-Dame de Paris, as well as many other great churches. Another popular style for churches was neo-Byzantine, as seen in the Sacré Cœur in Paris, the Basilique Notre-Dame in Lyon, and Notre-Dame-de-la-Garde in Marseille.

HOW TO ENJOY YOUR VISIT TO A FRENCH CHURCH

Much confusion can stem from the use of unfamiliar names to describe parts of a church; terms such as *nave, chancel, ambulatory,* etc. In order to clarify some of this confusion, below are several illustrations highlighting some of the major features of a church. Keep in mind that not all churches have all these features, and that there are significant variations in region and style.

This is a floor plan based on the Cathedral of Notre-Dame in Chartres, with some of the major features of cathedrals or other large churches indicated. (Note that not all these features appear at Chartres; this is an idealized cathedral used for illustration purposes only.)

First the worshiper entered the church through a doorway with a porch or narthex "A."

Usually above the narthex there is often at least one, sometimes two towers (B; Fr: *tours*). These functioned both as landmarks and watchtowers in isolated villages. Bells were added to call people to worship and warn of danger. They were usually the last part of a church to be built, often not added until centuries after construction was begun.

Beyond the narthex one enters the nave (Fr: *nef*) "C." This is the main body of the church and comes from the Latin word for *ship*. It represents the ship of salvation, Noah's Ark, and the invisible church of Christ to which all saved souls belong and where humans are protected from the storms of life and material temptations. In large churches there

may be more than one nave, and most have aisles (D) which are separated from the nave by pillars. The nave was both a place of worship and a general meeting place. Not until after the Reformation were seats added. Before then everyone had to stand and people often wandered around, even selling food and other goods in winter.

The nave is intersected by the transepts (E), which form the horizontal portion of the cross shape of the church. Where the nave and transepts intersect is the crossing (Fr: *croisée du transept*), typically the site of the altar (F; Fr: *autel*), where the death of Christ is reenacted in the sacrament of the Mass. There are also often various other side altars, in chapels (Fr: *chapelles*) or in the transepts. Until the 10th century, worshipers partook in communion before

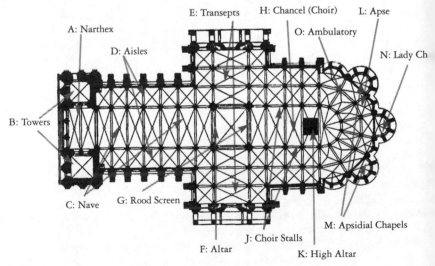

E: Transepts H: Chancel (Choir) L: Apse
A: Narthex O: Ambulatory
D: Aisles N: Lady Ch
B: Towers
C: Nave G: Rood Screen
M: Apsidial Chapels
F: Altar J: Choir Stalls K: High Altar

the altar, where they received both bread and wine. Later they received only bread. Originally this change seems to have come about to prevent drunkenness, but later it gained theological importance, as only priests, or men dedicated to God's service, were allowed to partake communion in both kinds.

Beyond the altar was a rood screen (G; Fr: *jubé*), which prevented ordinary people from entering the chancel or choir. Most of these in France were removed in the course of the 18th century; there are thus very few left—notably in the Cathédrale Ste-Cécile in Albi, in St-Etienne-du-Mont in Paris, and in Ste-Madeleine in Troyes. Behind the rood screen is the chancel or choir (H; Fr: *chœur*) where the choir, which consisted only of men, was located. They sat in choir stalls (J), which are often richly decorated with wood carvings.

Beyond the chancel was the high altar (K; Fr: *grand autel*) where the most solemn Masses were performed. In medieval churches the celebration of the Mass was the central event of the worship service.

The apse (L; Fr: *chevet*) is the rounded east end of the church, behind the chancel. Often it contained small apsidial chapels (M; Fr: *chapelles absidioles*), including the Lady Chapel (N) in churches not dedicated to the Virgin Mary. Many large churches have a walkway leading behind the choir, chancel, and the high altar. This is known as the ambulatory (O; Fr: *déambulatoire*) and was used, particularly in pilgrimage churches, to allow wor-

shipers to file past relics. (The veneration of relics was an important part of medieval piety. Relics were items of clothing and even the bodies or body parts of saints, or particularly sanctified Christians, many of whom were martyrs who had died for their faith. Miracles were often ascribed to relics, causing pilgrims to visit shrines and churches containing relics in search of healing.)

Other features not included in this idealized plan include the following:

The crypt (Fr: *crypte*), usually near or under the altar or even the high altar. Originally crypts were underground chambers where Christians met for worship in secret and buried their dead. Crypts are often the earliest part of a church building.

The vestry (Fr: *sacristie*), a small, and sometimes not so small, room where priests changed from their normal garb into ecclesiastical robes, which were selected on the basis of their color depending on the date according to the season in the church year. In liturgical churches, like the Roman Catholic Church, the Anglicans, or Church of England, and the Lutherans, services follow the traditional Christian year. This begins with Advent four weeks before Christmas. It continues with Lent, through Easter, and returns to a New Year the following Advent. Different colors, used for vestments and for covering the communion table or altar, represent the changing seasons as a visible sign to worshipers that constantly reminds them of an aspect of Christ's life.

Cloisters: to one side of large churches (especially monastery or abbey churches), usually the south side, one finds the cloisters. This is an enclosed rectangle with a high outside wall and roof, often with very beautiful stonework and ceiling vaulting, surrounding an open garden, usually a grassy lawn, that is enclosed by a low wall and pillars. Here monks and other clergy could walk in bad weather reciting the Scriptures or praying.

Chapter house (Fr: *salle capitulaire*): Cathedrals often have a chapter house, which is the meeting place of clergy during synods and other important functions. Here the business of a diocese was discussed.

The treasury (Fr: *trésor*) is where the treasures of the church are kept, including ancient crosses, scriptures and rare books, relics, and vestments. In some churches, the treasury is housed in a separate building, while in others, it adjoins the church itself.

THE FACADE

This is a picture of the west front or facade of Notre-Dame de Paris. Some of the more prominent features mentioned in the text are pointed out.

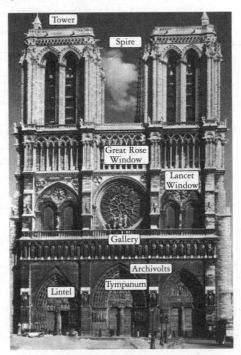

Part 3

CHRISTIAN HERITAGE SITES IN FRANCE

TOP 10 CHRISTIAN SITES IN FRANCE

1. ABBAYE DE FONTENAY: One of the best preserved medieval monasteries in France. A must for anyone interested in monasticism or medieval life in general.

2. MONT-SAINT-MICHEL: Perched atop a rocky outcropping off the Norman coast, the medieval monastery and village of Mont Saint-Michel is, after Paris, the most visited site in France.

3. CHARTRES CATHEDRAL: A masterpiece of Gothic architecture at its height, Chartres Cathedral is notable for its unity of style and its wealth of stained glass. If you can visit only one church during your stay in France, try to make Chartres the one.

4. NOTRE DAME CATHEDRAL: One of the earliest of Gothic cathedrals and an instantly recognizable symbol of Paris and France. The storied history of Notre Dame is a microcosm of Christianity in France: from religious center of a great kingdom, falling into neglect and ruin, pillaged and desecrated during the French Revolution, restored in the 19th century.

5. LES BAUX-DE-PROVENCE: On a rocky Provençal hilltop in a wild setting, the now-deserted village of Les Baux was a strong center of Protestantism before being demolished in the 17th century.

6. CARCASSONNE: A stronghold of the Cathar or Albigensian heresy in the Middle Ages, Carcassonne's walls are the best preserved medieval fortifications anywhere. Just outside the town is the Centre National d'Etudes Cathars (National Center for Cathar Studies).

7. ABBAYE DE TAIZÉ (Abbaye de Cluny—vicinity): One of the few Protestant monasteries anywhere in the world, Taizé stands as a monument to the power of the reconciling spirit of Christ. Begun as a refuge for Jews during the Second World War, the community is now an interdenominational and international community devoted to worship and prayer.

8. LE PUY-EN-VELAY: In a stunning physical setting high on a plateau, amid volcanic spires, the churches of Le Puy with their Romanesque and Byzantine style seem to transport us into a different world.

9. ABBAYE DE ST-BENOÎT-SUR-LOIRE: Like Notre-Dame, the Abbey of St-Benoît-sur-Loire presents a microcosm of the history of Christianity in France. The abbey church is one of the finest Romanesque churches anywhere. There is also the nearby Carolingian church at Germigny-des-Prés, with its stunning Byzantine ceiling mosaic.

10. CHÂTEAU DE VERSAILLES: The largest royal palace in Europe, the grounds and buildings are a testament to the cult of absolute monarchy, Louis XIV's desire to overawe his subjects into obedience, and to the very close relationship between the monarchy and the church.

KEY TO THE TEXTS

All entries in the Christian Travelers Guides are written according to the following outline.

PLACE NAMES: The name of each place is given in alphabetical order. Places are listed according to the local spelling, followed by the English spelling if needed, e.g., Marseille (Marseilles). The French practice has been followed in which, with place names including an article ("la," "le," or "les"), the article is ignored. Thus La Rochelle is listed under R, Le Puy-en-Velay under P, and so on. Places named after saints (e.g., St-Benoît-sur-Loire) are listed as if "saint" were spelled out.

BACKGROUND: The first few paragraphs in each entry provide a short history of the area explaining its religious, cultural, and intellectual significance.

PLACES TO VISIT: Individual sites are mentioned with recommendations about things that deserve close attention. Specific sites, such as churches or museums, are indicated in **BOLD PRINT**.

SPELLING AND DATES: In most cases, the French name and spelling of a particular person, place, or thing is used, followed by the English name in parentheses: Musée d'art chrétien (Museum of Christian Art). Rulers of France are referred to by the English version of their names; thus, Philip the Fair rather than Philippe le Bel. Most dates are A.D. and are given as a plain number, e.g., 800; only when there might be some doubt about the exact date are B.C. or A.D. used. Unless otherwise indicated, dates given for kings, popes, presidents, etc., are for their reigns or period in office rather than their life.

MAP OF KEY CHRISTIAN
HERITAGE SITES IN FRANCE

ENGLISH CHANNEL

BELGIUM

LUXEMBOURG

GERMANY

ATLANTIC OCEAN

SWITZERLAND

ITALY

SPAIN

MEDITERRANEAN SEA

Aire-sur-la-Lys
Douai
Amiens
Noyon • Laon
Rouen • Compiègne • Reims
Caen • Lisieux
Verdun • Metz
PARIS • Meaux • Châlons-en-Ch.
St-Thégonnec
Mont-Saint-Michel • Pontmain
Versailles • Wassy
Chartres • Fontainebleau • Domrémy • Rothau • Strasbourg
Troyes • Kaysersberg • Sélestat • Colmar
Sens • Abbaye de Clairvaux
Sablé-sur-Sarthe • Pontigny
Orléans • Auxerre • Abbaye de Fontenay • Ronchamp
Angers • Amboise • St-Benoît-sur-Loire • Dijon
Tours • Vézelay • Abbaye de Cîteaux
Chinon • Bourges • Beaune
Issoudun • Autun
Nevers
Poitiers
Abbaye de Cluny
La Rochelle
Royan • Oradour-sur-Glane
Marlieux • Annecy
Clermont-Ferrand • Lyon • Aix-les-Bains
St-Pierre-de-Chartreuse
Le Puy-en-Velay • Le Chambon-sur-Lignon
La Salette • St-Véran
Conques
Cahors
Montauban • Albi
Gaillac • Castres • St-Guilhem-le-Désert • Carpentras
Toulouse • Dourgne • Anduze • Avignon
Montpellier • Les Baux • Nice • Les Îles de Lérins
Pau • Arles • Aix-en-Provence
Bétharram • Carcassonne • Marseille
Lourdes • Ch. de Montségur
Ajaccio

AIRE-SUR-LA-LYS

ire-sur-la-Lys is a well-con-
served 17th- and 18th-century
town on the banks of the Lys. In
the GRANDE PLACE (1724) is the HOTÊL
DU BAILLAGE (16th century). There are
also many old town houses as well as a
Gothic church renovated in the 18th
century containing 16th-century frescoes
and 17th-century sculptures, though the
organ and apse were gravely damaged
during bombardments in 1944.

Aire-sur-la-Lys is best known as the
site of a famous pilgrimage to the statue
of Mary named NOTRE DAME PANETIÈRE
(Holy Mother of Bread). This curious
title was given to the statue when the
neighboring village of Thérouanne was
delivered from a famine. When
Thérouanne fell into ruin, the statue was
transferred to Aire. In 1641, Aire was
under siege and the people put the keys
to the town in the hands of the statue and
prayed for deliverance: the town was
indeed delivered. Aire was also spared the
ravages of the plague and again in 1849
the terrible outbreak of cholera. On
August 15 a considerable pilgrimage to
the statue takes place.

AIX-EN-PROVENCE

ix-en-Provence was founded by
the Roman general Sextius in
122 B.C. in order to protect the
Greek cities of the Mediterranean coast
from the barbarian tribes to the north.
He set up his camp near some thermal
springs, giving the city its name—
Aquae Sextiae, or the Waters of Sextius.
Twenty years later, when another barbarian tribe threatened to invade northern Italy through Provence, they were
stopped by the Roman general Marius
at Mont Ste-Victoire, just east of Aix.
Destroyed again by the invading Lombards in A.D. 574 and yet again by
marauding Saracens or Muslim Arabs in
A.D. 731, the city's fortunes revived in
the 12th century when the counts of
Provence made it their official residence.
For the rest of the Middle Ages, Aix
remained the center of intellectual and
cultural life in Provence, including a
university founded in 1413. Foremost
among the rulers of Aix was René, count
of Provence (1409–80), duke of Anjou,
Lorraine, Bar, and king of Naples. A
patron of artists and scholars, he established a brilliant court in Aix. When he
died, the county of Provence, and hence
the city of Aix, was incorporated into
the kingdom of France. The city was
largely rebuilt during the 17th century,
as magistrates in the *parlement* or
regional supreme court built themselves

luxurious town houses to go along with their country estates. The centerpiece of this urban planning was the Cours Mirabeau, a tree-lined boulevard named after the famous revolutionary. In the 19th century, Aix was home to the novelist Emile Zola and the Impressionist painter Paul Cézanne. Today, Aix remains an elegant alternative to the hustle and bustle of nearby Marseille, especially Vieil Aix (Old Aix), the area around the Cours Mirabeau. Aix is also a strong center for the Reformed church with a Reformed seminary and two lively Reformed churches.

PLACES TO VISIT

Aix's main point of interest is the CATHÉDRALE ST. SAUVEUR (Cathedral of the Holy Savior), which displays elements of all architectural styles from the 4th to the 16th century. The baptistery

FAMOUS NATIVE SONS OF AIX-EN-PROVENCE

EMILE ZOLA (1840–1902) was the preeminent French novelist of the later 19th century. In reaction against the Romantics, Zola founded a literary school which he called "naturalism." This meant that human life, activity, and attitudes were heavily influenced by their surroundings, including environment and heredity. He explores these issues in a series of 20 novels following the fortunes of the Rougon-Macquart family, the most famous of which is Germinal, which deals with the dark and depressing lives of coal miners. Zola was a leading supporter of Alfred Dreyfus in the divisive Dreyfus affair. In 1898 he wrote an open letter entitled J'accuse (I accuse) in a Parisian newspaper, condemning the conduct of the government, the Catholic Church, and the army. Zola was convicted of libel and imprisoned, before he escaped and went into a brief exile in England.

PAUL CÉZANNE (1839–1906) is often called the father of modern art, in that he attempted to combine naturalistic representation, personal vision, and abstract order. He was highly influential on later artists, including Henri Matisse (1869–1954), who admired his use of color, and on Pablo Picasso (1881–1973), who developed Cézanne's use of shapes into Cubism. A boyhood friend of Emile Zola, Cézanne later broke off relations with the author over a perceived slight in one of his novels. For a time, Cézanne was part of the Impressionist group, but gradually drifted away, arriving at an idiosyncratic use of color and representation of volume. Largely ignored and socially isolated for much of his career, in later life he was acknowledged as a legendary figure by a new generation of artists.

dates from Merovingian times (5th century) and was constructed from material salvaged from temples to Roman gods. The double nave displays Romanesque and Gothic styles side-by-side. In the nave as well is the cathedral's major artistic treasure, the *Tryptique du Buisson Ardent* (Triptych of the Burning Bush), which depicts King René and his wife Queen Joan kneeling in a scene with the Virgin Mary and Christ Child, along with the burning bush of Moses. This work was commissioned by King René in 1475 and painted by Jean Froment. It is illustrative both of René's patronage of the arts, and of the custom, seen everywhere in medieval cathedrals, of donors having themselves memorialized in the works they commissioned. The triptych is on display Tuesdays only between 3:00 and 4:00 P.M. when a guide explains the symbolism and hidden meaning. Next door to the cathedral is the tranquil Romanesque cloister.

AIX-LES-BAINS

Aix-les-Bains is a world-famous thermal spa and health resort and an international tourist center due to its picturesque location in the French Alps.

PLACES TO VISIT

One can take an alpine train up Mt. Revard giving a splendid view over the Alps (Mont Blanc) as well as the Jura mountain range. The THERMES NATIONAUX (National Spas) were constructed in 1860 and then in 1930–33, and they also contain the remains of Roman baths. Behind the Thermes, one can visit vast underground caves. The town also boasts the MUSÉE FAURE, which is home to a number of interesting 19th- and 20th-century paintings, notably works of Corot, Degas, Cézanne, Pissaro, and Sisley.

Nearby, you may visit ABBAYE DE HAUTECOMBE, which was founded in 1125 by St. Bernard, rebuilt in the 16th century, and completely renovated between 1821 and 1831. The abbey served as a burial place for the princes of Savoy, and 43 still repose there. Hautecombe has been an active monastery for over 870 years, except for a brief persecution during the Revolution. Benedictine monks replaced the Cistercians in 1922, and their Gregorian chants attract many visitors. The church itself can be visited with a guide, and one can admire the paintings, engravings, inscriptions, and richly ornamental nave.

AJACCIO

Surrounded by receding folds of rounded tree-covered hills and under the shadow of the rocky summit (snow covered in winter) of Mount Oro, Ajaccio sparkles with natural beauty as does the entire island of Corsica. As well as for its stunning natural beauty and ongoing struggle with Corsican nationalists, Corsica, and more precisely Ajaccio, is best known as the birthplace of undoubtedly the most famous figure in French history, Napoleon Bonaparte. Honored by most French people, perceived with awe by many Americans, he is remembered with hatred and scorn by England and the greater part of Western and Eastern Europe. He may have been an extremely talented military general, but he must be thought of with Hitler, as a terrible testimony to the way in which one individual's pride and lust for power can bring misery and destruction to so many others. Hundreds of thousands of European and French soldiers died in the Napoleonic wars between 1805 and 1815.

Napoleon was born on August 15, 1769, and entered military school at age ten. In 1793, he joined the French revolutionary army and, having shown great promise for planning and leadership, was given command of the French forces fighting the Austrians and Sardinians in 1796. He won a series of decisive victories, then led an expedition to Egypt, where France hoped to establish a base for striking at British troops in Africa and India. The mission was a military failure and cost the lives of thousands of Arab and French soldiers, not only to battle but also to an outbreak of bubonic plague. Antoine-Jean Gros's 1804 painting, *Napoleon in the Pesthouse at Jaffa* (Louvre), shows Napoleon touching the sores of a French soldier inflicted with the plague. The image of Napoleon reaching out with pity to the sick man is a direct allusion to Christ's healing powers as well as to the traditional belief in the divine touch of kings. By suggesting that the horrible means of war are justified by the noble ends of Napoleonic mercy and courage, the painting is thus an incredible example of the myth of nobility and heroism that was created around Napoleon even during his lifetime. In reality, the scene portrayed by Gros is completely fictitious. The truth is that Napoleon ordered the shooting of hundreds of prisoners whom he could not afford to house or feed.

One positive thing to come out of Napoleon's expedition to Egypt was the discovery, by French engineers, of the Rosetta stone that made it possible to read Egyptian hieroglyphics.

When Napoleon returned from Egypt in November 1799, he staged a coup d'état and made himself First Consul for life in the new republic. Despite retaining some of the reforms won by the revolution, and most notably bringing back religious tolerance for both Catholics and Protestants (all Christians had been severely persecuted in the years following the Revolution), Napoleon was not content to rule France; he must rule Europe as well. He proclaimed, and indeed crowned himself emperor in 1804 (celebrated in David's famous painting, *The Coronation of Napoleon*), and then went on to attempt to conquer Europe. After eight years of war, he was finally defeated at the battle of Leipzig in 1813 by the Allied forces of Prussia, Russia, Austria, and Sweden. Forced to abdicate, he was exiled to the island of Elba. In 1815, he managed to escape from Elba and regain power briefly during a second coup d'état known as the Hundred Days. He was defeated once and for all at the battle of Waterloo in June 1815 and this time exiled to St. Helena island, where he died in captivity six years later on May 5, 1821.

PLACES TO VISIT

MAISON BONAPARTE: Napoleon's birthplace and interesting Genoese-style house.

MUSÉE FESCH: Houses the most significant collection of Italian paintings besides the Louvre, including paintings by Titian, Botticelli *(Virgin with Garland),* and Bellini *(Mary with the Infant Jesus).*

PLACE MARÉCHAL-FOCH: Contains a marble statue by the sculptor Laborer of Napoleon as First Consul.

PLACE CHARLES DE GAULLE: Focal point of animation in the town and dominated by an equestrian statue (Byre, 1865) of Napoleon as emperor, surrounded by his four brothers.

VICINITY

PANORAMA OF AJACCIO: Follow the D11 past the Highland Hotel to have a tremendous view of the city with sea on one side and mountains on the other.

CHÂTEAU DE LA PUNTA: 13 kilometers N/NW. Built between 1868 and 1896 with materials recovered from the Tuileries (Louvre) fire of 1871. Paintings and furnishing d'époque to be viewed as well as another magnificent view of Ajaccio. If one follows the road up to the Pointe Pozzo di Borgo, the view is yet more extraordinary.

ALBI

S ituated on the banks of the River Tarn, and built in large part from pinkish brick made from the river's clay, Albi was in the 13th century one of the centers of the Cathar heresy. Although other towns were more important, Albi nonetheless became synonymous with the heresy, also known as the Albigensian heresy. In the early 13th century, the "Albigensian Crusade" was declared. The kings of France took advantage of the disorders to gain a foothold in Languedoc. Invading armies slaughtered heretics at Beziers, Carcassone, Minerve, and Lavaur. Although the area was purified by 1229, the Cathar heresy was not definitively stamped out until the Chateau de Montségur was conquered and its defenders burnt at the stake in 1244. The Albigensian Crusade stands out as one of the most violent episodes of the Middle Ages and of one of the vicious repressions of religious dissent. Though repugnant to us, it demonstrates the inextricable relationship of religion and politics in the Middle Ages, and the dangers of using force in matters of conscience. Albi's other major claim to fame is as the birthplace of Henri de Toulouse-Lautrec, the 19th-century painter of Parisian nightlife.

PLACES TO VISIT

Construction of the CATHÉDRALE STE-CÉCILE was begun in 1282 in the aftermath of the Albigensian Crusade as testimony to the might of the Church, which explains its fortresslike appearance. On the inside, it is elaborately decorated, most notably in an elaborately carved rood screen (*jubé*), one of the few to have survived. The rood screen shut the clergy off from the laypeople, graphically demonstrating the late medieval distinction between the clerical and lay worlds, and the clergy's separate and superior status as the custodians of the sacraments and as intermediaries between God and humanity. Besides the rood screen, on the west wall there is an elaborate 15th-century fresco depicting the Last Judgment and the ghastly punishments awaiting the damned. Unfortunately, the mural was partly disfigured during the installation of the great organ in the 17th century. Like other medieval depictions of the Last Judgment, this is an effort to reach a largely illiterate laity with the message of salvation. Once again, this demonstrates one of the central tenets of late medieval religion: that in order to attain salvation, people had to cooperate with God's grace in the form of good works and renunciation of sin. Depiction of the horrors of hell and the delights of heaven was seen as one of the most effective methods of achieving this.

HENRI DE TOULOUSE-LAUTREC (1864–1901). Born in Albi, Toulouse-Lautrec observed, participated in, and documented with great psychological insight the personalities and facets of Parisian night life and entertainment in the late 1800s. He was one of the first artists to display his work on posters, and his extreme simplicity in outline and movement and use of large color areas are premonitions of 1950s American pop art.

Next to the cathedral is the 13th-century PALAIS DE LA BERBIE, originally the bishops' palace. Like the cathedral it was constructed at least in part as fortress both to impress the locals with the Church's might and to provide a refuge if needed. Today it houses the MUSÉE TOULOUSE-LAUTREC (Toulouse-Lautrec Museum), containing the most important single collection of the painter's work, showing the seedy underside of 19th-century Parisian nightlife. The museum also contains a number of rooms dedicated to contemporary art: sculptures by Rodin, Maillol, and Drivier, paintings by Matisse, Sérusier, and Vlaminck.

VICINITY

NOTRE DAME DE LA DRÈCHE: five kilometers to the north on the D90, this church was built in 1863 in a style inspired by the CATHEDRAL ST. CÉCILE to replace a 13th-century edifice that had become insufficient due to the large numbers of pilgrims coming to pay homage to the statue of the Madonna, Notre Dame de la Drèche (Holy Mother of Light). In 1630 and then again in 1710, Albi was delivered from the plague after solemn prayers were offered in the name of the Madonna. For over a century, the pilgrimage has been taken up by the Franciscan order of the nearby convent.

AMBOISE

S ituated on the picturesque banks of the Loire River, Amboise is in the heart of the Loire valley château country and was strategically important because of an early bridge across the Loire and the presence of a commanding bluff. Clovis and the Visigothic king Alaric met here in A.D. 503. In the 15th and early 16th centuries, the kings of France largely governed the kingdom from a series of châteaux in the Loire valley, including the one at Amboise. This practice had the advantages of displaying the king and court to large numbers of his subjects, intimidating potentially rebellious nobles, and easing the provision of the royal court—it was easier to move the

court to the provisions than it was to move the provisions to the court. In addition, the Loire valley provided easy access to Paris, the largest city in the kingdom and its administrative heart, while still providing a luxurious backdrop to court life and easy access to the favorite sport of kings and courtiers—hunting in the surrounding fields and woods. Amboise figures in the Christian history of France primarily as the site of one of the key events which led to the Wars of Religion. In 1560, while the king and court were residing at nearby Blois, a group of 1,500 Protestant noblemen plotted to capture King Francis II (1559–60) and "liberate" him from his advisors, the staunchly Catholic

A

Guise family, led by the duke of Guise and his brother the cardinal of Lorraine. Moreover, the king, a sickly teenager, was married to Marie Stuart, daughter of a Guise princess and Queen of Scotland, better known no doubt as Mary Queen of Scots. Forewarned of the plot (the "Conspiracy" or "Tumult of Amboise"), the court took refuge in the château at Amboise. The plot was defeated, the conspirators were executed, and France began its downward spiral into a 35-year period of religious and civil war.

PLACES TO VISIT

The main attraction of Amboise, besides its setting below a bluff along the Loire River and its charming cobbled streets, is the CHÂTEAU, or what remains of it. The site of the château has been fortified since Gallo-Roman times. It was, however, in the 15th century that Amboise came into its own. King Charles VIII was born here in 1470, and he continued the construction begun by his father, Louis XI (1461–83). After his invasion of Italy in 1494, Charles returned to Amboise in 1496, where he died two years later after hitting his head on a door lintel (despite the fact that he was under five feet tall!) while in a hurry

to go see a tennis match. In the 17th century, and periodically thereafter, the château served as a prison. Most of it was torn down following the French Revolution, leaving primarily the TOUR DES MINIMES, LE BALCON DES CONJURÉS (the Plotters' Balcony), and the CHAPELLE ST. HUBERT. The circular Tour des Minimes was the original entrance to the château, leading from the town below up to the château itself, with its panoramic views of the town, the Loire, and surrounding countryside. Rather than a staircase, inside the tower is a circular sloping ramp which provided access to the château for horse-drawn wagons. The gallery overlooking the river known as the Plotters' Balcony gained its name during the events of 1560 when its iron balustrade served as a convenient gallows from which to hang approximately 1,200 of the conspirators. The CHAPELLE ST. HUBERT, named for the patron saint of huntsmen, lies across the garden, though in the 15th century it would have been connected to the château. Notable here is a fine example of Late Gothic or flamboyant Gothic architecture, are a stone carving above the door which depicts the conversion of St. Hubert, and above the carving the kneeling figures of Charles VIII and his wife

CLOVIS. King of the Barbarian tribe of Franks, 481–511. Converted to Roman Christianity c. 496, was baptized at Reims by St. Rémi, and is thus reckoned as the first Christian king of France.

Anne of Brittany. As a further testimony to the royal love of hunting, bronze antlers decorate the chapel's spire.

Also notable in Amboise is the manor house of CLOS LUCÉ, a short walk from the château. It was here that the great Italian artist, engineer, and inventor Leonardo da Vinci spent his last years, dying in 1519, having been lured to France by King Francis I (1515–74).

AMIENS

I n the mid-4th century, near the Roman settlement which would grow into the city of Amiens, a young Roman soldier took pity on a beggar freezing in the icy wind. Taking his sword, he cut his cloak in half and shared it with the unfortunate man. Later ordained as a priest, the former soldier later became bishop of Tours, and was canonized as St. Martin. Other than Christ himself, St. Martin was probably the most important religious figure in early medieval France. The city of Amiens itself became self-governing in the 12th century, and as the chief city of the surrounding province of Picardy, became an important economic center, renowned especially for its textile industries. After the death of Charles the Bold, duke of Burgundy (who ruled not only Burgundy but also Picardy and the neighboring Netherlands) in 1477, the province and the city were incorporated into the kingdom of France.

PLACES TO VISIT

Having suffered a great deal of damage during both World Wars and having been rebuilt largely in a sterile modern manner, there is really only one reason for visiting Amiens today: the CATHÉDRALE NOTRE-DAME. The largest church in France (the nave is 469 feet long and 140 feet high), it is a supreme example of Gothic architecture. Though it lacks the stained glass of Notre-Dame de Paris and Chartres, and the statuary of Reims, it nevertheless makes up for it in its impressive unity of style. Designed by Robert de Luzarches, it was begun in 1220 and substantially completed in 1269, an amazingly short period of time, as medieval cathedral construction goes. The only significant later addition was the spire, which was completed in 1533. Thus, it was able to escape later architectural styles which were incorporated into cathedrals which took longer to erect. On the outside note especially the west facade with its uneven towers, rose window, and the profusion of carvings around and above the three portals. The interior, by contrast, is impressive in its purity and simplicity, imparting a sense of light and calm. According to the 19th-century critic and writer Ruskin, the apse was "not only the best, but the very first thing done perfectly in its manner by northern Christendom." The 16th-century choir stalls are masterpieces of oak carving, showing more than 3000 scenes from the Bible and contemporary life (available by guided tour only). Likewise, on the right side of the choir screen, note the carved stone panels depicting the life of St. Firmin, the first bishop of Amiens. The cathedral treasury contains numerous silver and gold religious artifacts, as well as portions of what it is alleged to be John the Baptist's skull. Medieval Christians were very taken with the physical artifacts of Christ and the saints, from pieces of the cross to his crown of thorns, including physical remains, such as bones and hair. It was believed, not unreasonably in a largely illiterate age, that such physical reminders of the lives and sufferings of Christ and the saints would induce Christians to imitate them. In fact, many medieval churches and cathedrals were built precisely to house such relics.

After visiting the cathedral, you may wish to explore the Quartier St. Leu, just north of the cathedral. The atmosphere and architecture bear witness to Amiens' Flemish heritage, with its restored cottages and network of canals.

ANDUZE

One of the strongly Protestant towns of southern France, Anduze was a stronghold of the Huguenot revolt in the surrounding area of the Cévennes, known as the revolt of the Camisards, following the revocation of the Edict of Nantes.

PLACES TO VISIT

Anduze is home to the MUSÉE DU DÉSERT (Museum of the Protestant Struggle—they compared their trials to the wandering of the children of Israel in the desert), housed in the MAS SOUBEYRAN, or farmhouse of Pierre Laporte (also known as Rolland, 1675–1704), one of the leaders of the revolt. Every year on the first Sunday of September, a reunion which attracts Protestants from all over Europe is held here. In the afternoon, the events of the Camisard struggle are commemorated.

CAMISARD(S) is the name given to the revolt of French Protestants or Huguenots in the mountainous area of the Cévennes in south-central France in the aftermath of the revocation of the Edict of Nantes (1685). The revolt lasted from 1701–10 and required an army to repress, an army which was badly needed against France's foreign enemies in the War of Spanish Succession (1702–14).

ANGERS

Situated on the banks of the River Maine just five miles before its confluence with the Loire, Angers was, in the 12th century, capital of one of the most powerful rulers in Europe. In 1129, the count of Anjou, Geoffrey Plantagenet, married Mathilda, granddaughter of William the Conqueror, duke of Normandy and king of England. Geoffrey and Mathilda's son, Henry Plantagenet or Henry II of England, thus became ruler not only of England, but of Normandy, Anjou, Maine, and Touraine. Henry himself later married Eleanor of Aquitaine, the divorced wife of King Louis VII of France. The kings of England thus ruled a European empire which stretched from the English Channel to the Pyrenees. By comparison, the territories of the French kings to the east seemed insignificant, and Paris a mere overgrown village compared to Angers. By the early 13th century, most of this empire had been conquered by King Philip II (Philip Augustus) of France. Angers and the surrounding province of Anjou were in the possession of King René, also count of Provence and king of Naples. In 1471, the territory was incorporated into the kingdom of France.

PLACES TO VISIT

Angers's most notable sight is its CHÂTEAU, a masterpiece of medieval military architecture. It was built on the orders of King Louis XI (St. Louis) between 1228 and 1238 to prevent aggression by the neighboring duke of Brittany to the west. Connecting its 17 squat gray towers, one can stroll along the 3000-foot-long RAMPARTS, and climb the TOUR DU MOULIN for views of the town and the Cathédrale St. Maurice. Within the château walls are elegant gardens, but more importantly the TEINTURE DE L'APOCALYPSE (Apocalypse Tapestry). Created between 1375 and 1380, it was allowed to deteriorate, and in the 1840s was sold as a covering for transport wagons. The bishop of Angers rescued it, and it was restored in 1996. It is 16 feet high and was originally 550 feet long, of which about 330 feet remain. It depicts 70 scenes from the book of Revelation. You may want to bring your Bible, since while the biblical passages are given in French, the English "translation" is more of an explanation than a quotation. Its hallucinatory quality and horrific descriptions (including a seven-headed Satan and depictions of plagues) bear eloquent testimony to the apocalyptic expectations of the 14th-century mind, tortured as it was by the Black Death, religious schism, economic catastrophe, social dislocation, and endemic warfare.

The CATHÉDRALE ST. MAURICE, a Gothic structure built in the 12th and

13th centuries, is notable for its characteristic Angevin vaulting in the nave. This is a transitional stage between the round vaulting characteristic of the Romanesque style and the pointed arches of the Gothic. There is also a good deal of original stained glass (unusual considering the fragility of the material), including one showing the martyred St. Thomas à Becket, made shortly after his death in 1170. The rose window in the transept dates from the 15th century.

Across the river, in the district of Le Doutre, is the HÔPITAL ST. JEAN (St. John's Hospital). Founded by Henry Plantagenet in 1174, it was a hospital in the medieval sense rather than the modern one, and was used as a hospital until the 19th century. In the Middle Ages, a hospital was a refuge for the poor and sick, who had nowhere else to go, a place to die, rather than a place to be healed. They were often founded by a wealthy patron (such as Henry Plantagenet, or Nicolas Rolin, the chancellor of the duke of Burgundy who founded the famous hospices in Beaune in the 15th century), not only to succor the poor and sick, but also to assist in the patron's own salvation, since according to Catholic theology humans had to assist God's grace in attaining their salvation in the form of good works such as charitable acts like founding a hospital. Architecturally, the hospital shows the same characteristic Angevin vaulting as the cathedral, but its major interest lies in the fact that it now houses the MUSÉE JEAN LURÇAT (Jean Lurçat Museum). Named for Jean Lurçat (1892–1966), who discovered the Teinture de l'Apocalypse in 1938 and was inspired by it to take up the art of tapestry himself, the museum houses his modern response to the 14th-century work, *Le Chant du Monde* (Song of the World), which displays the contradictions of modern life.

ANNECY

Annecy is one of France's most popular resort towns, and it's not hard to see why. Situated in the French Alps, at the northern end of what is reputed to be the cleanest lake in Europe, Annecy, especially the *vieille ville* (old town), is often referred to as the "Venice of the Alps." An intriguing maze of narrow cobblestone streets, canals, flower-bedecked bridges, and brightly painted houses, Annecy seems more like a modern imitation of a fairytale village than a real town. It nevertheless holds interest for the Christian traveler on several points. It became the capital city of the counts of Geneva in the 10th century. The territory of the counts was absorbed into the duchy of

Savoy in the 15th century. Savoy was an independent state which straddled the Alps between Italy and France. Among the dukes' other possessions was the city of Geneva. When, under the influence of John Calvin, Geneva adopted the Reformation and broke away from the Roman Catholic Church in the 1530s, it also declared its independence from the duke of Savoy. Annecy was thus significant as both a political and religious counterweight to the Protestant and independent Geneva. In the 17th century, Annecy was the residence of St. François de Sales (1567–1622), one of the significant leaders in France of the Catholic religious revival known as the Counter-Reformation. In the 18th century, Annecy was notable for quite another reason, when it became the residence of a 16-year-old orphan from Geneva named Jean-Jacques Rousseau (1712–78). The teenager took up residence with the 28-year-old Madame de Warens, and the two soon became lovers. Rousseau, of course, would later go on to play a crucial role in both the secular and rational movement of the Enlightenment and in the formation of the Romantic movement, both of which questioned or rejected essential elements of Christianity.

PLACES TO VISIT

Annecy's major attractions are its natural beauty and its fairy-tale atmosphere, but there are several specific sights worth mentioning. THE PALAIS DE L'ISLE (Island Palace) is a small castle on an island in the river Thiou. Built in the 12th century, it has been at different times a mint, law-courts, a council chamber, and a prison. It now houses a small museum of the history of Annecy. Overlooking the old town is the CHÂTEAU of the counts of Geneva, first built in the 11th century, but extensively altered in subsequent centuries. The church of ST. FRANÇOIS contains the tombs of St. François de Sales and St. Jeanne de Chantal. The CATHEDRAL is an unexceptional 16th-century Gothic structure, in which Rousseau was once a chorister. The church of ST. MAURICE is interesting for its recently discovered 15th-century frescoes.

ST. FRANÇOIS DE SALES (1567–1622). Created bishop of Geneva in 1602, together with his friend St. Jeanne de Chantal, he founded at Annecy the Order of the Visitation, which emphasized teaching and caring for the sick. His *Introduction to the Devout Life* (1607) is a classic of Counter-Reformation Catholic spirituality.

JEAN-JACQUES ROUSSEAU (1712–78) was born in Geneva and orphaned at an early age. Shunted from relative to relative, he was largely self-educated and remained self-conscious about his humble origins. As a young man, he found his way to Paris, the center of the Enlightenment, where he became acquainted with many *philosophes*, including the eminent Voltaire. After a time, however, he came to distrust the Enlightenment's emphasis on human rationality. He came to believe that civilization corrupted humankind from a naturally good state. Among his many influential works were *The Discourse on the Origins of Inequality, The Social Contract* (his major political work), and his autobiographical *Confessions*. In his own day, he was best known for two of his later works: *Emile*, a novel which had as its focus the education of a young boy and grappled with the question of how to educate the young without corrupting them; and *Julie, or the New Heloïse*, a sentimental novel which emphasized the importance of pure and unreflective emotion over premeditated rational thought. Rousseau's political works were influential once the French Revolution had broken out, but cannot be said to have brought it about. He was also important as a progenitor of the Romantic movement in art and literature, with his adoration of nature, and his emphasis on the importance of feeling and emotion in contrast to the Enlightenment's emphasis on cold reason.

ARLES

Strategically situated on the banks of the River Rhône where it splits into two branches before entering the marshland of the Camargue to the south, Arles vies with Nîmes for the title "Rome of France." The site of an important Celtic settlement, Arles was taken over by Greek colonists in the 6th century B.C. Later, the city became an important post for Roman expansion into Gaul. Following his victory over the barbarian Teutons, the Roman general Marius used the captured tribesmen to dig a canal from Arles to the Mediterranean (closer to the city then than it is now), making Arles a Roman seaport of great importance in communication with Roman possessions in Spain. In 49 B.C., Julius Caesar built in Arles the fleet he used to conquer Marseille. As the network of Roman roads in Gaul expanded, Arles became an important crossroads and the capital of Roman Gaul. Emperor Constantine built a palace here, and in 314 held the first council of Christian bishops in Arles. As the Roman Empire crumbled, however, Arles lost much of its importance, and was isolated by the Camargue and the Rhône, an isolation which allowed the city to preserve much of its Roman heritage. In the 9th century, it became the capital of the kingdom of Arles, which included Burgundy and part of Provence. It was later incorporated into the Holy Roman Empire and then in the 13th century into the county of Provence, which in turn became part of the kingdom of France in 1482. In the 19th century, Arles was home to the Dutch painter Vincent van Gogh, who immortalized many of its scenes in his paintings.

PLACES TO VISIT

The most impressive legacy of the Roman heritage in Arles is without doubt the ARÈNES (Arena or Amphitheatre). Built around A.D. 75, it seated more than 20,000 spectators (and still does), was originally used for gladiator contests, and is now still used for bullfights and concerts. The seating area consists of two tiers, each composed of 60 arches. The floor is 150 yards long and as wide as a football field. As the Roman Empire crumbled in the 5th and 6th centuries, the Arènes was converted into a fortress, eventually with about 200 dwellings and a church inside it. Four defense towers (of which three still remain) were added in the 12th century.

Arles also was the site of an important ROMAN THEATRE (constructed in the 1st century B.C.), which may at one time have seated as many as 7000 people. Only a few tiers of seats remain. Of the stage, all that still stands are two tall pillars, which nevertheless give an indication of the size of the original structure.

All that remains of the PALAIS CONSTANTIN (Palace of Constantine), rebuilt in the 4th century A.D., are LES THERMES DE TROUILLE (the Trouille Baths), the largest Roman baths in Provence.

The MUSÉE D'ART CHRÉTIEN (Museum of Christian Art) is housed below a 17th-century Jesuit chapel, in a cellar known as the CRYPTOPORTICUS. Originally excavated as a foundation for the Roman forum above in the 1st century B.C., it is vast—295 feet long and

CONSTANTINE, Roman Emperor (306–37), defeated the last of his rivals in 312, whereupon he converted to Christianity. Under Constantine, Christianity went from being a proscribed and persecuted religion to being a permitted and officially favored religion. Under one of his successors, Theodosius (378–95), Christianity became the official and only legal religion of the Roman Empire.

197 feet wide—and was likely used as a granary. It was discovered when the chapel was built, but not excavated until the 20th century. The museum now houses an impressive collection of early Christian sarcophagi, some dating from the 4th century A.D., testimony to the early spread of Christianity in the area.

The CATHÉDRALE ST. TROPHIME was originally built in the Carolingian period (traces still survive in the lower part of the facade), but was substantially altered beginning in the 11th century. The church itself is dedicated to St. Trophime, a Greek who according to legend was sent by St. Peter to evangelize Provence, and who became the first bishop of Arles. In A.D. 597 St. Augustine (not the famous theologian and philosopher, who died in 430) was consecrated as the first archbishop of Canterbury and missionary to England by St. Virgil, the bishop of Arles. The west door is a masterpiece of Romanesque Provençal art, showing the Last Judgment. The interior features a Romanesque nave, a Gothic choir, and a 4th-century sarcophagus. Next to the cathedral is a beautiful Romanesque cloister, dating from the 12th–14th centuries, featuring elaborate stone carvings showing scenes from the Old and New Testaments, as well as from Provençal legends.

AUTUN

Situated on the edge of the region of forested granite hills known as the Morvan (from a Celtic word for "Black Hills"), Autun was one of the most important centers of Roman Gaul. Founded by the Roman Emperor Augustus in about 10 B.C. (and thus named Augustodunum, later contracted to Autun), the city was intended to be "a sister and rival of Rome itself," and to overawe and Romanize the Celtic Aedui tribe whose stronghold was at Bibracte on Mont Beuvray, 18 miles to the west. The new city was given a wall four miles in length and the usual public buildings of a Roman city. From the decline of the Roman Empire until the 12th century, Autun foundered under difficult conditions. In 1120, construction was begun on the Cathédrale St. Lazare to house the supposed relics of Lazarus, the friend whom Jesus had raised from the dead, which had been brought from Marseille shortly before. Autun thus became a significant pilgrimage site during the Middle Ages.

PLACES TO VISIT

The CATHÉDRALE ST. LAZARE, built between 1120 and 1146, is a fine example of Burgundian Romanesque style, although its exterior appearance has been altered by the addition of a Gothic tower and steeple in the 15th century, the addition of classical elements in the 18th century, and the two towers which were added in the 19th.

The major attraction of the cathedral, however, is the stone carving of the *Last Judgment* over the central doorway. Christ presides, while to his left the Archangel Michael disputes souls with Satan, who tries to cheat by leaning on the scales. Note the flames of hell tormenting the damned; while to Christ's right, the apostles look on as the saved enter heaven. This is another example of the tendency of medieval religion to deliberately stress the torments of hell and the delights of heaven in order to induce the good works necessary for salvation. This scene was carved by a prominent Burgundian sculptor named Gislebertus, who left his signature below the feet of Christ: *Gislebertus hoc fecit*—Gislebertus made this. That the cathedral was intended as a pilgrimage site is evident from its size—35 yards wide by 80 yards long. During the 18th-century movement known as the Enlightenment, the clergy of the cathedral dismantled Lazarus's tomb according to the rationalistic and secularizing tenor of the times. Finding the carving of the *Last Judgment* an inferior work, they plastered it over, inadvertently sparing it from destruction at the time of the French Revolution. In addition, carved capitals (many by Gisle-

bertus himself) showing biblical scenes adorn the top of many of the pillars. Most of the best capitals have been moved to the old chapter library *(salle capitulaire)* up the stairs on the right side of the choir, including a beautiful *Flight into Egypt* and an *Adoration of the Magi.*

Besides the cathedral, Gislebertus's work is also on display in the MUSÉE ROLIN, in the town house built by Nicolas Rolin, the chancellor of the duke of Burgundy in the 15th century. Here you can see Gislebertus's *Temptation of Eve,* which originally adorned one of the side doors of the cathedral, as well as the noted *Nativity* of the "Master of Moulins."

There are also reminders of Autun's Roman past. There are two gates which survive from the old Roman wall, the PORTE ST. ANDRÉ and the PORTE D'ARROUX. Just behind the train station, through the Porte d'Arroux, stands a ruined square tower, the remnants of the TEMPLE DE JANUS (the Temple of Janus). On the other side of town are the remnants of what was at one time the largest Roman theatre in Gaul, able to seat 15,000 spectators in its heyday. Now it is the site of a summertime play in which 600 locals in historic dress reenact the Autun's Gallo-Roman past.

AUXERRE

O ne of the oldest cities in France, Auxerre was originally an important stop on the Roman road from Lyon to Boulogne. Perched on a hillside overlooking the River Yonne, up until the 19th century,

Auxerre was a busy river port, but since the coming of the railroad, the town has slipped into semiobscurity.

PLACES TO VISIT

Auxerre is notable for two churches. The former CATHÉDRALE ST. ETIENNE (St. Stephen's Cathedral) is a cathedral no longer—the see was merged with Sens at the Revolution. Built over a period of three centuries, from 1215 to 1560, it is still unfinished, since the south tower was never completed. A flamboyant Gothic exterior is complemented by several notable works of art in the interior, including a stained-glass window showing Joan of Arc, a fresco of Christ on horseback, and a painting of the stoning of Stephen (Etienne), for whom the cathedral is named (Acts 7:54–8:1).

More unusual perhaps, because significantly older, is the ABBAYE ST. GER-MAIN, named after St. Germanus (A.D. 378–448), a native of Auxerre, its first bishop, and the successor of St. Martin in evangelizing Gaul. The first church on the site dated from the 6th century when Clotilde, the wife of Clovis, had built a church over the saint's tomb. This was expanded and renovated in the 9th century. The crypt, which housed the relics of the saint, dates mostly from the 9th century, but portions date from the original 6th-century structure, notably two oak beams which sit on Gallo-Roman columns, and a 5th-century monogram of Christ. The crypt also contains a raised cavity which was designed to hide the tomb and its treasures from raiding Vikings, as well as a false tomb to mislead the attackers. The crypt also houses frescoes—the oldest in France—depicting various bishops of Auxerre and the stoning of Stephen.

AVIGNON

Situated on the banks of the River Rhône, Avignon was a site of little importance in Roman times. Its major claim is that in the Middle Ages, it was home to the papacy, and therefore the capital of Christendom. In 1309, Pope Clement V (1305–16), a Frenchman, established the papacy in Avignon, partly to escape the feuding Roman noble factions which made Rome physically dangerous, and partly to patch up relations with King Philip IV (the Fair) of France who had been involved in a bitter dispute with the previous pope, Boniface VIII (1294–1303). Though not part of France until 1791, proximity eased communication between the popes and the French kings. For a period of almost 70 years (1309–77) seven popes (all of them French) reigned in Avignon. This period is known as the Avignonese Papacy or as the Babylonian Captivity, a reference to the 70 years that the children of Israel spent in captivity in Babylon. In 1377

Pope Gregory IX returned to Rome, but died shortly after his arrival. The newly elected pope, Urban VI, quickly alienated a number of cardinals with his plans for reform, and a number of them (mostly French) left Rome and elected a new pope, Clement VII, who returned to Avignon. From 1378 until 1415, Christendom was split in its allegiance between two popes (one in Rome and one in Avignon), and sometimes three, the result of a premature and ill-advised attempt to end the schism by the Council of Pisa in 1409. While the popes were resident in Avignon, the city became a European cultural center, home to a number of important artists who found patrons among the Church hierarchy, and most notably, to the humanist writer and poet Petrarch (1304–74), the coiner of the phrase "Babylonian captivity" and an ardent critic of corruption in the Church. With the end of schism, the new, single pope resumed his residence in Rome, and Avignon remained a papal possession governed by a papal legate until it was absorbed into France in 1791 during the French Revolution.

PLACES TO VISIT

Most notable among Avignon's sights is the PALAIS DES PAPES (Palace of the Popes). It is, in fact, two palaces. The PALAIS VIEUX or Old Palace is the northern part and was built by Pope Benedict XII (1334–42). Pope Benedict had been a Cistercian monk, and his austerity is evident in the design of this part of the palace, built as it is around a cloister as its courtyard. His successor, Clement VI (1342–52), was more lavish, and his PALAIS NOUVEAU reflects his more sumptuous style. During the French Revolution, the palace was looted and most of its interior decorations and furnishings were stolen or destroyed. As a result, little remains to remind us of the lavish lifestyles of 14th-century popes, bishops, and cardinals. There are, nevertheless, some reminders of their wealth and worldly concerns. On the second floor (to North Americans, first floor to Europeans), the Stag Room contains wall paintings of hunting scenes, while the ground floor contains the Grand Tinel, or Banqueting Hall, which measures 158 feet by 35 feet. Also on the second floor is the popes' bedchamber, which is painted with hundreds of small birds perched on trailing vines against a blue background. In contrast to the palace's interior, the grim and fortresslike exterior is a reminder of the difficult circumstances of the 14th century, and of the fact that the palace also needed on occasion to serve as a fortress to protect the popes.

Adjacent to the Palais des Papes is NOTRE-DAME-DES-DOMS CATHEDRAL, dating in large part from the 12th century, though with many later additions and alterations. Across the Place du Palais is the PETIT PALAIS (Little Palace), originally built in the 14th century as a cardinal's palace. It later became a bishop's palace and now houses a museum of medieval painting and sculpture, testifying to Avignon's

B

importance as a cultural center in the Middle Ages.

The old part of the city is also surrounded by walls or RAMPARTS which were intended to serve as a first line of defense. When the walls were restored in the 19th century, it proved impossible to excavate the surrounding moat. The walls, therefore, were much higher in the Middle Ages than they appear now.

Avignon is also the subject of a famous French folk song, "Sur le pont d'Avignon" ("On the Bridge at Avignon"). This refers to PONT ST. BÉNÉZET (St. Bénézet Bridge), which dates from the 12th century. According to local legend, Bénézet, a local shepherd boy, was commanded by heavenly voices to build a bridge across the Rhône at a spot shown him by an angel. No one believed him until he miraculously lifted a huge stone by himself. Given this evidence of divine favor, bishops gave money, donations flooded in, and volunteers formed a "Bridge Brotherhood." The bridge was completed in eight years, but its original 22 arches have been reduced to four by time and floods, with the result that the span now ends in the middle of the river.

LES BAUX-DE-PROVENCE

Perched on a rocky spur with commanding views of the *Val d'enfer* (Valley of Hell), from the 11th–14th centuries, Les Baux was the seat of one of the most powerful families in southern France. They claimed to trace their lineage back to Balthazar, one of the Magi who brought gifts to infant Christ, and accordingly their coat of arms featured the Star of Bethlehem. At one time, the town had a population of 6000 and was an important center of Provençal culture. The family died out in the 14th century, and Les Baux, along with Provence, was incorporated into the kingdom of France in the 15th century. During the Reformation and Wars of Religion of the 16th century, Les Baux, along with much of the rest of southern France, became Protestant under the Manville family. In 1632, King Louis XIII and Cardinal Richelieu, disturbed by both the independence of the Manvilles and their Protestant religion, decided to subdue it. The town's defenses were razed and the inhabitants fined a huge sum. From the 17th through the 19th centuries, it was largely deserted. In 1822, deposits of the mineral bauxite, from which aluminum is made and which is named after the town, were discovered nearby.

PLACES TO VISIT

Today Les Baux consists of two parts: the inhabited village, which is inhabited primarily by artisans and others who cater to the tourist trade; and the deserted Cité morte on the promontory above. In the inhabited village, note ST. VINCENT'S CHURCH, the site of a pageant performed by local shepherds at Christmas midnight mass. The MANVILLE HOUSE AND THE ADJOINING PROTESTANT CHAPEL, now in ruins, were built in the 16th century when the town was a Huguenot stronghold. On the chapel's window lintel, note the motto of the French Reformed Church, *Post tenebras lux* (After darkness, light). The CITÉ MORTE is notable for the ruins of the old fortress and commanding views of the surrounding countryside.

BEAUNE

Situated midway along the *Côte d'or,* or Golden Slope, Beaune is the center of the Burgundian wine trade. Vines had been planted here since Roman times, but during the Middle Ages, they were cultivated primarily by monks from local monasteries. Over time, much of this land came into the hands of local merchants, as monasteries and churches mortgaged them to finance their other activities. During the heyday of the dukes of Burgundy in the 15th century, Beaune was one of the chief cities of the duchy, and benefited from the patronage of Duke Philip the Good, and his chancellor Nicolas Rolin (1377–1461), who endowed the HÔTEL-DIEU to care for the poor and sick. Today, surrounded by its medieval walls, Beaune still derives its livelihood from its surrounding vineyards and the associated tourist trade.

PLACES TO VISIT

The HÔTEL-DIEU, which together with the Hospice de la Charité forms the Hospices de Beaune (Beaune Hospital), was founded in 1443 by Nicolas Rolin and his wife Guigone de Salins, to care for the sick and poor. In typical medieval fashion, this was a work of charity which benefited both the recipients and the donors, who were performing a good work which aided their salvation. Rolin, of humble origins from nearby Autun, rose to the rank of chancellor in the service of the duke of Burgundy, one of the most powerful rulers of the late 14th and early 15th centuries. While enriching his master, he

B

also amassed wealth and power for himself. Whether the hospital was founded out of guilt or out of a genuine desire to help the poor is impossible to say. He endowed the hospital with some of his vineyards around the town, a practice followed over the centuries by other benefactors. Today, the hospital (no longer at this site) is funded by the produce of 143 acres of Burgundy's finest vineyards. The wine from these vineyards is auctioned every November, and the bottles bear the name of the benefactor who left the land to the hospices. With its steep and colorfully tiled roofs and elegant decoration, the Hôtel-Dieu is a masterpiece of the Late Gothic style, built to display the generosity of its founder. Of note in the interior are the pharmacy, the kitchens, the nuns' quarters, and the GRANDE SALLE DES MALADES (Great Hall of the Sick). The Grande Salle also contains one the great masterpieces of Late Gothic painting, Rogier van der Weyden's *Polyptych of the Last Judgment,* painted between 1443 and 1451, and commissioned by Rolin himself. The central panel shows Christ presiding, with the Archangel Michael weighing souls. On the right, we see the Virgin Mary and six apostles, along with Nicolas Rolin, Duke Philip the Good, Bishop (later Cardinal) Jean Rolin (the chancellor's son), and Pope Eugenius IV. On the left, we see John the Baptist and six apostles; the duchess of Burgundy; Guigone de Salins, the chancellor's wife (partly hidden); and Philipote Rolin, the chancellor's daughter, who died in the hospital. The Hôtel-Dieu functioned as a hospital for over five centuries, housing patients until 1971.

BOURGES

Situated at almost the exact geographic center of France, and the capital city of the old province of Berry, the origins of Bourges are very ancient. Its site, on the promontory between two rivers and surrounded by marshes, gave the settlement military importance, and as Avaricum it was the stronghold of the Gallic tribe of the Bituriges. Conquered by Julius Caesar, who reportedly massacred its 40,000 inhabitants, it became an important administrative center in the Roman province of Aquitaine. From late Roman times, it was governed by its archbishops, until purchased by King Philip I of France in 1101. It was governed by a succession of younger sons and brothers of kings, the most notable of whom was Duke John (1340–1416), son of King John II (the Good, 1350–64). Duke John sought to turn Bourges into a cultural center to match the Dijon of the rival dukes of Burgundy. He was responsible for commissioning one of the masterpieces of medieval illuminated manu-

B

scripts, the sumptuous *Très riches heures du duc de Berry* (The Book of Hours of the Duke of Berry). This tradition of artistic patronage was carried on by Jacques Cœur (1394/1400–1455), an international merchant and financier, the wealthiest of his day, and finance minister to King Charles VII (1422–61). At the nadir of France's fortunes during the Hundred Years' War (1337–1453), the insane Charles VI (1380–1422) was forced to sign the Treaty of Troyes (1420). This treaty disinherited his own son (later King Charles VII, 1422–61), who ruled a rump kingdom from Bourges, earning him the derisive nickname, "the King of Bourges." Roused into action by Joan of Arc after 1429, however, Charles VII and the French managed to turn the tables on the English, who were expelled from France by 1453, except for the Channel port of Calais. Both Charles VII and his son, Louis XI (1461–83), who was born in Bourges, often resided here. The town's university, founded in 1463, became an important center of legal studies, and in 1531 numbered among its students a still Catholic native of Picardy in the north, named John Calvin. Today, the old town, largely undisturbed by the passage of time, is a maze of twisting cobblestone streets bordered by half-timbered houses (more than 400 remain).

PLACES TO VISIT

Apart from the medieval ambiance, and the **PALAIS JACQUES CŒUR**—which incidentally the financier never got to enjoy fully, since it was still under construction at his disgrace and imprisonment in 1451—Bourges's major attraction is the **CATHÉDRALE ST. ETIENNE** (St. Stephen's Cathedral), which along with the cathedrals in Chartres, Amiens, and Notre-Dame in Paris, is one of France's most magnificent Gothic cathedrals. Built on the site of four previous churches, construction was begun in 1192 and completed in 1224, although there have been many additions and renovations since. It was apparently modeled on Notre-Dame in Paris, but shows several design advances, apparently due to the desire of Archbishop Henry de Sully to build a church that would outshine that of his Parisian rivals and colleagues. The cathedral has no transept, or cross-aisle, and the central aisle or nave is much higher than that of Notre-Dame, while the four side aisles are lower. The overall impression is of vast length and height, an impression which is strengthened by the abundance of stained glass, dating from the early 12th (from the earlier church) through the 17th centuries. Unlike the cathedral at Chartres, Bourges was never an important pilgrimage site, but seems to have been intended as an educational experience, which helps to explain the abundance of stained-glass windows, which were seen as the books of the illiterate. Fulfilling the same educational function is the sculpture of the Last Judgment above the main door on the huge west

B

facade, which shows sinners (among them bishops and archbishops) being cast into Satan's open mouth, while the saved are led into Paradise by St. Peter. Also of note on the exterior are the row of two-tiered flying buttresses (necessary to support the high walls of the nave), and the unequal towers, with the south tower being built in the 16th century to replace the original, which collapsed in 1506.

BÉTHARRAM

Bétharram is most famous for its world-renowned *grottes* (caves) which comprise five different levels of underground chambers routed out at different stages by the waters of the underground river. The caves present a living and incredible demonstration of erosion and the deposits which create stalactites and stalagmites.

Much less well-known, even by the many thousands of visitors to nearby Lourdes, is a sight of great devotion, the church NOTRE-DAME DU BEAU RAMEAU (good branch). The original "good branch" church was erected in the 16th century after a local girl had fallen into the river Gave, and praying to God, had found a providential branch in her hand. Since then, a new church has been added to the original chapel to hold the body of St. Michel Garicoïts, a local priest who died in 1863 and was canonized in 1947. The Catholic Church canonizes a person (officially sanctions intercessory prayers offered to them) when the Vatican has decided that the person is definitely residing with Christ

in heaven. Though many saints were canonized in the early centuries, the Catholic Church only systematically recognizes those saints canonized since 1534, a date decided by a decree issued by Urban VIII in 1634.

Michel Garicoïts was born in 1797 at Ibarre, near St. Palais. Too poor to pay for theological studies, he accessed the ministry by becoming a servant of the bishop of Bayonne, a position which allowed him to attend seminary classes. Having taken orders, he was sent to the empty seminary of Bétharram. It was here that he founded the Fathers of the Sacred Heart, an order dedicated to the evangelization of the dechristianized rural communities. Within ten years, the order had 50 monks and 15 lay brothers who worked tirelessly in bringing the gospel back to the surrounding communities.

In the chapel NOTRE DAME DU BEAU RAMEAU, one can visit his tomb as well as his cell. There are also the CHAPELLES DU CHEMIN DE CROIX (two chapels dedicated to Christ's ascent to Calvary).

CAEN

Chief city of lower Normandy, Caen was the favorite residence of Duke William of Normandy, who after his successful invasion of England in 1066, became better known as William the Conqueror. Caen suffered terrible damage during World War II. The first bombs fell on the city on D-Day itself (June 6, 1944), and a fire raged for 11 days. Liberated by Canadian forces on July 9, the city was then bombarded by the Germans for a month, while the residents huddled for protection in the Abbaye aux Hommes, a local hospital, and a rock quarry.

PLACES TO VISIT

The two major religious sites in Caen are the ABBAYE AUX HOMMES (Abbey for Men) and the ABBAYE AUX DAMES (Abbey for Women), both excellent examples of Norman Romanesque architecture. William the Conqueror had married a distant cousin, Mathilda of Flanders, which had incurred the displeasure of the pope, because Church law forbade such marriages between relatives without special permission. The pope excommunicated William and Mathilda, and placed Normandy under an interdict, which meant that the sacraments could not be administered while the interdict was in effect—no one could be baptized, married, buried, confess, or receive Mass. In 1059, Bishop Lanfranc was able to have the interdict lifted, provided the duke and duchess show their contrition by the founding of the two abbeys. The ABBAYE AUX HOMMES, with its adjoining EGLISE ST. ETIENNE (St. Stephen's Church), was begun in 1066 and completed in 1078. The original Romanesque towers were topped by Early Gothic spires in the 13th century. The church was the burial place of William the Conqueror, but his grave was desecrated and his remains scattered in 1562 by Protestants during the Wars of Religion, and again in 1793 during the French Revolution. His grave is now marked by a plain marble slab near the altar. At the other end of the old town stands the ABBAYE AUX DAMES, with its adjoining church, the EGLISE DE LA TRINITÉ (Trinity Church), founded in 1062 by Duchess Mathilda as a nunnery for noble women, a purer example of Norman Romanesque architecture than the Eglise St. Etienne. This church was her burial place, but like her husband's, her grave was desecrated in the 16th and 18th centuries.

CAHORS

Occupying a defensible site formed by a loop in the River Lot, the origins of Cahors go back to Gallic times. It rose to prominence, however, in the 14th century as the birthplace of Jacques Duèze, who became, as John XXII, the second Avignon pope (1316–34). As pope, he founded a university, and the city became an important banking center, largely due to the influence of its native son. When the papacy returned to Rome, however, Cahors receded into semiobscurity, a blow which was compounded by the city's cession to England by the Treaty of Bretigny in 1360. In the 16th-century Wars of Religion, Cahors was a Catholic stronghold in largely Protestant southwestern France, resulting in its sack in 1580 by a Huguenot army led by Henry of Navarre (the future Henry IV). Cahors was also the birthplace of Clément Marot (ca. 1496–1544), a famous printer, musician, and lyricist, whose musical settings of many of the Psalms were very popular among the Huguenots, and whose setting of the Doxology is still widely sung today. Cahors is also the birthplace of Léon Gambetta (1838–82), perhaps France's most famous republican statesman. Almost every town in France has a street named after him. In a famous speech in 1868, he indicted the imperial regime of Napoleon III, and when war broke out with Prussia and the emperor was captured at the defeat of the French at Sedan, Gambetta took the leading role in proclaiming the republic and forming a provisional government. With Paris under siege, it was essential that an army be raised in the unoccupied provinces, and as the principal delegate, Gambetta was floated out of Paris in a hot air balloon so that he could proceed with the task of recruiting soldiers. Despite French efforts, the provisional government had to sign an armistice in January 1871. It was in the years immediately following the peace treaty that Gambetta played his most significant part in making France a republic for good. The majority of the national delegates were monarchists and were ready to restore constitutional monarchy to France. However, there were two candidates to the throne, the elder and younger branches of the Bourbons, and they could not decide who should be king. Taking advantage of this rivalry, Gambetta was able, with supreme political skill, to push ratification of the republic through the weary assembly. The republican constitution of 1875 formed the basis of the French Third Republic until its demise in 1940. In the Place Briand is a monument of Gambetta by Falguière.

PLACES TO VISIT

Foremost among Cahors's attractions for the Christian traveler is the Romanesque CATHEDRALE ST. ETIENNE (St. Stephen's Cathedral). Built in the 12th century and substantially rebuilt between 1200 and 1500, it was the first church in France to be roofed with a dome, or in this case, two large cupolas, showing the Byzantine influence present in much of southern France, as do the frescoes on the interior of the cupolas.

CLÉMENT MAROT (1496–1544) was court poet under King Francis I (1515–47). Previously, he had been secretary to the king's sister Marguerite, well-known for reforming religious ideas and sponsorship of the reforming group at Meaux. As court poet, he wrote poems celebrating various political and cultural events. But his real significance lay in his religious sympathies. Several times he was imprisoned or exiled for his Protestant sympathies, before gaining official pardon. He lived for a time in Geneva, but found life there not to his liking. He died in the Italian city of Turin in 1544. His most significant accomplishment was his rendering of the Psalms into French verse. Many of these verse translations of the Psalms were set to music, primarily by Louis Bourgeois (ca. 1510–ca. 61). The best-known of these is the doxology "Praise God From Whom All Blessings Flow," still widely sung today. Marot's Psalms served the Huguenot movement in France as sources of inspiration and comfort throughout the Wars of Religion, the revocation of the Edict of Nantes, and the years of the "Desert" when Protestant worship was illegal in France.

CARCASSONNE

Occupying a strategic spot on the route between Toulouse and the Mediterranean, Carcassonne has been a strongly fortified site since Roman times. Like much of Languedoc, including Albi and Beziers, Carcassonne was a stronghold of Catharism or Albigensianism in the 12th and 13th centuries. In 1209, the city was besieged and conquered by the notorious and brutal Simon de Montfort, and was absorbed into the kingdom of France with the rest of Languedoc. In 1240, the townspeople rebelled, but were repressed by Louis IX (St. Louis), who ordered the town's defenses razed and sentenced the inhabitants to seven years' exile. They were allowed to return, but on the

C

condition that they settled only on the far bank of the River Aude, today's VILLE BASSE (Lower town). The king then restored the fortifications (the CITÉ), both to assure the loyalty of his new territories and to defend against invasion from Spain. During the Hundred Years' War with England, the Lower town was burnt to the ground, while the Cité survived unscathed. After the 17th century, the fortifications were no longer needed for border defense and fell into disrepair and were on the point of being demolished in the 19th century. They were saved, however, by the Romantic movement's fascination with all things medieval, and the writer Prosper Mérimée persuaded the government to restore them, a project carried out by Viollet-le-Duc, the architect who was responsible for restoring many of France's medieval monuments, including NOTRE-DAME DE PARIS. As a result, Carcassone retains a great deal of its medieval atmosphere.

PLACES TO VISIT

The CITÉ is the largest and best preserved example of medieval military architecture in Europe. It consists of a double set of walls, and was reportedly modeled on fortifications in Palestine that St. Louis had seen while on a Crusade. Parts of the inner wall (ENCEINTE INTÉRIEUR) go back to the Visigoths of the 6th century. The outer walls (ENCEINTE EXTÉRIEUR) were begun by St. Louis and finished by his son Philip III (the Bold). The Cité also includes the CHÂTEAU COMTAL (Castle of the Counts), built in the 12th century by the town's ruling family, the Trencavels, who were dispossessed in the 13th century by de Montfort and St. Louis. Perhaps of more interest is the church of ST. NAZAIRE, with its Romanesque nave, Gothic transepts and choir, and its remarkable stained glass, especially the rose windows of the transepts. On the south side, a stone carving illustrates one of the 13th-century sieges of the town, while the south transept contains the tombstone of Simon de Montfort, though his actual body was later moved.

For more information on the Cathars or Albigensians, you might want to pay a visit to the CENTRE NATIONAL D'ETUDES CATHARS in the Château Villegly in Conques-sur-Orbiel, eight kilometers northeast of Carcassonne.

CARPENTRAS

Capital of the region of the Comtat Venaissin, a papal possession until the time of the French Revolution, Carpentras thus benefited from the residence of the papacy in Avignon (1307–77).

PLACES TO VISIT

For the Christian visitor, the main site to see in Carpentras is France's oldest synagogue, built in 1367 and rebuilt in the 18th century. At a time when the secular rulers were expelling Jews from their kingdoms—England in 1290, France in 1306, Spain in 1492—the popes afforded Jews in their territories a significant amount of protection, though they were confined to a ghetto known as *la carrière*. When Provence was incorporated into the kingdom of France in the 15th century, Carpentras became a major Jewish center. Within the synagogue are a kosher oven for unleavened bread and purification baths.

CASTRES

Built on the banks of the Agout River, Castres is a pretty town with many old houses lining the river. It is a good place from which to visit the Lacaune Mountain range and the Montagne Noire. Castres is the birthplace of Jean Jaurès (1854–1914) and the PLACE JEAN JAURÈS in the center of town has a statue of Jaurès by Puech. Jaurès was one of the great socialist figures in French history, and his influence helped to form the strong socialist element which goes a long way to explaining why France is still very much a socialist country today. Jaurès did not share all of Marx's ideas, and he was strongly criticized by Marxist socialists for taking the defense of Alfred Dreyfus, a middle-class officer, in the infamous Dreyfus affair. A member of the Chamber of Deputies, Jaurès was one of the political figures who came out most strongly in favor of the wronged Dreyfus: He published *Les Preuves,* a book denouncing the evidence and calling for a retrial. His courageous stand for justice caused his defeat in the parliamentary elections of 1898. As World War I approached, Jaurès, a pacifist, preached strongly for reconciliation with the Germans. This stand caused his death: In 1914, he was assassinated by a young fanatic who believed his efforts to secure peace were playing into Imperial Germany's hands. On the very day of his assassination, he was considering an appeal to President Woodrow Wilson for help in solving the crisis.

Castres is also home to the MUSÉE GOYA, specializing in Spanish painting and containing a remarkable collection of Goya's works including *Self Portrait, The Disasters of War,* and *Francisco del Mazo,* among many others.

LE CHAMBON-SUR-LIGNON

Le Chambon is not perhaps figured in most guidebooks and may seem a rather out-of-the-way place to visit. Surrounded by mountains and extinct volcanoes, subject, as a local saying goes, to "nine months of winter," and exposed to the icy blasts of the Mistral (northerly wind chasing the clouds away and bringing a wind-swept cold), it is indeed a rugged place in the winter months.

However, it was here in this small village, a faithful Huguenot stronghold since the revocation of the Edict of Nantes in 1685, that took place an amazing effort to shelter Jewish refugees during the German occupation of France from 1940–44. There are many episodes of individual bravery and self-sacrifice during the Resistance, but perhaps few so collective in their scope as that of Le Chambon. The pastor André Trocmé, Protestant minister in Chambon, persuaded the whole village to shelter Jews even though they were under constant threat from the Vichy and German forces stationed at Le Puy. Indeed, in 1943, the village had come to be known as "that nest of Jews in Huguenot country." The Vichy officials knew of the presence of the Jews, as did the German troops and even the Gestapo. However, apart from a failed attempt by the Vichy officials in 1941 to deport the refugees (Trocmé was able to warn the village in time to let all the Jews escape to the outlying forests), neither the German army nor the Gestapo came in to round up the Jews they knew were there. How is this explained? It may have been partly due to the fact that André Trocmé was a committed pacifist and the village thus confined their resistance to helping the victims rather than attacking the enemy. It was certainly due in some measure to the German commander of the local occupying forces, Major Schmehling, a devout man who deeply admired Trocmé and his colleagues and who convinced his superiors and the Gestapo to put off their raids until it was too late. Yet, in the light of the killings and mass deportations that were occurring all over France at the same time, one can only say that the sparing of Le Chambon was miraculous.

PLACES TO VISIT

One can visit the **PROTESTANT TEMPLE** where André Trocmé preached his sermons of encouragement, returning often to the parable of the Samaritan and the Sermon on the Mount, his two favorite passages of the New Testament, and reminding his congregation of what Moses says in Deuteronomy 19, that if one does not prevent innocent blood from being shed, "the guilt of bloodshed will be upon you." One can also visit the **PRESBYTERY** where Trocmé and his wife themselves hid a number of Jews all through the occupation, and the cemetery where Trocmé and many of the villagers who helped hide the Jews are buried.

CHARTRES

Situated on the Eure River, east of Paris in the rich agricultural region of the Beauce, Chartres is a charming town, with narrow cobbled streets winding among quaint houses. What sets this town apart from dozens of similarly charming towns in France, however, is the cathedral, **NOTRE-DAME DE CHARTRES** (Our Lady of Chartres). If you are able to visit only one church during your visit to France, try to make Chartres the one. The present cathedral is the most recent of several to have stood on this spot. Some authorities maintain that the site of Chartres has been sacred since Druidic times, but others claim that there is no real evidence for it. There has likely been a church here since the evangelization of Chartres in the 4th century by St. Adventinus. We know that the church at Chartres has been dedicated to Mary since at least the 8th century, and likely much earlier, making it one of the first in France to be so dedicated. In 858, after the church had been pillaged and burnt by raiding Vikings, Charles the Bald, Charlemagne's grandson, presented the church with the *Sancta Camisia,* the veil believed to have been worn by Mary when she gave birth to Jesus. (Some sources indicate, however, that it was the veil worn at the Annunciation.) The increasing importance given to Mary through the 12th and 13th centuries combined with the belief that relics provided a tangible link to the saints to make Chartres an increasingly important pilgrimage center. These beliefs were confirmed in the minds of the inhabitants of Chartres in 911 when the Viking chieftain Rollo besieged the town. The bishop ordered the relic to be paraded on the city walls, and the besiegers fled. In the 10th and 11th centuries, Chartres also became an intellectual center of the first rank. In 980, the famous scholar Fulbert came to teach in the cathedral school from Reims where he had been a pupil of Gerbert of Aurillac, later Pope Sylvester II. The school at Chartres was one of a series in northern France which dominated medieval intellectual life until eclipsed by the University of Paris toward 1200, such as those at Reims and Laon. Fulbert was also bishop of Chartres until his death in 1028, and it was during his reign that the cathedral was once again destroyed, this time by fire, on September 7, 1020. Fulbert solicited funds from all over Europe to build a more magnificent replacement in Romanesque style. This structure was in turn enlarged and modified over the years. During the night of June 10, 1194, most of the city of Chartres was destroyed by fire, and Fulbert's cathedral was badly damaged. It was believed all had been lost, most significantly the *Sancta Camisia.* Three days later, however, three smoky and hungry priests emerged from the crypt, where they had taken refuge along with the relic. This was taken as a miracle and a sign from the Virgin to build an even grander cathedral. Construction began almost immediately and was largely completed by 1223, although the cathedral was not formally consecrated until 1260. One of the noteworthy aspects about the construction of Chartres Cathedral was its widespread support. It attracted support from the wealthy and powerful—King Philip Augustus donated the funds for the north porch, his son Louis VIII for the north rose window, and St. Louis the rood screen, for example—but also from ordinary people. The citizens of Chartres volunteered their time and labor to haul the stone from the quarry five miles away. Many of the stained-glass windows were donated by the craft guilds in Chartres. Thus many windows contain everyday scenes portraying the trade of those who donated them, such as masons, cobblers, and car-

penters, to name only a few. Amazingly, the cathedral has survived the centuries virtually unscathed. In the 18th century, the cathedral clergy decided to "modernize" it. They removed some of the choir windows and replaced them with plain glass, and the rood screen donated by St. Louis was demolished and replaced by a wrought iron grille. At the time of the Revolution, the cathedral treasure was confiscated and a wooden statue of the Virgin was publicly burned in front of the cathedral on December 20, 1793. It was further proposed to destroy all the statuary, and even to demolish the cathedral itself! Fortunately, bureaucratic inertia set in, and the most anti-Christian phase of the Revolution soon passed, sparing the cathedral for posterity. In 1836, the wooden roof of the cathedral fell victim to a fire, and was replaced by a metal roof. During World War II, the stained glass was dismantled and stored, to be reinstalled after the war.

PLACES TO VISIT

The CATHÉDRALE NOTRE-DAME DE CHARTRES is distinguished from most other churches in France (and Europe) by several important factors. The first is the purity of its Gothic style. Because it was substantially built in such a short period of time (about 30 years), one vision and one style were largely preserved throughout. It was also built at a time when Gothic architecture was at a peak. The basic structural problems which had begun to be solved with the construction of St. Denis and Sens about a century

C

earlier were now worked out. Architects were able to concentrate on the refinements and bring the Gothic style to a peak of development, before the intricate ornamentation of the flamboyant style. Thus, one's attention is drawn to the lightness and airiness of the structure, its sense of soaring space (which after all is the point of the Gothic style) rather than to its ornamentation, rich though it is. Another distinguishing factor is the stained glass, notable for its vastness (almost 30,000 square feet), its quality, and its age—almost all the glass dates from the 12th and 13th centuries. A Gothic cathedral is really a sermon in stone, full of symbols and allusions in glass and stone, in much greater detail than can be given here. If at all possible, try to time your visit to coincide with the tours given by Malcolm Miller, an expatriate Englishman who has made decoding Chartres cathedral his life's work, and is recognized worldwide as the leading authority. He conducts tours between April and January at noon and 2:45 P.M., Monday–Saturday. No two tours are the same; it is therefore worthwhile to try to take in both on any given day. For more information, contact the tourist office.

The Exterior

The west facade is notable for several reasons. First, the royal portal or three doorways, which was one of the few parts salvaged from Fulbert's earlier cathedral, and was built between 1145 and 1155. The tympanum above the central door features Christ triumphant at the end of time, with the symbols of the four Evangelists (or gospel writers), with a frieze of the apostles on the lintel below. The standing figures at either end of the apostles are Enoch and Elijah, who will return to convert humanity before the Last Judgment. Around Christ on the archivolts are angels, and the 24 elders of the Apocalypse playing musical instruments. On the right, the tympanum shows Christ as a child with Mary. The two-layered frieze on the lintel below portrays the Annunciation and birth of Christ, and his presentation in the temple, while the archivolts feature figures representing the seven liberal arts. (Mary was associated with wisdom and learning, especially appropriate to an important intellectual center such as Chartres.) On the left, the tympanum features Christ's Ascension. Beneath, angels descend from heaven to foretell his return. The archivolts display the signs of the zodiac with their appropriate monthly activities. The doors are flanked by statues representing Christ's forbears, the kings and queens of Judah and priests and prophets of the Old Testament. Above these flanking statues, and below the lintels described above, is a frieze with almost 200 carved figures showing scenes from the life of Christ. Above the great rose window is a gallery with statues of 16 kings of Judah. The lower parts of both towers were likewise salvaged from the previous structure, and are largely Romanesque in style. The south tower (on your right as you

C

face the cathedral) at 106 meters (348 feet) is the tallest Romanesque tower in existence. The taller north tower (115 meters—377 feet) was topped by a flamboyant spire in 1506. Another distinguishing characteristic of Chartres Cathedral are its north and south porches, at either end of the transept. In most churches, these entrances (where they exist) are very much poor relations of the showpiece west facade. Not so in Chartres, where they rival the Royal Portal. Both were constructed between 1200 and 1225, and are thus governed by the same style and vision. In comparison to the serene and rather static Romanesque sculptures of the west front, the sculptures here are Gothic style—more realistic and expressive, and standing further away from the structure. The ruling theme of the north porch is foretelling of Christ and his church, culminating in the coronation of Mary by her Son, in the tympanum above the central door. On the lintel below are depicted Mary's death and burial, and on the surrounding archivolts are depicted angels, Old Testament prophets, and queens of Judah. On the doorjambs on either side are statues of various biblical persons, including Simeon holding the Christ Child, John the Baptist holding a lamb, Abraham preparing to sacrifice Isaac, Moses holding the tablets of the Law, and King David. Above the left door, the tympanum shows the Adoration of the Magi, and the lintel displays the Nativity and

the Annunciation to the Shepherds. The jamb figures are probably Isaiah and Daniel (with scrolls), the Annunciation, and the Visitation of Mary and Elizabeth, her cousin and mother of John the Baptist. The right bay features in the tympanum the suffering of Job, while the lintel shows the judgment of Solomon. The jamb figures include Balaam standing on his donkey, Joseph, and the Queen of Sheba come to sample the wisdom of Solomon. On the south porch, the story is continued with Christ triumphant in earth and heaven. In the central bay the central jamb figure is Christ trampling a lion and dragon, the forces of evil. On either side are the apostles. The tympanum is the Last Judgment, with Christ displaying his wounds flanked by Mary and John. Below, on the lintel, the central figure is St. Michael, holding the scales of judgment. On his right are the saved being led into Paradise by an angel, while on his left the damned are being led by demons into hell, depicted as an open mouth. The left bay is dedicated to the martyrs of the Church with the instruments of their deaths. The lintel displays the stoning of Stephen, the first martyr, while the tympanum is dedicated to Christ, the supreme martyr. The right bay features other important figures of the early church, including St. Jerome pointing to his Latin translation of the Bible, known as the Vulgate, and Pope Gregory the Great, with the Holy Spirit perched on his shoulder, inspiring his Church reforms. The lintel features St. Nicholas and St. Martin performing their acts of charity.

The Interior

The dimensions of the interior were largely determined by the size of the previous church, whose foundations were retained. The nave is the widest in France at 16 meters (53 feet) between the pillars. It is interesting to note that the floor is gently sloped from back to front to assist in the cleaning of the cathedral. People would often spend the night in the cathedral to seek healing; the floor was simply sluiced with water which would then run out the front doors. In the middle of the nave is a circular maze, set out in colored stone. It was probably a penitential exercise to be followed on their knees by penitents. The choir screen is a Late Gothic work, dating from the 16th century, whose elaborate carvings detail the lives of the Virgin Mary and of Christ. The Baroque altar dates from the 18th century and depicts the Assumption of Mary. The real glory of the cathedral interior, however, are the stained-glass windows, more

than 160 of them. Most of them date from the 13th century, though the lancet windows of the west facade were salvaged from the previous church. In general, the windows illustrate scenes from the Bible and lives of the saints. The windows were meant to be "read" in greater detail than can be conveyed here. As mentioned above, many windows were donated by craft guilds who immortalized their contributions in scenes depicting their trades. The stained glass at Chartres is especially notable for its deep blue color, achieved nowhere else. Especially famous is the Notre-Dame de la Belle Verrière (literally, Our Lady of the Beautiful Window, more commonly called the Blue Virgin) in the south ambulatory. Though part of a 13th-century window, these particular panels date from about 1180. The cathedral's treasury is in the Chapelle St. Piat, a 14th-century addition to the apse. Here may be seen the *Sancta Camisia*. The crypt contains portions of a 4th-century Gallo-Roman wall and well, a 9th-century inner crypt, and the Romanesque chapels from Fulbert's cathedral.

CHINON

This small, picturesque town on the banks of the River Vienne, a tributary of the Loire, is dominated by the ruins of the château perched on the bluffs above. It is famed as the place where Joan of Arc first

encountered the dauphin, later King Charles VII, in 1429. Discouraged by English victories in the Hundred Years' War and by his father disinheriting him in favor of the English king, Charles languished in indolence. Until, that is,

C

an illiterate peasant girl from Lorraine, who believed she had a divine mission from God to save France, encountered the dauphin in Chinon. Thinking to have a little fun with her, Charles got someone else to wear his robes while he attempted to remain anonymous among a crowd of 300 nobles. Joan unhesitatingly picked the true dauphin out from among the crowd, informing the astonished ruler, "You are the heir of France and true son of the king, Lieutenant of the King of Heaven who is King of France." Charles, to the bewilderment of his nobles, listened to Joan's pleas and gave her an army to command, which was the turning point of the Hundred Years' War. A century earlier, in 1308, the Grand Master and 140 leading Knights Templar were imprisoned here for a year before being burnt at the stake in Paris on trumped-up charges of sexual immorality and heresy, at the insistence of King Philip IV (the Fair) and with the connivance of Pope Clement V,

the first Avignon pope. Chinon is also renowned as the birthplace of François Rabelais (1495–1553), a physician and humanist scholar, whose ribald books *Gargantua* and *Pantagruel* deflated and criticized the hypocrisy and pedantry of the official religion of his day.

PLACES TO VISIT

Despite its historic significance, there is little left to see or visit in Chinon today. In the old town, which has retained much of its medieval flavor, one can see at the **GRAND CARROI** (crossroads) the well-head which Joan of Arc is reputed to have used in dismounting from her horse on that fateful day in 1429. The **CHÂTEAU**, now in ruins, is where Joan actually met the dauphin. One can also climb the **TOUR COUDRAY** (Coudray Tower) where the Templars were kept prisoner. The 14th-century **TOUR DE L'HORLOGE** (clock tower) contains a small Joan of Arc museum.

FRANÇOIS RABELAIS (ca. 1495–1553) was born near Chinon. Educated in a monastery, he served for a while as a priest before undertaking a medical education at Montpellier. He practiced medicine in Lyon, but his real fame was as a popular author. His most famous works concern the adventures of the giant Gargantua and his son Pantagruel. Realizing that corrupt and outmoded institutions were more susceptible to laughter and ridicule than to frontal attack, the giants' adventures mercilessly satirized Rabelais's and the humanists' favorite targets: the scholastic thought of the universities, religious hypocrisy and corruption, and the ignorance and superstition so prevalent in everyday life. His stories are often hilariously funny, and just as often raunchy and crude, delighting in sensual pleasures. Despite running afoul of religious and political authorities, Rabelais benefited from powerful protectors.

CHÂLONS-EN-CHAMPAGNE

(CHÂLONS-SUR-MARNE)

Situated on the banks of the river Marne in the midst of the wide-open plains of Champagne, Châlons was first inhabited during Roman times, on an island in the river. It was near Châlons (the exact site is in dispute) in 451 that a Roman army defeated the Huns of Attila, who had given up conquering Paris because of the intervention of St. Geneviève. Throughout the Middle Ages, Châlons was governed by its bishop, one of the peers of France, and it became an administrative and industrial center of some importance. During the Wars of Religion of the 16th century, Châlons remained loyal to King Henry III and the Protestant Henry IV, despite the fact that it was an overwhelmingly Catholic town. Besides this, the duke of Guise, the leader of the Catholic League, was the military governor of the province of Champagne, and almost the whole of the province followed Guise in his rebellion against the king. In Châlons, Protestants and Catholics seem to have been able to put aside their differences in the interests of relatively peaceful, if not always harmonious coexistence.

Today, it suffers somewhat, at least from a touristic point of view, from the ecclesiastical and architectural glory of Reims to the north, and the charms of the well-preserved old town of Troyes to the south. Nevertheless, it remains a pleasant stop with peaceful canals meandering among half-timbered houses.

PLACES TO VISIT

The CATHÉDRALE ST. ETIENNE (St. Stephen's Cathedral) was begun in 1235 on the site of a church which had been destroyed by fire in 1230. Built in the current Gothic style, it nevertheless sports an incongruous classical facade added in the 17th century. In the interior, the cathedral boasts many fine examples of medieval and Renaissance stained glass, with green hues characteristic of Champagne, as opposed to the blues seen in Chartres. Purer in style is the nearby church of NOTRE-DAME-EN-VAUX, begun in Romanesque style in the 12th century and completed in Early Gothic in the 13th. The bell tower boasts a carillon of 56 bells, considered the greatest in Europe. Like the cathedral, Notre-Dame-en-Vaux has some superb examples of stained glass, notably in the north aisle and the rose windows. Adjoining the church is the MUSÉE DU CLOÎTRE DE NOTRE-DAME-EN-VAUX (Cloister Museum), which contains important examples of Romanesque sculpture dating from the 12th century.

CÎTEAUX, ABBAYE DE

Few places in France can rank with Cîteaux in sheer importance for the history of Christianity in the Middle Ages. In 1098, a group of disaffected monks from nearby Cluny, led by St. Robert of Molesme, founded a new monastery in the middle of what was then a vast wilderness. They were upset by what they saw as the luxurious lifestyle at Cluniac monasteries, and by the wealth and power of the abbots of Cluniac monasteries, especially the abbot of Cluny himself, who was one of the most powerful men in Europe. They resolved to return to the original intent of the Benedictine Rule with its emphasis on poverty and manual labor, again in contrast to Cluny, where the emphasis was on elaborate ritual. The real growth of the resulting Cistercian order, however, came through the tremendous influence of St. Bernard of Clairvaux (1090–1153), who entered the Abbey of Cîteaux in 1113. In 1115, there were five Cistercian houses, by St. Bernard's death in 1153 there were 343, and by 1300 there were around 700. The Cistercians would build only on undeveloped land, and they therefore played an important role in the economic and agricultural expansion of medieval Europe. Nevertheless, as in any organization with high ideals, over time, the Cistercians became lax and fell away from those ideals. The order was therefore reformed in the 16th, and again in the 18th century. In line with the anticlerical, and sometimes anti-Christian tenor of the French Revolution, the Abbey of Cîteaux was suppressed in 1790 when the revolutionary government confiscated the lands of the Catholic Church. In the 19th century, the Cistercians once again took up residence there.

PLACES TO VISIT

Unfortunately, there is little left to see at Cîteaux today. Most of what remains was built in the 18th century, but there is a disused 12th-century chapel and the remnants of a Gothic cloister.

CLAIRVAUX, ABBAYE DE

Like Cîteaux, Clairvaux is enormously significant for the history of Christianity in France and in Europe, but there is little left to testify to this importance. Founded by St. Bernard of Clairvaux (1090–1153) as a daughter house of Cîteaux, the monastery itself was constructed between 1135 and 1145, displaying the plainness and austerity characteristic of the Cistercians, as opposed to the elegance and sumptuousness of the Cluniacs.

PLACES TO VISIT

Most of the **ABBEY** as it appears now was constructed in the 18th century, when Clairvaux had become enormously wealthy and luxurious. Only a vaulted cellar and part of the church date from the 12th century. In the early 19th century, the abbey was converted into a prison.

CLERMONT-FERRAND

Formed by the union of the two rival towns of Clermont and Montferrand in 1630, Clermont-Ferrand is today perhaps best known as the headquarters of the Michelin Tire empire, and as the gateway to the neighboring mountains of the Massif Central, especially the Puy de Dôme, the extinct volcano which looms over the city. The Gallic tribe of the Arverni (who gave their name to the surrounding region of Auvergne) had their fortress or *oppidium* of Gergovia near Clermont. It was the leader of the Arverni, a Gallic chieftain named Vercingetorix, who handed Julius Caesar one of his few defeats in March of 52 B.C. Later that summer, however, Caesar returned to defeat him and his Gallic tribesmen. Vercingetorix was captured and kept a prisoner in Rome for six years before being strangled. It was in Clermont that in November of 1095 Pope Urban II, a former Cluniac monk, proclaimed the First Crusade to recover the Holy Land from the Muslims. His message was heard by a vast crowd which responded by crying out "Dieu le veut!" ("God wishes it!").

C

Three years later, a Christian army would conquer Jerusalem, setting a pattern that would be repeated numerous times over the next several centuries. Clermont-Ferrand was also the birthplace of Blaise Pascal.

PLACES TO VISIT

The old part of Clermont is known as LA VILLE NOIRE (the black town), not because it is dirty, but because it is built of the local black volcanic rock. Within the *ville noire,* note the equestrian statue of Vercingetorix by Bartholdi (the sculptor of the Statue of Liberty) at one end of the Place de Jaude. There are two churches worth seeing in Clermont which display the evolution from Romanesque to Gothic styles. The older of the two is NOTRE-DAME-DU-PORT. Built of yellowish sandstone in around 1150, it displays the Romanesque, with its round arches and feeling of solidity, solemnity, and mystery. Note the intricately carved capitals on the columns of the raised choir. Standing in contrast in style and building material is the nearby CATHÉDRALE NOTRE-DAME-DE-L'AS-SOMPTION, begun in 1248. Built of the local black volcanic basalt, which makes for a dramatic contrast with the colorful stained-glass windows, it is the most important Gothic structure in Auvergne. The two spires are the work of Viollet-le-Duc in the 19th century. The strength of the black stone allowed the columns of the nave to be slimmer than usual, increasing the sense of height and the typical Gothic illusion of being swept up to heaven, as opposed to the more earthbound feeling of the Romanesque. The stained-glass medallions, dating from the 12th to 15th centuries, are copies of those in the Sainte-Chapelle in Paris.

BLAISE PASCAL (1623–62) was a brilliant mathematician and scientist and inventor of a calculating machine, a kind of primitive mechanical computer. Following a mystical experience, which he called his "night of fire," Pascal turned away from science to devote himself to God. He believed that science, while important in revealing the truth about God's creation, ultimately availed nothing for human happiness or salvation. He became a key supporter of the Jansenists against the Jesuits and most of the Catholic hierarchy. He died before he could write his masterpiece, which he believed would have a profound impact in turning people toward God, but many of his notes have come down to us in the form of his *Pensées* (Thoughts), among the most famous of which is: "The heart has its reasons, which reason does not know" ("Le cœur a ses raisons que la raison ne connaît point").

CLUNY, ABBAYE DE

Throughout the Middle Ages, whenever the Church fell away from its high ideals, reform came from within the monastic orders. Nowhere is this truer than in the case of Cluny. The Abbey of Cluny was founded in 910 by Duke William of Aquitaine in what was then a remote region of Burgundy. Cluny was intended by its first great abbot, St. Odo, as a revival of the strict observance of the Benedictine Rule. Independent of local political and ecclesiastical control, the abbots of Cluny acknowledged only the authority of the pope. Very quickly the Abbey of Cluny inspired imitators, and daughter houses were founded all over Europe—within several centuries there were 3000 Cluniac monasteries. They were organized in hierarchical and centralized fashion, with the abbot of the mother house at Cluny firmly in charge. The order, and its abbot, soon became extremely wealthy and powerful, as evidenced by the abbot's palatial residence in Paris, the Hôtel de Cluny. A number of popes were Cluniac monks, including Urban II who proclaimed the First Crusade in 1095, and the abbots of Cluny were among the most important figures in Christendom, including such figures as St. Hugh, St. Mayeul, and Peter the Venerable. It is not too much to say that Cluny was indispensable to the moral and religious revival of the high Middle Ages which did so much to shape the western world. Unlike the later Cistercian order, itself founded by Cluniac dissidents, which emphasized simplicity, austerity, and manual labor, the Cluniac order emphasized the communal prayer and worship of monks in sumptuous settings. It is therefore not surprising that the order failed to live up to its high ideals over the long term. In the 16th century, the position of abbot was in the power of the king to bestow *in commendam,* which meant that the titular abbot received the revenue and prestige of the position, but had nothing to do with the day-to-day affairs of the monastery. In the 17th century, both great cardinal-ministers of French kings, Cardinals Richelieu and Mazarin, would hold the title.

PLACES TO VISIT

In keeping with the Cluniac emphasis on elaborate worship, the EGLISE ABBATIALE (Abbey Church), built between 1088 and 1131, was the largest church in Christendom until the completion of the present St. Peter's in Rome in the 16th century. And even then, St. Peter's is only about 20 feet longer. Unfortunately, little remains of either the abbey or the church. It was sacked during the religious wars of the 16th century, and was finally disbanded in 1790 during the French Revolution. The church was demolished in order to use the stone as building material. All that remains are the south arms of the transepts, an octagonal belfry known as the CLOCHER DE L'EAU BÉNITE (Holy Water Tower), and the smaller CLOCHER DE L'HORLOGE (Clock Tower). The 13th-century FARINIER, or granary, contains some of the sculptures salvaged from the church, while a small museum, the MUSÉE OCHIER, contains some religious paintings and sculptures, and the remnants of the abbey library. Of the abbey itself, all that remains is the cloister, enclosed by 18th-century buildings, now a technical college.

VICINITY

Just a few miles from the world-famous Cluny stands another monastery, perhaps less well-known, but no less significant in the history of Christianity in France: the abbey of TAIZÉ. In 1949, Taizé became the site of the first Protestant monastery since the Reformation. A Swiss Reformed theology student, Roger Schultz, bought a large uninhabited house in Taizé in 1940 with the intention of helping those suffering under the German occupation. Alone, he sheltered Jews, resistants, and refugees for two years, but in 1942 was arrested by the Gestapo and sent back to Switzerland. After the war, Schultz returned, this time with three other students, and the four of them founded a sort of community where the day was marked by sung offices and prayer. Lit-

tle by little, the small group increased in size and became more and more monastic in its lifestyle. On Easter morning 1949, the seven men there pronounced their vows of poverty, chastity, and obedience, and set about inventing a new monastic rule, and an original liturgy. There is one fundamental difference between the monks of Taizé and those of other orders: they all support themselves through a job in the world: there are businessmen, artists, laborers, doctors. The Taizé monks now number over 50, with another 20 or so in missionary work among the disinherited all over the world. Being one of the rare Protestant monasteries in the world, Taizé attracts men from all over Europe and even from North America. This diversity in nationality is also reflected in a striking diversity in denomination: there are Lutherans, Presbyterians, Episcopalians, etc. Indeed, the fundamental mission of the Taizé is the reconciliation of the different Christian churches. Catholic and Orthodox monks have since established small communities in the area and participate in the celebration of offices at Taizé.

The church in which the offices are celebrated, L'EGLISE DE LA RÉCONCILIATION, a simple concrete structure, was built in 1962 by young German volunteers as a symbol of retribution for the devastation their countrymen inflicted upon Europe. During the week, offices are at 7:00 A.M., 12:00 P.M., and 7:00 P.M.; on Sundays at 8:30 A.M., 11:30 A.M.,

4:30 P.M., and 8:00 P.M. The traditional Taizé worship consists of simple one-line songs of praise sung in many different languages and repeated many times. Through the repetition of simple words, worshipers are drawn into God's presence. This sort of meditative common prayer is often sung long into the night.

Individuals and families are welcome to visit the monastery at any time.

One can attend worship services or "meetings" Monday through Friday from 10 A.M.–12 P.M. and 5–7 P.M. You may also make a weeklong stay. You should plan to arrive between 2 and 4 P.M. on Sunday for a weeklong stay. Meals and lodging are provided for weekly residents. To contact Taizé or find out more about them, simply do a web search with the word *Taizé.*

COLMAR

nce the capital of Upper Alsace, now the prefecture of the department of Haut-Rhin, Colmar traces its roots back to the Middle Ages when it rose to prosperity on Alsace's wine trade. It is situated in the foothills of the Vosges Mountains in the heart of the picturesque Alsace wine country. Occupied by Germany between 1871 and 1918, Colmar stuck aggressively to its French identity. Heavily damaged during the two World Wars, the central part of the town has been meticulously restored, resulting in a charming town of crooked cobblestone streets and half-timbered Alsatian houses, complete with brightly colored pastel plaster, painted shutters, and flower boxes. Especially attractive is the area near the River Lauch, known as *La petite Venise* ("Little Venice"). Colmar is also notable as the birthplace of Frédéric Bartholdi (1834–1904), sculptor of the Statue of Liberty.

PLACES TO VISIT

Colmar is especially notable for several pieces of Late Gothic art. Of these, the most notable is RETABLE D'ISSENHEIM (Issenheim Altarpiece). Painted around 1512 by Matthias Grünewald for the abbey at Issenheim, 22 kilometers south of Colmar, it found its present home in the MUSÉE UNTERLINDEN (Unterlinden Museum) when the abbey was suppressed at the time of the French Revolution. A polyptych, or multipaneled painting, the central panel displays the Crucifixion when closed. In typical Late Gothic style, Christ is shown on the cross in the fullness of horrific suffering, ribcage distended, hands turned upwards with fingers splayed in pain. Below, the fainting Mary is supported by St. John, and Mary Magdalene looks on, seemingly both repulsed by the physical horror and attracted by the love displayed by Christ on the cross. On the other side of the central panel, John the Baptist

C

points to the dying Christ. The central panel is flanked on the left by St. Sebastian, and on the right by St. Anthony. Below is the Entombment of Christ. When opened, according to the Church calendar, other panels depict the Annunciation, the Resurrection, Mary and the Christ child, and other biblical scenes. One of the great masterpieces of medieval religious art, the Issenheim altarpiece shows the realistic techniques of Renaissance art (anatomy, perspective, and the natural world) applied to the religious subjects of Gothic art, bringing to a new level the emphasis on Christ's suffering and death, which was one of

the major themes of late medieval Christianity. Besides the Issenheim altarpiece, the museum also contains several notable late medieval works of art.

Not far away, the EGLISE DES DOMINICAINS (Dominican Church) contains, besides some notable stained glass, another significant masterpiece of late Gothic religious art, the MADONNA OF THE ROSEBUSH, painted in 1473 by the Colmar native Martin Schongauer (1445–91).

The MUSÉE BARTHOLDI (Bartholdi Museum) commemorates the life achievements of the sculptor born in Colmar in 1834.

COMPIÈGNE

George Bernanos's (one of France's best-known 20th-century authors, and a man of faith) famous play, *Dialogue of the Carmelites,* popularized the story of the 16 Carmelite sisters from Compiègne, guillotined in 1794, and proclaimed "blessed" by the Church in 1906. In 1792, the sisters had prayed they might be sacrificed to appease God's anger at France and the Church, which they believed he was pouring out in the violence and religious persecutions of the Revolution. Arrested in 1794 and tried in Paris for fanaticism, defined by the judge simply as "their attachment to puerile religious beliefs," the sisters were condemned to death. On hearing

the sentence, their faces lit up with joy: God had accepted their sacrifice. The sisters went to their deaths singing and with such joy that the ceremonial drums were not beaten. The 16 sisters are buried in the Picpus cemetery in Paris.

Compiègne was occupied by the Germans from August 31 to September 12 in 1914, then, recaptured, became the French headquarters from spring 1917 to spring 1918. The town was badly damaged during both wars, particularly the Soférino area, which was entirely reconstructed after World War II.

PLACES TO VISIT

LE CHÂTEAU DE COMPIÈGNE was one of the favorite places of residence of

GEORGES BERNANOS (1888–1948) was one of France's leading Catholic writers of the 20th century. As a novelist, he explored the struggle between good and evil, particularly within the individual soul. This is exemplified in his best-known work, *Journal d'un curé de campagne (Diary of a Country Priest,* 1937), which was made into a film in 1951 by the French director Robert Bresson. Somewhat mystical in his views, for Bernanos, the supernatural was never far removed from everyday life. He was also intimately involved in current affairs. He spoke out powerfully against the materialism of modern life. He also wrote against the Fascists in the Spanish Civil War, and especially the church leaders who supported them. He condemned the Munich agreement of 1938, and discouraged by current events, he went into exile in Brazil with his wife and six children. He was an early supporter of General Charles de Gaulle, leader of the Free French forces during the Second World War. His return to France in 1945 brought disillusionment with the lack of a spiritual revival. He lived in Tunis until shortly before his death, when he returned to France. Shortly before his death, he completed the *Dialogue des Carmélites (Dialogue of the Carmelites),* dealing with the nuns of Compiègne martyred during the French Revolution. This was later made into an opera by Francis Poulenc.

both Napoleon I and III. The apartments have been restored exactly as they were under the First and Second Empires, displaying much of the original furniture. The chateau houses the **MUSEUM OF THE SECOND EMPIRE** as well as the **MUSEUM OF THE EMPRESS**, which holds many souvenirs of the Imperial family. The chateau is also home to the **COACH AND AUTOMOBILE MUSEUM**, which displays many of Renault's and Citroen's first cars as well as some sumptuous 18th- and 19th-century coaches.

VICINITY

CLARIÈRE DE L'ARMISTICE: eight kilometers east. It was here on November 11, 1918, that the armistice which brought World War I to a close was signed by Marshal Foch and the Germans. Ferdinand Foch (1851–1929) was the greatest military planner in World War I and distinguished himself in the Battle of the Frontiers and then the "Miracle of the Marne." Given the command of the Allied French and British forces, he orchestrated the final Allied attack starting in August 1918. In World War II, after the French were decisively beaten in the Battle of France (1940), the French delegate was forced to come here to sign the German's terms of peace, or rather occupation.

C

CHÂTEAU DE PIERREFONDS: 14 kilometers southeast. Though this castle may seem medieval in appearance, it was in fact constructed almost entirely in the 19th century by the famous architect Viollet-le-Duc (1814–79). The first edifice on the site dates back to Charlemagne's times, but the castle was rebuilt during the Hundred Years' War with England, only to be dismantled in the 17th century by Louis XIII. It was Napoleon III who commissioned Viollet-le-Duc to rebuild a medieval castle which would be an impressive setting in which to receive guests.

CHÂTEAU DE BLÉRANCOURT: 31 kilometers northeast. In World War I, Anne Morgan used the castle as a hospital, and it then became the central site of relief for the civilian population. After the war, Morgan worked on organizing a museum dedicated to the combined history of France and America. She gave the château and exhibition to the state in 1929, which renamed the building MUSÉE NATIONAL DE LA COOPÉRATION FRANCO-AMÉRICAIN. The museum documents and illustrates the long relationship France and America have had, including the Louisiana Purchase, emigration to America, and cooperation in the two World Wars.

CONQUES

A tiny medieval town, situated on the steeply wooded gorge above the river Dourdou, Conques was an important stop on the medieval pilgrimage route between Le Puy-En-Velay and Santiago de Compostela in northwestern Spain, the most important pilgrimage site in medieval Europe. Conques was also a pilgrimage site in its own right. The reason for the town's existence in the first place is the Abbaye Ste-Foye, founded by a hermit named Dadon who settled in the area around 800 and founded a Benedictine monastery. In the mid-9th century, one of the monks stole the relics of St. Foy

from the church at Agen. St. Foy was a young Christian girl martyred in Agen near the beginning of the 4th century. Her relics were reputed to be able to cure blindness and liberate captives. The abbey was sacked by the Huguenots in the 16th century and languished until restored in the 19th century through the activism of Prosper Mérimée.

PLACES TO VISIT

The EGLISE STE-FOY (St. Foy Church) was the abbey church, and as it now stands, it was built between 1045 and 1060, and is an outstanding example of Romanesque architecture. In striking contrast to the austere exterior, above the west door is an elaborate tympanum, which still has traces of its original coloring. It shows the Last Judgment, with Christ in the center, flanked by the hermit Dadon and the Emperor Charlemagne, while St. Foy kneels in supplication. To the right are represented the horrors of hell, including one scene where demons shove sinners into the throat of hell, to be welcomed by Satan himself. Inside, the major attraction is the TRÉSOR (Treasury). Its most precious possession is the reliquary of St. Foy. Made of wood and covered with beaten gold, it was assembled over the centuries; the head dates from the late Roman Empire, while the gold and engraved crystal date from the Merovingian period (7th–9th centuries). Near the end of the 10th century, the statue was refurbished and adorned with enamel and precious stones. During the Middle Ages, it would have been on display in order for pilgrims to venerate the saint. An account dating from 1010 gives an idea of the impact of the reliquary on pilgrims: "The crowd of people prostrating themselves on the ground was so dense it was impossible to kneel down.... When they saw it for the first time, all in gold and sparkling with precious stones and looking like a human face, the majority of the peasants thought that the statue was really looking at them and answering their prayers with its eyes." Besides St. Foy, the treasury also possesses several other significant reliquaries, including one thought to have been presented to the monastery by Emperor Charlemagne.

The village of Conques itself is mainly contained within its medieval walls, parts of which still stand, along with three of its gates. Most of the houses date from the late Middle Ages. On top of the hill is the new EUROPEAN CENTER FOR MEDIEVAL ART AND CIVILIZATION, with continual exhibits and displays.

DIJON

Situated at the northern end of the great Burgundian wine-growing district of the Côte d'Or, Dijon began life as a relatively insignificant Roman settlement known as Divio. It was converted to Christianity in the 2nd century by the martyr St. Bénigne, in whose honor a monastery was founded in the 6th century. Chief town of the barbarian kingdom of Burgundy, it only became prominent, however, in the 11th century when it became the capital of the duchy of Burgundy. When the last native duke died in 1364, Charles V (the Wise), king of France (1364–80), ensconced his younger brother as duke.

This was Duke Philip the Bold (1364–1404). He and his successors (John the Fearless, 1404–19; Philip the Good, 1419–67; and Charles the Bold, 1467–77) became the most powerful rulers in Europe. Through marriage and inheritance, they also became rulers of large parts of the Netherlands, which were the industrial and commercial heartland of medieval Europe, giving the dukes fantastic wealth and power. They used these to establish Dijon and the ducal court as the preeminent cultural center in northern Europe, attracting artists, musicians, and writers from all over Europe. They also used their wealth and power to establish their diplomatic and military might, playing an important role in the Hundred Years' War. At a time when Charles VI of France (1380–1422) was completely mad, John the Fearless established himself as the key player in the kingdom, before he was murdered in 1419. While the dauphin, later Charles VII, disinherited by his father in favor of the king of England, cowered in Bourges, the dukes of Burgundy far exceeded the kings of France in power and wealth, despite their technical status as inferior vassals. It was Philip the Good who sold Joan of Arc to the English to be executed as a witch, before changing sides and supporting Charles VII, which changed the course of the war. Following the end of the Hundred Years' War in 1453, Charles the Bold attempted to continue his predecessors' independent policy but came up against the wily Louis XI of France (1461–83). Charles was killed in battle at the siege of Nancy in 1477. Louis XI managed to seize the duchy of Burgundy, but most of the Netherlands escaped his grasp and went to Charles's daughter, Mary of Burgundy. Mary subsequently married the Holy Roman Emperor Maximilian of Habsburg. The Burgundian inheritance therefore lay at the base of the rise to power of the Habsburg dynasty in the 16th century. Upon Burgundy's annexation to the kingdom of France, Dijon became the seat of a *parlement* (or regional supreme court) and the Burgundian estates, or regional representative assembly. As a result, it attracted judges, lawyers, nobles, and statesmen, who graced the city with their stylish *hôtels particuliers* or town houses throughout the 17th and 18th centuries. During the Wars of Religion, Burgundy and Dijon were firmly controlled by the Guise family in the interests of the Catholic League. Dijon was one of the last cities in France to recognize as legitimate king the former Huguenot Henry IV, holding out even longer than Paris.

PLACES TO VISIT

Dijon's most important site is the PALAIS DES DUCS (Ducal Palace). Abandoned after the death of Charles the Bold in 1477, it fell into disrepair before being renovated in a classical style to serve as the seat of the estates of Burgundy. Part of the palace still serves as

Dijon's city hall. The only parts remaining from the earlier period are the Tour Philippe-le-Bon and the Tour de Bar in the east wing, which now houses the MUSÉE DES BEAUX-ARTS (Fine Arts Museum). On the first floor, the SALLE DES GARDES, or former Banqueting Hall, bears witness to Dijon's artistic prominence. The most important works are two tombs *(tombeaux)*, those of Philip the Bold by Claus Sluter and Claus de Werve, and of John the Fearless and his wife Margaret of Bavaria. Both tombs were originally in the Chartreuse de Champmol (see below), but were desecrated and despoiled in the Revolution, before being restored in their new location in 1827. The tombs demonstrate both the wealth and power of the dukes, and the flamboyant and often excessive modes of devotion characteristic of the late Middle Ages. The tomb of Philip the Bold contains statuettes of forty members of the ducal household and monks of various orders, while a statue of the duke lies above with angels supporting his helmet and a lion lying at his feet. The tomb of John the Fearless is similar in style, with a procession of hooded mourners around the base. There are also two magnificent altarpieces. One, sculpted by Jacques de Baerze and painted by Broederlam, depicts the saints and martyrs. The other shows the Crucifixion and has more of Broederlam's paintings on the reverse sides of its panels. There is also a notable portrait of Philip the Good by the famous Flemish master Rogier van der Weyden, a student of van Eyck and teacher of Hans Memling.

The CHARTREUSE DE CHAMPMOL (Charterhouse of Champmol) lies about 1,500 meters west of the city center along Avenue Albert Ier past the railway station. Founded in 1383 by Philip the Bold, this monastery was intended to serve as his dynasty's burial place, a sort of Burgundian St. Dénis. The monastery was despoiled during the French Revolution, and little remains. It is now the site of a psychiatric hospital. There is, however, a sculpture of the PUITS DE MOISE (Moses' Well) by Claus Sluter. This was originally the pedestal of a sculpture of Calvary, and contains six great statues of Moses and other prophets looking outwards from a hexagonal base. Sluter was a native Dutchman who worked in Dijon between 1385 and 1404. Sluter was also responsible for the PORTAIL DE LA CHAPELLE (chapel doorway), which also remains, and contains sculpture portraits of Philip the Bold and his wife, Margaret of Flanders.

CATHÉDRALE ST. BÉGNINE (St. Bégnine Cathedral) is unexceptional except for its typically Burgundian brightly colored tile roof and its circular 11th-century crypt, which contains the remains of the tomb of St. Bégnine.

EGLISE NOTRE-DAME (Notre Dame Church) is a fine example of 13th-century Burgundian Gothic architecture. The unique west facade contains rows of spectacular gargoyles, many of them original. The clock tower contains a famous mechanical clock, carried off from Courtrai in the Netherlands by Philip the Bold in 1382. In the interior there is a famous 11th-century statue of the Black Virgin.

DOMRÉMY-LA-PUCELLE

On January 6, 1412, a young girl was born to a prosperous peasant in Domrémy-la-Pucelle. Named Jeanne (Joan), as a young girl she heard voices she attributed to St. Catherine, St. Margaret, and St. Michael, urging her to deliver France from its misery and from English oppression. French fortunes were then at their nadir during the Hundred Years' War. With some difficulty, she convinced her local lord that her visions were genuine. Leaving the nearby town of Vaucouleurs on February 23, 1429, over the next fifteen months she searched out the dauphin in Chinon, relieved the siege of Orléans, fought her way to Reims where the dauphin was crowned Charles VII, was captured by the Burgundians, turned over to the English, and burned as a witch in Rouen. Known as *La Pucelle* (the Maid), Joan of Arc's career and campaigns were the turning point in the Hundred Years' War, rousing the despairing Charles VII into action, and stirring feelings of French patriotism in the campaign to expel the English. Although largely ignored after her death (her successes and victories were an embarrassment to Charles VII and the nobility), she has repeatedly served as a symbol of French patriotism and resistance to foreign rule. Interestingly, she was not canonized by the Catholic Church as St. Joan until the 1920s, when the French needed a national symbol of resistance and hope in the aftermath of the catastrophic First World War.

PLACES TO VISIT

The MAISON NATALE (birthplace) of Joan of Arc, though often restored, still stands. A simple stone cottage, once used as a cowshed, it now adjoins a small museum devoted to Joan's career and memory. The VILLAGE CHURCH, though much altered since Joan's day, still houses the 12th-century font at which Joan was baptized. Two kilometers southwest of Domrémy is Bois Chenu, where Joan heard the saints' voices calling her to her divine mission.

This is now commemorated in the elaborate and ornate **BASILIQUE DU BOIS CHENU** (Basilica of Bois Chenu), built in 1881, to assuage French national pride in the aftermath of the disastrous defeat at the hands of the Prussians in 1871.

DOUAI

An old Flemish trading town, Douai was heavily damaged in both World Wars. Because of the valuable nearby coal fields, it was occupied by the Germans for most of the First World War (1914–18). Nevertheless, through extensive restoration, Douai has managed to retain much of its medieval and 18th-century Flemish flavor. Its main point of historic and religious significance, however, is its connection to England, specifically to English Catholicism. In 1568, at a time when it was illegal to be a Catholic in England, the exiled Cardinal Allen founded a Jesuit college in Douai to train English Catholic priests, anticipating the day (never realized) when England would be restored to the Catholic Church. Many of these "seminary priests" returned surreptitiously to England to succor English Catholics, or "recusants" as they were known. Many of them paid with their lives. It was also in Douai that an English Catholic translation of the Old Testament was published in 1609, which when put together with a translation of the New Testament published in Reims in 1582, is known as the Douai Bible, an English Catholic counterpart of the Protestant King James Version, published in 1611. The Jesuit college was closed during the Revolution.

In 1815, a British soldier who had come over for the Battle of Waterloo found a small nonconformist evangelical group and put them in contact with the Baptist Society of Evangelization. A Swiss Baptist, Henri Pyt, arrived to promote the Baptist faith and founded a small community from which is descended the current *Association des Eglises baptistes de France* (Association of French Baptist Churches). In 1832, the Baptist convention at Boston established a church at Douai, and there is still today a small Baptist community with their church in the rue de la Comédie. There are around 3000 Baptists today in France.

Occupied for the whole of World War I, Douai was systematically destroyed as the Germans retreated. It then suffered heavily again in World War II. The bell tower on the Hôtel de Ville was replaced in 1954.

PLACES TO VISIT

HÔTEL DE VILLE (City Hall) contains a celebrated **BEFFROI** (belfry, or bell tower) built in 1390, celebrated by Victor Hugo

D

in the 19th century and painted by the Impressionist Corot. The belfry also contains a famous carillon of 62 bells. The MUSÉE DE LA CHARTREUSE (Charterhouse Museum) in a former Carthusian monastery houses an important collection of paintings by French, Flemish, and Dutch masters, including Rubens, van Dyck, Rodin, and Douai's own native son Jean Bellegambe (1470–1534). The museum houses Bellegambe's most famous work, his *Polyptique d'Anchin* (Polyptych of the Trinity) which combines medieval themes with Renaissance decoration (columns and shells) and Flemish realism.

DOURGNE

Two kilometers northeast of this out-of-the-way village are hidden the vast buildings of two Benedictine abbeys. L'ABBAYE ST. BENOÎT D'EN CALCAT was erected in 1896 and observes the primitive rule restored in France in 1850. The architect of the monastery and splendid Roman-style church completed in 1936 was an anonymous monk. The monks of d'En Calcat are renowned for the beauty of their Gregorian chants, which can be heard at the regular offices of the day. Just a few hundred meters away stands another abbey, L'ABBAYE SAINTE-SCHOLASTIQUE, designed and constructed between 1891 and 1927 by the same monk. The pair of abbeys constitute the most important monastic construction of the 20th century.

FONTAINEBLEAU

The royal palace or *château* at Fontainebleau was constructed by King Francis I (1515–47) and reflects the influence of the Italian Renaissance, with which Francis was much taken. It was also Napoleon Bonaparte's favorite residence.

Pope Pius VII stayed in the château when he came to France for the crowning of Napoleon as emperor in 1804. Though it was thanks to Napoleon that France renewed relations with the pope and returned, at least officially, to being a Christian nation, these measures were certainly more politically than personally motivated. Himself a religious skeptic, at the coronation ceremony, Napoleon showed a blatant disrespect for the head of the Church, and thus symbolically for the notion of the state being subject to the laws of Rome, when he took the emperor's crown from the pope's hands and crowned himself. This disrespect was evidenced once again in 1809 when Napoleon arrested Pius VII for refusing to allow the Catholic Church at Rome to become both temporal and spiritual subject of the Empire. The pope was held in captivity for over four years, the last two of which were spent at the château in Fontainbleau. It was also at Fontainbleau on April 6, 1814, that Napoleon abdicated and gave his farewell address to his men.

One can visit the sumptuous NAPOLEONIC APARTMENTS furnished in Empire style as well as the MUSÉE NAPOLEON.

FONTENAY, ABBAYE DE

Founded in 1118 by St. Bernard of Clairvaux, Fontenay was one of the earliest daughter houses of the Cistercian order. It was built according to Cistercian specifications in a remote and undeveloped location in western Burgundy, and in a plain and austere style, which contrasted with the wealth and sumptuousness of the Cluniac order. The monastery prospered until the 16th century, when it suffered under Huguenot attacks. It was also affected by the practice of *commendam*. Under this, according to the tenets of Gallicanism, abbots were appointed by the king "in commendam," for the sole purpose of garnering the revenue; the actual administration of the abbey was left in the hands of poorly paid and often unqualified substitutes. Dissolved at the time of the Revolution in the late 18th century, it was used as a paper factory until 1906, when it entered private hands and was restored to the state one sees now. Fontenay is one of the best preserved medieval monasteries in France, despite the fact that its refectory or dining hall was destroyed in 1745. No one who is interested in monasticism or medieval life in general should miss it.

PLACES TO VISIT

EGLISE ABBATIALE (Abbey Church), constructed between 1139 and 1147, is an excellent example of Cistercian plainness and austerity. Lit only by windows in the square apse, it is completely unadorned

GALLICAN/GALLICANISM is the system or belief in the semi-autonomous nature of the Catholic Church in France. According to its tenets, the Church in France was self-governing in terms of personnel, finance, and administration, while subject to Rome in matters of doctrine. According to Gallicanism, bishops and other important clergymen were appointed by the king and consecrated by the pope. Those who upheld the power of Rome were known as ultramontanists, because they looked across the mountains, into Italy, for authority.

both inside and out. One can also visit the plainest Romanesque cloisters, dormitory, scriptorium (where monks laboriously copied manuscripts), and chapter house (where meetings were held), as well as the kennels, bakery, forge, dovecote, abbot's residence, infirmary, and prison.

GAILLAC

G

The small town of Gaillac formed around an important abbey founded in the 7th century, which is also famous for a sparkling white wine developed by the monks. Gaillac is the birthplace of St. Emilie de Vialar (1797–1856), founder of the Sisters of St. Joseph of the Apparition. While still very young, she was inspired by St. François Xavier and wished to become a missionary. When she had brought up her three brothers, she started the new order in a small building at the end of the Cours Gambetta. In 1835, she and three others went to Algeria as missionaries, and later founded hospices and girls schools in Tunisia, Malta, and Jerusalem. Penniless but never discouraged, she died in 1856 and was canonized in 1951.

ISSOUDUN

PLACES TO VISIT

BASILICA OF NOTRE DAME DU SACRÉ CŒUR (Our Lady of the Sacred Heart Basilica), erected in 1864, is interesting in the history of Catholic churches in that no statue, miracle, or apparition of any kind lies behind its construction. Instead, it came to be because of an idea of the local parish priest of the 19th century, Father Jules Chevalier. His idea was that the heart of Christ, the Son, can refuse nothing to his mother Mary, thus the hope behind prayers offered up to the Virgin Mary. Abandoned in a church by his parents, Chevalier felt called to the ministry early in life and entered the modest seminary at Bourges at eighteen. Ordained in 1854, he was sent to Issoudun, a dying parish where just 30 of the 12,000 inhabitants attended Mass, and just one participated in the Easter communion. Issoudun is a shocking example of the dechristianization that took place not just in the cities but in the country as well in the years following the Revolution. Despite the barren environment, Chevalier set to work to reconvert the parish, and in 1864, the current basilica was constructed from the gifts of locals and other Catholics inspired by his new devotional idea.

KAYSERSBERG

Situated in the heart of beautiful Alsace wine country, where the Weiss River flows out of the Vosges Mountains into the lowlands of Alsace, Kaysersberg is a picturesque village, which, as its name indicates, reflects the German heritage of both the town itself, and of the surrounding province of Alsace. In the late Middle Ages, it was part of a group of Alsatian cities called the Decapolis, whose purpose was to maintain the privileges of urban dwellers against the exactions of feudal lords. Its main claim to fame, however, is as the birthplace of Albert Schweitzer (1875–1965), physician, theologian, philosopher, organist, humanitarian, and Nobel Peace Prize laureate. Born at a time when Alsace was part of the German Empire, Schweitzer was educated in both France and Germany, and by the age of 30, had established an international reputation as a theologian and as an organist, especially as an interpreter of the works of Johann Sebastian Bach. In 1902, he took up a theology position at the University of Strasbourg. Based on his reverence for life, he determined to become a medical missionary, and studied medicine in Strasbourg from 1905–13. He established a hospital at Lambaréné in French Equatorial Africa (now Gabon) with money raised from organ recitals, and in 1913 took up residence there, and expanded the hospital over the years. During World War I (1914–18) he was interned as a German national, but returned to Africa in 1924. In 1952, he won the Nobel Peace Prize, using the prize money to further expand the hospital and establish a leper colony. He was also a renowned writer on theology and philosophy. His most famous work is *The Quest for the Historical Jesus* (1906), in which he criticized 19th-century theologians for ignoring the Jesus of the Bible and retaining only those characteristics which fit into their notions of who Jesus should be.

PLACES TO VISIT

Next door to SCHWEITZER'S BIRTHPLACE at 12 rue du Général de Gaulle is the MUSÉE ALBERT SCHWEITZER (Albert Schweitzer Museum). While in Kaysersberg, be sure to see the ruins of the 20th-century fortress, the fortified bridge, the charming half-timbered houses, and the church, which contains an impressive 16th-century altarpiece.

LAON

Situated on a rocky ridge 100 meters above the surrounding Picard plain, Laon provides commanding views of the surrounding countryside. Laon was first fortified in late Roman times. For a time under the later Carolingians, Laon served as the capital of France, before Hugh Capet moved to Paris in the 10th century. During the intellectual revival of the 11th and 12th centuries, the cathedral school at Laon was one of the foremost centers of learning in northern Europe. Until the 12th century, Laon was ruled by its bishop, before bloody riots by the townspeople, and the assassination of Bishop Gaudry in 1111, resulted in self-government by the town's citizens. Among Laon's natives are the 17th-century painters the Le Nain brothers, and the Jesuit missionary Jacques Marquette (1637–75), who explored much of the Mississippi valley.

PLACES TO VISIT

The HAUTE VILLE (upper town) has preserved much of its medieval heritage, including its ramparts or walls, which provide stunning views of the surrounding countryside. Laon was once the site of two abbeys and numerous churches, giving the town the name *la montagne*

couronée (the crowned mountain). Of these churches, only three remain. At the western end of the *haute ville* is ST. MARTIN, a massively buttressed early Gothic structure, built in the 12th century, and a remnant of a famous abbey. Note especially the carving on the facade of St. Martin dividing his cloak. Near the eastern end of the *haute ville* is the Romanesque octagonal CHAPELLE DES TEMPLIERS (Templars' Chapel). Laon's major attraction, however, is the CATHÉDRALE NOTRE-DAME (Notre-Dame Cathedral). Built between 1160 and 1235 in a pure early Gothic style, it is unusual in possessing four towers, rather than the usual two on the west front. The two towers of the facade feature colossal carvings of oxen, which according to legend hauled the building stone to the site of their own accord. The facade is unusual in that it is deeply recessed. Among the sculptures are figures representing the liberal arts, reflecting the importance of the cathedral school as a center of learning in the

CAROLINGIAN(S). Ruling dynasty of France from 751 to 987. Founded by Pepin the Short (751–68), it reached its greatest height under Charles the Great or Charlemagne (768–814), when it took in most of current-day France, Germany, and northern Italy. Charlemagne was crowned Roman emperor by the pope on Christmas Day, 800. After Charlemagne's death in 814, his empire fragmented as his successors fought with each other and dealt with foreign pressure, particularly from the Vikings and Magyars (or Hungarians). The empire split into two halves: West Francia, which would eventually evolve into the kingdom of France; and East Francia, which would become the Holy Roman Empire, based in Germany.

Middle Ages. Above the main portal is a carving of the coronation of the Virgin, while the south portal features the Last Judgment. The huge interior (120 yards long by 33 yards wide at the transepts, and 26 yards high) is notable for its sense of space and light, and its elegant rose windows.

LISIEUX

Lisieux is the birthplace of St. Thérèse de Lisieux or St. Thérèse de l'enfant Jésus (1873–97), one of the most well-known saints recently canonized by the Catholic Church. At just ten years of age when she was very sick, she had a vision of the Virgin Mary, and was healed at the instant. She decided at this point that she wanted to join the Carmelite order, the strictest of religious orders, and because of her evident faith and ardent desire, was allowed to enter at just 15 though the regular eligible age is 21. However, she caught tuberculosis, and after much suffering, she died at just 25. When she died, people discovered that she had written the story of her spiritual life, which she called "Story of a Soul," in school notebooks. Though naïve in style, her writing had a profound spiritual inspiration and message, precisely that God is above all a God of love who desires not the death of the sinner but rather his salvation. Thérèse Martin was canonized St. Thérèse de Lisieux in 1925, and the story of her soul is now translated into over 50 languages.

PLACES TO VISIT

Her TOMB is in the CARMELITE CHAPEL and to the northeast of town is LA MAISON DES BUISSONNETS, where Thérèse Martin grew up and where she had the miraculous vision. In 1952, a MONUMENTAL BASILICA dedicated to St. Thérèse was consecrated. The basilica lies to the southeast of town.

LOURDES

This small town in the High Pyrenees is today the site of one of the world's most important pilgrimages to the cult of the Virgin Mary. Many miracles have been attested here, and over 50 million people a year from all five continents visit the site, hoping for healing, for a conversion experience, or simply to express their devotion to Mary. It is in the summer months that the great national and international pilgrimages take place.

The pilgrimage arose from the repeated apparitions in 1858 of the Virgin

Mary to an extremely poor girl named Bernadette Soubirou. The first vision came on February 11 at the Grotte (cave) de Massabielle: it was a woman bathed in white light and smiling. Bernadette had 17 more visions at the cave over the following months. The vision revealed a mountain spring and instructed her to tell the Church to build a chapel at the cave. Bernadette, who became a novice at the Sisters of Charity convent in Nevers, faced much opposition from the Church and other pretenders, but after four years of investigation, it was finally concluded that the Virgin Mary had indeed appeared to this humble girl. Then, seven years later, Pope Pius IX declared authentic the testimony of Bernadette. A sanctuary was constructed and then a basilica was consecrated in 1876. The pilgrimage was born and miracles started to be observed. The Church asked for the cooperation of doctors in determining the veracity of miracles, and in 1885 a bureau of miracle verification was created. Since its creation, over 60 miracles have been officially recognized by doctors. What is a miracle for the doctors? The disease or illness from which a person suffered must be incurable or extremely hard to heal; all known medical treatments must have been tried and failed; before the pilgrimage, the sick person must have shown no signs of recovery; and finally, the healing must be sudden, complete, and definitive.

PLACES TO VISIT

With the growing importance of the site, another church, the **BASILICA OF THE ROSARY,** was built in 1889 in Romano-Byzantine style and has two curving approach ramps. Then, in 1959, the largest underground sanctuary in the world (it seats up to 30,000), the elliptical **ST. PIUS X UNDERGROUND BASILICA,** was constructed. In 1988 the **CHURCH OF ST. BERNADETTE** was dedicated, built in a thoroughly modern style. Underneath the **UPPER BASILICA** are the **CRYPT** (the site of the first chapel), a place for prayer and meditation and the **GROTTO OF MASSABIELLE** (Grotto of Miracles), the site of the first apparition of the Virgin. Here are the springs which Bernadette later discovered, the waters of which are highly sought after in the form of both baths and drinking fountains. Overlooking the basilicas and the spring are the **STATIONS OF THE CROSS,** a symbolic reenactment of Christ's journey to Calvary.

LYON
(LYONS)

Situated at the confluence of the rivers Rhône and Saône, Lyon vies with Marseille for the title of France's second city. An important interchange for more than 2000 years, Lyon is currently a cultural, industrial, and financial center second only to Paris. The site of a Celtic settlement, in 43 B.C. it was established as Julius Caesar's base for the conquest of Gaul and renamed Lugdunum, or "hill of the crow." With its position at the meeting of two major rivers, Lugdunum was also made the hub of the Roman road system in Gaul, establishing for the settlement an important role in transportation and communications which has persisted into the 21st century. The city became the capital of the Roman province of the Three Gauls, which took in most of what is now eastern France, and complemented the older Roman province (or Provence) centered in Narbonne.

Lyon is also one of the oldest Christian sites in France. In the 2nd century A.D., Christianity had made a number of converts in the city. In A.D. 177, faced with hostility from the non-Christians and the potential for mob violence, the governor martyred a number of Christians, notably St. Pothinus and the slave woman St. Blandina. Some twenty years later St. Irenaeus—an early Christian theologian and apologist, combatant of the Gnostic heresy, and bishop of Lyon—was also martyred here. Throughout the Middle Ages, Lyon remained subject to its bishops, until it was incorporated into the kingdom of France in the early 14th century. In the 12th century, Peter Waldo or Valdez, native of Lyon, founded the "Poor of Lyon," or Waldensians.

During the 15th and 16th centuries, Lyon experienced a rebirth of sorts. Situated on the main route into Italy, Lyon was the portal through which the cultural movement of the Renaissance entered France from Italy. It became an important financial center, outstripping Paris in this respect, as Italian bankers set up shop and lent money to the French kings. It also became a center of the new printing industry, and was the home base of many of the most important publishers of the day, including Claude Nourry, the publisher of Rabelais; Etienne Dolet, the publisher of Marot; and Henri Estienne. In the 15th century as well, Lyon became the center of the French silk industry, as silkworms were smuggled from China. It was during this period that Vieux Lyon (Old Lyon) took on the elegant aspect it retains today. Wealthy bankers, merchants, and financiers built elegant town houses (hôtels) for themselves in flamboyant Gothic and later in Renaissance styles. In the mid-16th century, Lyon was a hotbed of Calvinism, which appealed especially to workers in skilled trades such as printers and silkweavers. During the first religious war, in 1562, Lyon was one of the cities seized by Huguenot forces. Thereafter, it was a stronghold of militant Catholicism. It suffered its own St. Bartholomew's Massacre in 1572, and was one of the strongholds of the Catholic League.

During the French Revolution, Lyon supported the moderate Girondins against the more radical Jacobins during the Reign of Terror. As a result, the city was conquered after a two-month-long siege, and thousands of its citizens were executed and parts of the city razed. In the 19th century, Lyon continued to prosper, largely due to the invention of the power loom by native son Joseph Jacquard. Industrialization, however, produced labor unrest, and in 1834 there was an uprising of silk workers or "Canuts," which was forcibly repressed at the cost of several hundred lives. During World War II, Lyon was a center of the Resistance.

Lyon remains prosperous and important, a center of French and European finance and industry. It is also renowned as the gastronomic capital of France, home of many of the most important chefs, including Paul Bocuse.

PLACES TO VISIT

Lyon's Roman past remains visible atop the COLLINE DE FOURVIÈRE (Fourvière Hill), the site of Roman Lugdunum. The name derives from the Latin for old forum (*forum vetus*). It is accessible by a steep walk or by a funicular which leads to the BASILIQUE NOTRE-DAME DE FOURVIÈRE. Most notable among the Roman remains are two theatres, one which seated about 10,000 (equal to that at Arles), and a smaller Odeon, which while less well preserved boasts a mosaic floor, and which is still used for cultural events. On the hill, there is also the MUSÉE DE LA CIVILISATION GALLO-ROMAINE (Museum of Gallo-Roman

Civilization), which contains an extensive collection of artifacts. Most notable among these are the *Table Claudienne* (Claudian Tables), on which are inscribed the words of a speech of the Roman Emperor Claudius (born in Lyon), in A.D. 48 in which he granted full rights of Roman citizenship to the inhabitants of Gaul. The BASILIQUE NOTRE-DAME, very similar in its neo-Byzantine style to SACRÉ CŒUR in Paris, was indeed built under similar circumstances. Closed by the convention in 1793, Pope Pius VII celebrated the first Mass of reconciliation on returning to Italy from the crowning of Napoleon. In 1852, a huge statue (20 feet tall) of the Virgin Mary was inaugurated, and the whole city was lit up with candles. During the Franco-Prussian War, the prelate of the chapel made a vow to erect a new Basilica to Notre Dame de Fourvières if the town was spared a German assault. It was and in 1872, construction started and the new basilica was consecrated in 1896, though the statue remained in the old chapel. It also served the purpose of demonstrating the continuing wealth and power of the Roman Catholic Church in the face of the secularizing policies of the Third Republic, instituted in the wake of the French defeat. The church is notable mostly for its extravagant interior decoration in marble and mosaics. Adjacent to the basilica is an 18th-century chapel with an adjoining terrace which provides superb views of the city, the rivers, and on a clear day, the Alps, including Mont Blanc.

Below Fourvière, wedged between the hill and the river Saône, is VIEUX LYON (Old Lyon), where Lyon's glorious medieval and Renaissance past is on display in the form of elegant town houses and narrow cobblestone streets. Many of the courtyards are connected to nearby alleys by narrow covered passages called *traboules,* from the Latin *trans ambulare,* to "walk through." Originally built to protect delicate and expensive silk cloth from the elements while in transit, during World War II, the *traboules* enabled the Resistance to escape arrest, since the occupying Germans would get lost in the mazelike network. The CATHÉDRALE ST. JEAN (St. John Cathedral) was begun in the late 12th century and largely completed by the 15th. It suffered extensive damage at the hands of the Huguenots in the 16th century and of the revolutionaries in the 18th. Its elaborately decorated west facade contains 280 carved medallions. Inside, the chancel and apse are in a Romanesque style typical of the Rhône valley, while the nave is Early Gothic. The glass in the chancel dates from the 13th century, as do the rose windows in the transepts. In the north transept is a 14th-century astronomical clock which reenacts the Annunciation at noon, 2:00, and 3:00 most days.

Across the Saône from Vieux Lyon is the PRESQU'ÎLE (Peninsula), the modern city center. Among its attractions is the MUSÉE DE L'IMPRIMERIE (Printing Museum), which displays some of the first books ever printed, including a page from a Gutenberg Bible printed in 1455. There is also the MUSÉE DES TISSUS (Fabric Museum), which houses an extensive display of Oriental and European silks. The MUSÉE DES BEAUX-ARTS (Fine Arts Museum) is the second largest art museum in France, behind only the LOUVRE. Housed in a 17th-century former Benedictine abbey, it contains an extensive collection of Egyptian, Greco-Roman, and Gallo-Roman antiquities. There is also an impressive collection of French, Italian, Dutch, and Spanish old masters, including *The Ascension* by Perugino and *The Adoration of the Magi* by Rubens. The museum also houses works by Impressionists, including Monet and Chagall. The former cloister houses an extensive sculpture garden with numerous works by Rodin.

PLACE BELLACOUR: The buildings lining the square were razed by the Convention troops and the facades you see today were built in 1800. In the center of the square is a classical equestrian statue of Louis XIV (1825).

RUE DE LA RÉPUBLIQUE: The magnificent 19th-century facades of this the main avenue of Lyon help to give Lyon its elegant and majestic character. At the corner of the rue Gaspain stands a monument to Lyon's martyrs of the Resistance (1948).

PLACE DES TERREAUX: Contains a splendid fountain by Bartholdi of four bounding horses representing four springing rivers.

PLACE DES JACOBINS: Contains a beautiful fountain by Desgeorges (1886), ornated with statues of the four artists: Delorme, Audran, Coustou, and Flandun.

PARC DE LA TÊTE D'OR: Created in 1856, this large lovely park offers a moment of quietness away from the hustle and bustle of the town center.

PALAIS DU COMMERCE ET DE LA BOURSE: Constructed by Dardel from 1855 to 1860, it was here that President Carnot was assassinated as he left the palace on June 24, 1894.

PALAIS DE JUSTICE: Impressive and stately building built by Baltard in 1835.

LÉRINS, LES ILES DE

Site of an important early monastery founded by St. Honorat in 410, the two islands of St. Marguerite and St. Honorat were an important center of learning in the Dark Ages. Among those who studied here were St. Loup, Bishop of Troyes; and St. Patrick, patron saint of Ireland. Devastated by Saracen raids, the monastery was abandoned in the 10th century and was refounded in the 12th.

PLACES TO VISIT

L'ÎLE ST. HONORAT: Site of a monastery since the 4th century. The 18th century saw the community of monks fall into rapid decline, and in 1788 on the eve of the Revolution, with only three monks left, the pope secularized the island. As with all the land the church possessed, St. Honorat was confiscated under the Revolution and was sold to an actress. The island then passed into the hands of an English Anglican minister, who sold it to an anonymous party in 1859. Great no doubt was his surprise when he learned that the anonymous party was none other than the bishop of Fréjus. The island was conferred on a group of Benedictine monks from Sénanque (southeast of Avignon), and in 1872, the community was definitively established. A new monastery was constructed in neo-Romanesque style as a sort of reliquary which encloses the remains of the old cloister, refectory, and chapter room. A sizeable community of monks occupy the monastery today and live principally from cultivating wine grapes. The visit of the monastery is reserved to men, but the rest of the island is open to all and offers much scenery as well as a magnificent view of the French coastline.

L'ÎLE ST. MARGUERITE: Made famous as the site of the prison which held the prisoner "Masque de fer" (the

Man in the Iron Mask), and also the marshal Bazaine, condemned for treason during the Franco-Prussian war, the prison also held Huguenot pastors who were imprisoned after the revocation of the Edict of Nantes in 1685. In 1950, a HUGUENOT MEMORIAL remembering six pastors who died in the prison was constructed in one of the cells.

MARLIEUX

In the middle of this isolated marshland arise the buildings of a lonely Trappist monastery, NOTRE DAME DES DOMBES. Established by about 50 monks from another Trappist monastery at Grignan in 1863, the desire was to found an abbey "right in the middle of this empire of fever," so called because of the marshy surroundings. The buildings of the abbey were finished in 1865. The monastery played a heroic and tragic role in the Resistance during World War II. Starting in 1940, the abbey hid machinery, fuel, and arms for French Resistance fighters. Denounced in late 1941, the monks were interrogated by the Germans. On December 8, they threatened to shoot one of the monks, Father Bernard. He responded: "Go ahead! I believe in the resurrection of the dead." Tortured and deported to Buchenwald, then Bergen-Belsen, he died in 1944. On May 19, 1944, the SS once more invaded the abbey, which was by this time hiding many resistors and Jews. Two monks were gunned down, but the lives of all the other occupants were saved by an attack by Resistance guerillas which forced the Germans to retreat. The monastery received the *Légion d'honneur* (Legion of Honor) and *Croix de Guerre* (Cross of War) for its heroic efforts.

MARSEILLE
(MARSEILLES)

Founded as Massilia by Greek colonists around 600 B.C., Marseille is presently France's third largest city (after Paris and Lyon) and is famous (or infamous) for its pollution, corruption, and organized crime. It has been an important seaport since its foundation, when it controlled the trade from the interior of Gaul and from as far away as Britain, via the Rhône River. The city's Greek inhabitants controlled a series of trading outposts, making it a rival of the North African city of Carthage. By the late 2nd century B.C.,

Marseille had formed an alliance with Rome, which allowed its continued self-government and control of the Rhône trade, as well as serving Rome as an important link in its communications with its possessions in Spain. However, in the civil war between Julius Caesar and Pompey, Marseille chose to support Pompey (the eventual loser). In 49 B.C., the city was conquered and sacked by Caesar, losing its commercial preeminence to Arles and nearby Fréjus. According to legend, the Christian heritage of Marseille is very ancient. Supposedly, after Jesus' death Lazarus and Mary Magdalene fled to Marseille. Regardless, there is concrete evidence of Christian activity in Marseille at a very early date. In the late Roman Empire, Marseille was famous as a center of culture and learning. During the 9th and 10th centuries, the city was attacked repeatedly by Saracen Muslim raiders. Its commerce would not revive until the Crusades of the 11th and 12th centuries, when it became the jumping-off point for Crusader fleets from France. In 1249, the rich port city provided St. Louis (Louis IX) with all the galleys he needed to transport his army for the Seventh Crusade. Marseille remained one of the chief seaports of the Mediterranean, along with its Italian rivals Genoa, Pisa, and Venice. Previously an independent city, though sometimes subject to the counts of Provence, Marseille was annexed to the kingdom of France in 1482. This revived its moribund commerce, as it now became the chief Mediterranean seaport of a large and powerful kingdom. The inhabitants of Marseille *(les Marseillais)* have shown a stubborn independence through the centuries. During the Wars of Religion of the 16th century, the town's economic and governing elite used the disorder and chaos of the wars to reestablish the city's independence, and the town was one of the very last to submit to Henry IV in 1595, long after Paris had done so. Under Louis XIV, Marseille's rebellious ways continued: in 1660 Louis XIV, the Sun King, was able to enter the city only through a breach in its walls. He subsequently built the fortress of St. Nicolas both to guard the harbor and to keep an eye on the inhabitants. In 1720, Marseille witnessed the last major outbreak of bubonic plague, or Black Death, which had terrorized Europe since the original pandemic in 1348. During the French Revolution, continuing its fiercely independent ways, Marseille was a hotbed of radical republicanism, and was the site of many bloody battles during the Revolution. The Reign of Terror was more vicious and continued longer in Marseille than almost anywhere else. While a contingent of 500 Marseillais were on their way to join the Army of Rhine in 1792, they popularized a patriotic marching song, eventually adopted as France's national anthem, *La Marseillaise*. The city underwent much expansion during the Restoration and the second Empire, and in the 20th century has seen the influx of a very large immigrant population. Perhaps due to its 2000-year history as a seaport and thus its constant contact with foreigners, Marseille has avoided some of the tensions that have arisen between French people and immigrants, evidenced by the growth of Jean Marie Le Pen's National Front party, which in the last national elections won nearly 20 percent of the vote. With France's acquisition of colonies in Algeria and elsewhere in Africa in the 19th century, Marseille's commerce revived once again, and it remains the largest port in the Mediterranean.

PLACES TO VISIT

Although not renowned as a tourist mecca, Marseille does have its points of interest for the Christian traveler. Foremost among these is the BASILIQUE ST. VICTOR (St. Victor Basilica). A Christian settlement had grown up across the VIEUX PORT (Old Harbor) from the old Greco-Roman city. It was here that St. Victor, the patron saint of sailors and millers, himself a Roman soldier, is said to have been martyred in the early 4th century by being slowly ground to death by two millstones. A fortified abbey was built in his honor in the 5th century. This structure was destroyed by Saracen raiders in 923, but was rebuilt beginning in 1040, and renovated in the 14th century. Its major interest lies in the crypt and catacombs below, which contain an extensive collection of early Christian art, including decorated sarcophagi, and the remains of many saints and martyrs. Every February 2 the arrival in Marseille of Lazarus and Mary Magdalene is celebrated at St. Victor.

Marseille's cathedral is NOTRE DAME DE LA MAJOR. There are actually two cathedrals here, the older Romanesque edifice and a newer one in a neo-Byzantine style. Subject of much dispute because it hides the beautiful older building, the new cathedral was finished in 1852. It was built from red marble and from green Calissanne stone from Florence and is in the shape of a Latin cross. Inside are statues of the four gospel writers and in the nave a marble sculpture of Christ and St. Veronica.

To the east is the restored 17th-century hospice, LA VIEILLE CHARITÉ, an example of the Counter-Reformation Church's commitment to charitable foundations. Its east wing now contains LA MUSÉE ARCHÉOLOGIE MÉDITERRANÉENNE (Mediterranean Archaeological Museum), which houses an important collection of Egyptian, Etruscan, and Roman artifacts. To the south, beyond St. Victor, is the church of NOTRE-DAME DE LA GARDE, also built in a 19th-century neo-Byzantine style. Perched on a hill overlooking the Vieux Port and giving a view of the whole city as well as the port, the islands (Château d'If and Frioul), and the rocky white hills that surround the city inland, Notre-Dame de la Garde is the symbol of Marseille. When you arrive, either by sea or by land, you can

M

immediately recognize Marseille by the statue of the Virgin Mary atop the basilica which dominates the city. Protectress of the city and especially its sailors, she is affectionately known as "La Bonne Mère" (The Good Mother), which is appropriate for Marseille since "Mère" is a pun on "Mer," meaning sea. The site of a chapel since the 13th century, the present basilica dates from 1864. Built in green, white, and red Calissane stone from Florence, the basilica is of Romano-Byzantine inspiration. The dome measures over 100 feet high and the statue itself 30 feet. Notre Dame was the site of a battle between German and Algerian forces in World War II, and the church bears the marks of German machine gun fire on the left side. One enters the church by splendid bronze doors, and inside is much beautiful marble and many lovely mosaics. The walls of the chapel are covered with ex-voto offered especially by sailors in thanks for the protection of La Bonne Mère.

Marseille's ancient heritage is evident in several other museums. The Palais de la Bourse (old stock exchange) now houses a MUSÉE DE LA MARINE (Maritime Museum). Immediately behind this is the JARDIN DES VESTIGES (Garden of Ruins), which holds the excavated ruins of Greek and Roman fortifications. Just behind the *Hôtel de Ville* (City Hall) is the MUSÉE DES DOCKS ROMAINS (Roman Docks Museum) on the site of the old Greco-Roman harbor, discovered in 1947. Adjacent, in the Centre Bourse, is the MUSÉE D'HISTOIRE DE MARSEILLE (The Marseille Historical Museum), which contains a 3rd-century Roman ship, excavated in 1974. Another ship, this one 2,500 years old, was discovered in 1993.

LA CANEBIÈRE is the central avenue of Marseille as well as the symbolic heart of the city. On the left (coming from the Vieux Port) is LA BOURSE (1860), where Alexander I of Serbia and Louis Barthou were assassinated on October 9, 1934. At the top of the Canebière, one arrives at the Eglise St. Vincent de Paul, also known as LES RÉFORMÉS (the Metro stop bears the name Réformés). Inspired by 13th-century Gothic style, the church was erected in 1849–90.

MEAUX

Situated in the middle of the loop in the middle of the river Marne, Meaux, though not especially important today, holds a significant place in the Christian history of France. In the early 16th century, the bishop of Meaux, Guillaume Briçonnet, was one of the leading advocates of religious reform in France. He attracted to Meaux a group of humanists and reformers who believed in the importance of reform. Among these were the humanist Jacques Lefèvre d'Etaples, who translated portions of the Psalms into French, and Guillaume Farel, who while resident in Geneva persuaded a young writer and theologian named John Calvin to stay and help him reform that city. Protected, at least for a time, by their connections with Marguerite de Navarre, sister of King Francis I, and herself an accomplished writer and scholar, the "Circle of Meaux" testifies to the widespread perception that in the 16th century, the Catholic Church had gone seriously astray and that some kind of reform was necessary. The only question was whether or not this could be achieved from within, or whether the church would be fractured. With the revolt in Germany of Martin Luther (many of whose ideas were similar to those of the "Circle of Meaux"), these ideas now became dangerous, and by the late 1520s these reformers and their ideas had been declared heretical. Some of them, like Lefèvre, maintained their loyalty to the old church, while others, like Farel, left the Catholic Church entirely. Largely because of this heritage, Meaux attracted a large and militant Huguenot community, and was the site of considerable tension and violence between the supporters of the two churches in the 1540s and 1550s. In 1572, Meaux was the site of a particularly bloody massacre of Huguenots in the wake of the St. Bartholomew Massacre in Paris. The city was a stronghold of the Catholic League and was one of the last holdouts against Henry IV. In the 17th century, the bishop of Meaux was Jacques-Bénigne Bossuet, one of the most famous and powerful clergymen of the day. Tutor to Louis XIV's eldest son, the grand dauphin, the "Eagle of Meaux" was famous as a moving and eloquent preacher and writer. A firm supporter of the divine right of kings, he nevertheless upheld the power of the pope against Gallicanism.

PLACES TO VISIT

The CATHÉDRALE ST. ETIENNE (St. Stephen's Cathedral) was built between the 12th and 16th centuries in a mixture of Gothic styles. Only one of the projected two towers was completed, but this one is almost 200 feet high. Above the central door of the flamboyant west front is a depiction of the Last Judgment, while above the north door is a statue of St. Stephen and a bas-relief with scenes of his life. The interior is vast and solemn. Bossuet is buried in the choir, though his monument is in the north nave aisle. To the north of the cathedral is the PALAIS EPISCOPAL (Bishops' Palace), with its 12th-century chapel. It now houses the MUSÉE BOSSUET (Bossuet Museum).

METZ

So close to Germany, Metz was inevitably the site of many bloody struggles in France's long history of war with its neighbor. In the Franco-Prussian War of 1870–71, Metz was surrendered to the Germans after the inept Marshal Bazaine had failed to halt the invading armies. In the armistice treaty, the city was lost to the new German Empire, and over a quarter of the population fled, many to nearby Nancy. In the years leading up to World War I, Metz became the greatest fortified camp in the world, and in 1914, Metz was the starting point of the Schlieffen Plan which, had it not been for the incredible defense put up by Marshal Joffre at the Miracle of the Marne, would have succeeded. At the end of the war, Metz was reincorporated into France and became part of the Maginot Line. However, in World War II, the Germans captured Metz once again, and the people suffered greatly from the German occupation: 10,000 were deported, and many were enrolled by force in the Wehrmacht. Due to the Maginot fortifications, it took the Allied armies over ten weeks to overcome the German defenders in the autumn of 1944. The city was finally liberated on November 19.

PLACES TO VISIT

ESPLANADE: Opening onto a terrace which affords a lovely view over the Moselle River, the esplanade features a statue of Marshal Ney and also a bust of the 19th-century poet Paul Verlaine (1844–96), a native of Metz. Verlaine is perhaps most widely known for the homosexual relationship he had with the young poet Arthur Rimbaud which ended in Verlaine's being shot in the hand by his partner and being sent to jail for two years. What is perhaps less known is that Verlaine had a conversion experience while in jail and wrote some of the most poignant spiritual and devotional poetry that exists in the French language. Even before his conversion experience, Verlaine had rejected the cold materialism and cult of form of the Parnassian school, and all his poetry is characterized by the sense that something more than mere sensuality is needed by the human soul.

EGLISE ST. THÉRÈSE: In the south end of town, this modern church (1956) is worth the visit for its interesting concrete structure.

MONT-SAINT-MICHEL

Perched on a rocky outcropping several hundred yards off the Norman coast, the abbey-fortress of Mont-Saint-Michel is, after Paris, the most visited place in France, and one of the truly unforgettable sites in the world. If at all possible, therefore, try to visit it in off-season, when it is not over-run by hordes of tourists. Failing that, try to arrive early enough that you can beat the crowds.

The religious connotations of the site predate the arrival of Christianity. Previously known as *Mont-Tombe* (Tomb Mountain), it was presumably one of the places where, according to Celtic mythology, the souls of the dead were transported by an invisible ship. Previously connected to the mainland, in the 7th century a giant wave cut it off, surrounding the 294-foot-high rock with mud flats. The site is subject to dramatic tides, varying by up to 45 feet, and rushing in at up to 15 miles per hour. In addition, the mud flats surrounding the island can often be the consistency of quicksand. For these reasons, it is not advisable to explore the flats on your own.

In A.D. 708, St. Aubert, bishop of nearby Avranches, experienced a series of visions from the Archangel St. Michael, commanding him to erect an oratory on the site. At first Aubert did not believe him, but after the third vision he carried out the angel's wishes. This small chapel was soon replaced by a Carolingian church in the 10th century, and in turn by a Romanesque Benedictine abbey built in the 11th and 12th centuries. This structure was partly destroyed by fire in the 13th century and was replaced by a complex of buildings known as *La Merveille* (The Marvel). In the early 13th century, Mont-Saint-Michel passed from the hands of the dukes of Normandy (who were also the kings of England) into the hands of King Philip Augustus of France. During the Hundred Years' War (1337–1453), it was practically the only place in northern and western France to remain in French hands, twice resisting English sieges. In the 15th century, the chancel collapsed, and was replaced by a flamboyant Gothic chancel and steeple. By the 17th century, the abbey had fallen into disrepute for the monks' lax lifestyle, and the Benedictines were

M

replaced by the more austere Congregation of St. Maur. By the time of the French Revolution, the island had been turned into a prison. In 1874, the site was officially recognized as a national monument, and in 1969, a small group of Benedictines (three monks and three nuns) returned to live on the site.

PLACES TO VISIT

From the causeway which connects the island to the mainland, one enters the town through the *Porte du roi* (King's Gate) and proceeds up the *Grande rue* to the steep staircase (the *Grand Degré*), which leads up to the abbey. On the right are the lodgings of the abbot's guard and the ramparts built in the 15th century to fight off the invading English. Of the five towers, the TOUR DU NORD is the highest. Near the base of the *Grand Degré,* a plaque records that on May 8, 1532 (the spring feast of St. Michael), Jacques Cartier was commissioned by King Francis I to explore the shoreline of Canada. The ABBEY itself consists of the church and the complex of buildings known as LA MERVEILLE. The CHURCH itself becomes even more impressive when one considers that it is built on only a few square yards of flat rock at the very top of the island. All the rest had to be supported on foundations built onto the steep sides of the *mont,* with the granite laboriously carved to

match the contours of the slopes. The CHURCH consists of two parts: the nave and transepts are in a massive Norman Romanesque style, constructed in the 11th and 12th centuries, while the chancel, completed in 1521 to replace the original choir which collapsed in 1421, is in a flamboyant Gothic style, complete with flying buttresses topped with pinnacles. The spire was added in 1895 and topped with a gilded statue of St. Michael. The buildings of LA MERVEILLE incorporate the north face of the mont, and were built in the 13th century. The CLOISTERS boast 277 slender columns of pink granite, and offer spectacular views of the sea below. From the REFECTORY, or dining room, lit by its recessed windows, one can descend to the crypts and chapels below, which support the complex. The SALLE DES CHEVALIERS (Knights' Hall) was originally the scriptorium, or copying workshop. In 1469 King Louis XI founded the Order of St. Michel, to compete with the English Order of the Garter and the Burgundian Order of the Golden Fleece. The meetings of the order, which was limited in membership to the high nobility of military distinction, met here. There is also the SALLE DES HÔTES (Guest Hall), a masterpiece of high Gothic, which evokes memories of Mont-Saint-Michel's esteemed list of guests over the centuries.

MONTAUBAN

S ituated on the right bank of the Tarn River, the extensive use of pink brick and the terraced facades directly over the Tarn give Montauban a grand and distinctive aspect. Opposite the PONT VIEUX, a brick bridge constructed between 1306 and 1316, stands an impressive group of bronze figures by the native sculptor Bourdelle (1861–1929). In the Promenade Foucault, one finds another sculpture by Bourdelle, the MONUMENT AUX MORTS DE 1914–18. The MUSÉE INGRES, another native of Montauban, is housed in an old bishop's palace, a vast structure dating back to 1659. The museum holds some of Ingres's most important works, as well as many of his sketches and works of other painters which put Ingres's work in context, both historically and in relation to other 19th-century painters such as Delacroix, David, and Géricault.

Montauban has been a Protestant stronghold ever since the Reformation, and in the 19th century, THE INSTITUT JEAN CALVIN played a very important role in training pastors during the Protestant *Reveil* (Revival). Adolph Monod, one of France's great Protestant preachers and theologians, taught at the seminary in Montauban from 1836–47. The *Reveil* took place between 1818 and 1840, and as with John Wesley in England, was characterized by a return to the historic theology of Calvin, Luther, and the first Reformers. During the 18th century, the Protestant Church as well as the Catholic Church was deeply influenced by Enlightenment notions of a deist "natural religion" in which Christ ceased to be Savior and Son of God. The *Reveil* was engineered by both foreign evangelists, mostly from Britain and Switzerland, and by Frenchmen such as the Monod brothers (Adolph and

M

JEAN-AUGUSTE-DOMINIQUE INGRES (1780–1867). Along with David, Ingres was one of the great neo-classical painters of the 19th century. His work is characterized by a perfectly smooth surface created by infinitely fine brushwork which lends an almost photolike quality to his paintings, and also by the choice of heroic and historical subject matter (Napoleon had Ingres do a number of paintings for him). Where Ingres differed from David was in the subversion of perfect anatomical precision to the use of exaggerated form and line for the sake of esthetic effect.

Frédéric) and Antoine Vermeil. In the tradition of the *Désert* churches, much of the preaching was done in the open air using portable pulpits. The *Reveil* met with moderate success but at least had the result of reintroducing Protestantism into areas where it had been completely eradicated by the 100 years of persecutions that followed the revocation of the Edict of Nantes.

MONTPELLIER

ontpellier, a lively and cultured university town, is young by French standards. Its origins date to the 8th century when it was founded in the course of Charles Martel's struggles against the Muslim Saracens. By 1000, it was a bustling center of commerce, connected to the Mediterranean by the Maguelone lagoon. Sometime before 1000, Jewish and Arab physicians began to teach pupils in Montpellier, a situation which was regularized when a medical school was formally recognized in 1221, and a university founded in 1289. Henceforth, the university was famed for its medical school, a reputation which persists today. At one time ruled by the kings of Aragon, then by the king of Mallorca, Montpellier passed permanently into the hands of the kings of France in 1349. Among its most prominent residents were the Italian poet, scholar, and humanist, and father of the Italian Renaissance, Francesco Petrarca or Petrarch (1304–74), who studied at the university, and François Rabelais, who received his medical degree here in 1537.

During the 16th century, Montpellier became a Huguenot stronghold, and suffered extensive destruction during the Wars of Religion. In 1622, the town was subdued by Louis XIII and its defenses destroyed. In 1844, the English reformer John Darby came to Montpellier and started a number of "assemblies of brothers" in the regions surrounding Montpellier, many of which, including one in Montpellier itself, still exist today.

PLACES TO VISIT

The major attraction is the picturesque narrow streets and aristocratic town houses of VIEUX MONTPELLIER (Old Montpellier), also known as *"Lou clapas"* ("heap of stones"). The city boasts two important art museums: the MUSÉE FABRET has important works by French painters including Delacroix and Courbet, as well as 17th-century Dutch and Flemish paintings, while the MUSÉE ATGER has drawings by Watteau, Fragonard, and Caravaggio. The unexceptional CATHÉDRALE ST. PIERRE (St. Peter's Cathedral) dates from the 14th century. Near the cathedral are two towers which are all that remain of the city walls which were demolished by Louis XIII in the 17th century as punishment for the town's Protestant religion and stubborn rebellion. Adjoining the old town is the **PROMENADE DE PEYROU**, a jewel of 18th-century town planning. At one end of the promenade is an **ARC DE TRIOMPHE** (triumphal arch) erected in 1691 to honor Louis XIV. This arch contains two reliefs in honor of the Sun King: one commemorates the construction of the Canal du Midi, which linked the Atlantic and Mediterranean, while the other commemorates the revocation of the Edict of Nantes in 1685.

MONTSÉGUR, CHÂTEAU DE

I t was on this remote mountain peak that the last bloody act of the Albigensian Crusade was carried out. Around 1200, the Cathars built a castle here to replace an earlier ruined stronghold. As their persecution intensified, about 400 Cathars faithful took refuge here. On March 2, 1244, the château was conquered. Given two weeks to recant their beliefs, about 200 refused. On March 16, they were burned in a mass execution at the *Camp des Crémats* (the Field of the Burnt Ones). Legend has it that before the castle fell, the Cathar leader entrusted four *perfecti* with their treasure, which supposedly included the Holy Grail.

PLACES TO VISIT

The **CHÂTEAU** which one sees today was built after the bloody events of 1244. The **MUSEUM** in the village below displays artifacts from the castle.

NEVERS

B ernadette Soubirou, the girl who witnessed the apparitions of the Virgin Mary at Lourdes, came to Nevers in 1866 to the **ST. GILDARD CONVENT**, at first to escape people's curiosity, and then to become a sister. She suffered from terrible asthma attacks and died at just 35. Her body, exhumed three times and untouched by decay, reposes in a glass coffin in the chapel of the convent. The chapel is open daily.

143

NICE

Nice refused to come under the jurisdiction of the count of Provence, Louis d'Anjou, in 1388, and it was only in 1860 that the town came back to France, after a plebiscite showed an overwhelming desire to return. It is now the major city on the Côte d'Azur (French Riviera).

PLACES TO VISIT

PLACE MASSÉNA: The focal point of the town, the square has a pleasing architectural ensemble of arcades and facades, created in 1835. The FONTAINE DU SOLEIL (1956) was designed by Janniot. From the square, the Avenue de la Victoire, shaded by magnificent poplars, takes you to the station.

PROMENADE DES ANGLAIS: This famous spot for strollers has a lovely view out to the Estérel and Cape Ferrat. Under the ramparts lies an interesting little aquarium.

MUSÉE MASSÉNA: Built at the end of the 19th century for the grandson of the famous marshal, the museum features early religious art of Nice, many interesting pieces from the First Empire, and also collections of Chinese, Arabian, and Byzantine jewelry.

MUSÉE MATISSE: Housed in the Villa des Arènes, the museum features an interesting variety of the artist's work.

MUSÉE MARC-CHAGALL, avenue Docteur Menard and boulevard Cimiez, was designed to display works by the famed Russian Jewish artist Marc Chagall (1887-1985). His 17 wonderful paintings depict the essential message of the Bible, Jewish life, and folklore. His works are an illustration of the biblical message in an incredible way, making a visit to this museum a must for all Christian visitors to France.

EGLISE DE CIMIEZ (Cimiez Church): The entire ceiling of the church is decorated with 19th-century artwork.

EGLISE RUSSE (Russian Church): Constructed in 1912 in the style of the Yaroslav church in Moscow, and decorated with remarkable icons, the church is a testimony to the wonderful variety that exists in Christian architectural styles throughout the world.

VICINITY

Fourteen kilometers north of Nice is the town of VENCE, site of 11 churches and chapels, of which the most famous is without doubt the most recent. The CHAPELLE DU ROSAIRE was designed and decorated by Henri Matisse as a gesture of thanks to the Dominican nuns of the village who had nursed him during an illness. He had begun by agreeing to design some stained-glass windows, and ended up designing nearly everything inside and outside, including vestments and liturgical objects. Completed in 1951, the chapel is an important piece of modern religious art. Visits are just Tuesdays and Thursdays, late mornings and afternoons.

Henri Matisse (1869–1954), was the leader of the Fauvism (*fauve* literally means "wild beast") movement in painting, a group of young artists who reacted against the pointillism of men like Seurat and opted for swirls and slabs of expressive and realistic color. From a bourgeois background and of an extremely hard-working rational temperament, Matisse settled into a sort of modern classicism in an evident attempt to please the art public which was understandably tired of attempts to shock it. Though he was bedridden for many of his last years, he continued to paint from a crayon attached to a long pole, producing some of the most daring and serenely optimistic work of his life.

NOYON

oyon's present status as a sleepy provincial town belies its long and important history. One of the oldest cities in France, Noyon had a Christian bishop as early as the 6th century. In 768 Charlemagne was crowned king of Neustria (the largest of the Frankish kingdoms) in Noyon, while in 987 Hugh Capet was crowned king of France here. Noyon's most famous native was the Protestant reformer John Calvin, born here in 1509. His father, Gérard Cauvin (Calvin is a Latinized form of the family name), was the son of a boatman, and a local official of some importance. He intended his son John to enter the Catholic Church, and to this end secured for him a position in the cathedral at a young age. Such practices were common at the time. A position would be purchased on behalf of a young boy.

The revenue from this position would be used to finance his education, and then, he would enter the church, whereupon the revenue from the position would provide his income. It seems, however, that Calvin's father had some sort of disagreement with the cathedral clergy, and as a result, his plans for his son changed. He was sent off to school in Paris, and then ultimately to law school. It was as a young man in law school that Calvin underwent the religious experience which would change not only his life, but Christianity itself and the course of European history. In 1534 he went into exile in Basel, Switzerland, where he intended to reside and research and publish scholarly works. In 1536, however, he made one last trip to Noyon to wind up some family business. It was on his way back that he detoured through Geneva and was

N

persuaded to stay and take an active role in reforming the church there. With the exception of two years in Strasbourg from 1538–40, he would spend the rest of his life in Geneva. He died in 1564. Noyon was heavily damaged during both World Wars—indeed, it was occupied by the Germans from 1914–17—but has been extensively restored.

PLACES TO VISIT

The **CATHÉDRALE ST. ELOI** (St. Eloi Cathedral) is an excellent example of the transition from Romanesque to Gothic. This is the fifth church to stand on this site, and was built between 1150 and 1220. As one of the earliest attempts at what would become the Gothic style, it combines rounded and pointed arches, with the soaring nave typical of Gothic churches. Next door are remains of a 13th-century cloister, and a Renaissance library that contains a 9th-century illuminated Bible (guided tours only; apply in advance at the tourist office). Among the 15th-century buildings restored in the 20th century is Calvin's birthplace (on the street named after him) which now houses the **MUSÉE JEAN CALVIN** (John Calvin Museum).

NÎMES

Whether they know it or not, the city of Nîmes is commemorated every time someone puts on a pair of blue jeans. For it was in this ancient city that the heavy blue cotton fabric originated. Hence it was known as *"de Nîmes"* (from Nîmes), from which the word *denim* derives.

Nîmes's real attractions, however, lie elsewhere: in its wealth of well-preserved Roman ruins, and in its Protestant heritage. There was a Roman settlement here as early as the 2nd century B.C., along the main Roman road from Italy to Spain. It was not until the reign of Augustus, however, that Nîmes became prominent, for Augustus made Nîmes into a colony for settling the veterans of his campaign in Egypt against Mark Antony and Cleopatra. This is still commemorated in the coat of arms of the city, which features a crocodile chained to a palm tree. With the decline of the Roman Empire, it was sacked by Vandals (A.D. 407), occupied by Visigoths (A.D. 470) and Muslim Moors from Spain (724), and conquered by Charles Martel (737). Until 1185 it formed part of the kingdom of Aquitaine, and from 1185 to 1299 it was part of the county of Toulouse. In 1299 it became part of the kingdom of France, following on the heels of the Albigensian Crusade. In the 16th century, Nîmes was a Huguenot stronghold. In 1567, in a massacre known as the *Michelade,* the Huguenots killed Catholic priests and notables. After the Edict of Nantes was revoked in 1685, large numbers of Protestants from Nîmes joined the Camisard revolt.

Nîmes was home to one of the great figures of French Protestantism, Charles Babut (d. 1916), known as "The Saint of Nîmes." In 1905, the assembly that led to the formation of the *Fédération protestante de France* met in Nîmes. It was also the birthplace of Alphonse Daudet.

PLACES TO VISIT

The major attractions in Nîmes are the remains of the Roman past, rivaled in France only by those in nearby Arles. Chief among these is the massive amphitheater known as **LES ARÈNES**. Able to seat more than 20,000 people, it dates from the 1st century A.D., and although the amphitheater in Arles is slightly larger, the one in Nîmes is better preserved. During the city's occupation by the Visigoths, it was transformed into a fortress. Up until the 18th century, it was used as a squatters' settlement and was home to more than 2000 people, who often used the stone to build their own dwellings. Restoration was undertaken in the early 19th century. It is still in regular use, notably for bullfights, reflecting the influence of nearby Spain. There is also the **MAISON CARRÉE**, a 1st century B.C. Roman temple, which despite its name ("Square House") is a rectangular structure of harmonious proportions. It is, in fact, the purest and best preserved Roman temple anywhere. During the height of the classical revival style in the 18th century, it served as the model for the church of the **MADELEINE** in Paris. Thomas Jefferson admired the columns so much that he had them copied for the Virginia State Capitol in Richmond. The Roman watchtower known as the **TOUR MAGNE** stands atop the Mont Cavalier, named after Jean Cavalier, a leader of the Camisard rebels who submitted to government forces in Nîmes in 1704. The tower may be ascended and offers fine

ALPHONSE DAUDET (1840–97) is one of the most endearing, touching, and funny writers of 19th-century French literature. Though "realist" in his depiction of everyday life in Provence of the Third Republic, he does not fall into the dark pessimism which Emile Zola seems to revel in, but rather has a beautiful sense of the joy and pain of life, and of the marvelous qualities of the human spirit created in God's image. Daudet dreamt of being a "salesman of happiness," and, similar in many aspects to Dickens, he succeeds in bringing to life with humor and emotion the impressions and sensations of his native Provence. Some of his most well-known works are *Le Petit Chose* and *Tartarin de Tarascon*.

views of the city, and on a clear day, of the distant Pyrenees.

In the center of the PLACE DE LA LIBÉRATION is the magnificent FONTAINE DE NÎMES by the famous sculptor Pradier. The SQUARE DE LA COURONNE figures a statue of the celebrated writer Alphonse Daudet (1840–97), born in Nîmes. The splendid EGLISE SAINT PAUL (St. Paul's Church), built in the mid-19th century, contains some marvelous frescoes by the Flandrin brothers.

ORADOUR-SUR-GLANE

O n June 10, 1944, just shortly after the D-Day landings, a German SS division that was moving towards the front and was harassed by Resistance fighters took revenge by massacring the 642 innocent inhabitants of the village. The burned-out walls were left as a reminder of the brutal act.

ORLÉANS

S ituated on the right bank of the river Loire at its northernmost point, Orléans has long been important for its position at a strategic crossing of the Loire and its proximity to Paris. Site of an important Celtic settlement destroyed by Julius Caesar in 52 B.C., it was reestablished by the Romans and remained Aurelianus, the origin of the current name. It narrowly escaped destruction by the Huns in 451 as its bishop, St. Aignan, successfully organized the town's defense. For a time in the 10th and 11th centuries, it served as the capital of the early kings of the Capetian dynasty. From the 14th through 18th centuries, it and the surrounding territory were periodically granted as an *appanage* to the younger sons or brothers of the king. (An *appanage* was a territory given to a younger son or brother of a king to govern, both as a way of spreading royal influence in an age of poor communications, and to occupy these princes with jobs worthy of their high rank.) Orléans real moment in the sun occurred, however, during the Hundred Years' War. With the English in control of most of northern France, and the dauphin (Charles VII) languishing in Bourges, in October 1428 Orléans came under siege by the English. Had it fallen, the English could quickly have taken control of most of the rest of France. It was at this point that Joan of Arc roused the indolent dauphin into action. Joan and the relieving army entered Orléans on April 29, 1429. The siege was lifted in eight short days, and Joan was able to lead the dauphin and an army to Reims, where he was crowned. More than anything else, the lifting of the siege of Orléans represented the turning point in the Hundred Years' War. At the beginning of the Wars of Religion, Orléans was taken by the Huguenots, who wrought significant damage to the city. The throne of France came back to the Orléans line when Louis Philippe became king in 1830 after the "Glorious Revolution" and the flight of Charles X and the Bourbons. It was occupied by the Prussians in 1870–71, bombed by Italian forces in 1940, and bombed by the U.S. army in 1944. Since World War II, the old city has been extensively restored. Orléans was also the birthplace of Charles Péguy.

PLACES TO VISIT

Everywhere one turns in Orléans, one is confronted by Joan of Arc, *la Pucelle* (the Maid). The **CATHÉDRALE STE-CROIX** (St. Croix Cathedral) features a series of stained-glass windows

CHARLES PÉGUY (1873–1914) was a Christian poet, philosopher, socialist, and patriot, who, despite the intense anticlericalism of the late 19th and early 20th centuries, stood firm in his faith. Paul Claudel, another great figure of 20th-century literature and man of faith, wrote in 1907: "It required heroism of a young man to believe all alone a ridiculed doctrine, to dare to face up to the arguments, the insults, the blasphemy which filled the books, the streets, and the newspapers, to resist even his friends, and to hold onto his faith as one against a storm." Yet, more than just resisting the storm, Charles Péguy fought against it and, through his integrity and action, testified to the power of his faith. He was one of the principal leaders in the battle to establish Dreyfus's innocence, and it was he who convinced many of his socialist friends to join the defense of Dreyfus. In 1900, he began publishing the *Cahiers de la quinzaine (Biweekly Notebook),* which had a profound influence on French intellectual life. He went on to publish a number of meditative Christian poems including *Mystère des Saints Innocents (Mystery of the Holy Innocents),* and in his final years, *Eve* (1913), a four-thousand-line poem in which Péguy views the human condition in the perspective of the Christian revelation. When World War I broke out, Péguy went to fight as a lieutenant and was killed in the first battle of the Marne.

devoted to her exploits. The cathedral is otherwise an unexceptional melange of styles and periods. Begun in high Gothic style in the 13th century, it was largely destroyed by the Huguenots in the 16th. What you see now is mostly a composite Gothic style built between the 16th and 19th centuries. When Orléans opened its gates to Henry IV in 1594, he (the newly converted former Huguenot) began the cathedral's reconstruction as a reward to the town's inhabitants. In the center of town in the PLACE DU MARTROI stands a splendid equestrian statue of Joan of Arc by the sculptor Foyatier (1855). Much of the square was severely damaged during 1940, but it has been supremely well restored in 18th-century style, especially the two pavilions on the south side. Nearby is the MAISON DE JEANNE D'ARC (Joan of Arc house), a 20th-century reconstruction of the house in which she lodged while in Orléans. It now houses a Joan of Arc museum. Closer to the river is the church of NOTRE-DAME-DES-MIRACLES (Our Lady of Miracles), a modern church on the site of an earlier church, where Joan and the citizens of Orléans gave thanks for their deliverance before a 5th-century statue of the Virgin. This statue was used as firewood to roast a piece of mutton by Huguenot soldiers in the 16th century, thus displaying their contempt for what they saw as Catholic "idolatry." The MUSÉE DES BEAUX-ARTS (Fine Arts Museum) is home to a decent collection of paintings from the 17th through 20th centuries, and is housed in the Hôtel des Crénaux, a mixture of flamboyant Gothic and Renaissance styles. The Renaissance Hôtel Cabu (built in 1530, gutted in 1940, and since restored) contains the MUSÉE HISTORIQUE (History Museum). The main attraction here is a series of magnificent Gallo-Roman bronzes discovered in a nearby sandpit in 1861. Apparently they had once adorned a pagan temple and were hidden by the pagans in the 4th century to prevent their destruction by Christians.

The CENTRE CHARLES PÉGUY is housed in a Renaissance mansion, the Hôtel Euverte Hatte, and commemorates his life and achievements.

PARIS

Introduction

Paris is not only the largest and most important city in France, it is also one of the most important cities in European history and civilization. A visitor could easily spend weeks exploring all its attractions: its churches, monuments, and museums. This entry is not intended to substitute for an all-purpose guide to the city. Rather, it is intended to guide the Christian visitor to the sites especially important for the history of Christianity in France (for good or ill) and to relate them to the Christian heritage of France, Europe, and the Western world in general. Thus, much is omitted which features prominently in other guides: for example, the Eiffel Tower, the Arc de Triomphe, restaurants, shopping, and fashion.

Origins and Early History

The name of the city derives from the Celtic tribe of the Parisii who established their stronghold on the island in the Seine River now known as the Ile de la Cité. Though the Parisii were politically weak, their settlement thrived as a commercial and economic center. In 52 B.C. a Roman settlement known as Lutetia was established on the site and expanded from the island to the left bank of the Seine. Nevertheless, Paris remained a center of secondary importance in Roman Gaul. Little remains of Paris's Roman past: notably the amphitheater of the Arènes de Lutèce and the baths under the Hôtel de Cluny. For the next three centuries, until the incursions of the Germanic invasions, Paris remained under Roman rule. The area was partially Christianized by about A.D. 300. Its first bishop was St. Dionysius (St. Denis), who was martyred during the persecution of the Emperor Decius. Legend has it that the actual killing took place at Montmartre ("Mont des Martyres" or "Martyrs' Mountain") by beheading, whereupon the saint picked up his head and walked to the town of St. Denis where he finally

expired. Thus the traditional portrayal of St. Denis carrying his head in his hands. A monastery and basilica were erected to his memory, and for more than a millenium, the kings and queens of France were buried at St. Denis. Denis became the patron saint of France, the abbot of St. Denis became one of the most powerful figures in France, and the monks became the custodians of the cult of royalty. In 451, the city was threatened with attack by the Huns under their bloodthirsty leader Attila. The city was allegedly saved by the intervention of St. Geneviève (423–512), who persuaded the inhabitants not to flee but instead to stay and pray for deliverance. Attila bypassed the city and was defeated shortly thereafter near Châlons-sur-Marne. In 508, the city was conquered by the Frankish king Clovis, who made it his capital. St. Geneviève also persuaded the newly converted Clovis to build a church on the current site of the Panthéon, atop the hill which bears her name, the Montagne Ste-Geneviève.

The Middle Ages

As the Frankish kingdom disintegrated and fragmented through civil war, Paris remained a focal point of conflict, and the city continued to grow on both banks of the river. Under the Carolingians, the political center of gravity came to rest further east, along the Rhine, especially after Charlemagne established his imperial capital at Aachen (French: Aix-la-Chapelle). Nevertheless, Paris retained its economic importance and by about the year 800 boasted a population of around 20,000 people, which made it a huge city by the standards of the day. Throughout the 9th and 10th centuries, Paris was repeatedly sacked and pillaged by invading Vikings and Norsemen, before they converted to Christianity and settled around the mouth of the Seine in Normandy. Paris's political importance declined as Charlemagne's empire fragmented amid civil war among his successors. Paris was nominally the capital of the kingdom of West Francia, but the king of France (as he was becoming known) often controlled no more than a small area around the city, the Ile de France. Politically, he was overshadowed by a handful of powerful noblemen, most notably the duke of Normandy to the north. This began to change in 987 with the election of Hugh Capet as king to replace the defunct Carolingian dynasty. For the next three centuries, his successors of the Capetian dynasty patiently expanded their power base and territory. It was during this time that Paris really developed into the important world capital which it has continued to be to this day. Increasingly, Paris became the royal residence and headquarters of the civil service. The king took up residence in the palace on the Ile de la Cité (now the Palais de Justice) and in the fortress of the Louvre. King Philip Augustus (1180–1223) built new walls to accommodate the expanding city. His grand-

son, Louis IX (St. Louis; 1226–70), further embellished the royal palace, adding the Sainte-Chapelle, and granted self-government to the city. The trade guilds of Paris elected the mayor (*prévôt des marchands,* or provost of the merchants). The most important and influential of these guilds was that of the watermen, reflecting the importance of river commerce. Thus it was that the arms of the city of Paris feature a boat with the motto *Fluctuat nec mergitur*— "She is buffeted but does not sink." During the High Middle Ages (10th–mid-14th centuries), Paris also became a leading cultural and intellectual center. The cathedral school of Paris was one of a series of important schools in northern France, including those of Laon and Chartres. By about 1200, however, the schools and teachers of Paris became recognized as preeminent and had begun to function as a single entity—the University of Paris—a fact which was formally recognized in 1215. In 1253 a canon of Notre-Dame Cathedral named Robert de Sorbon established a residential college for poor university students. His establishment became known as the Sorbonne, the most prominent of a number of colleges which made up the university. The name "Sorbonne" is often (and mistakenly) used as a synonym for the University of Paris. The University was the most important center of learning in medieval Europe, attracting students from all over, and boasted among its faculty the most important philosophers, theologians, and teachers of the day, including Thomas Aquinas (1227–74).

At this time, the city was divided into three distinct districts. The Cité, on the Ile de la Cité, was the center of government and the church, housing the royal palace and the cathedral. The right bank (*rive droite*) was the center of commerce and business. The left bank (*rive gauche*) or Latin Quarter (*quartier latin*) was home to the university and its ancillary services—bookstores, taverns, boarding houses, etc.

As the chief city of the kingdom, Paris suffered tremendously during the Hundred Years' War (1337–1453). During the initial stages, after King John II (the Good; 1350–64) had been captured by the English at the Battle of Poitiers (1356), and the kingdom had suffered the disastrous effects of the Black Death, the citizens of Paris rebelled against royal authority under the leadership of Etienne Marcel, a cloth merchant and *prévôt des marchands* (mayor) of Paris. Marcel was assassinated in 1358 and the rebellion forcibly repressed. King Charles V (1364–80) shifted the main royal residence in Paris to the newly expanded and fortified Louvre. In the 1420s, following the disastrous defeat by the English at Agincourt (1415) and the humiliating Treaty of Troyes, Paris suffered the lowest ebb of its fortunes. The city was under English occupation, and there are stories of wolves prowling the streets eating corpses. Joan of Arc

attempted unsuccessfully to retake the city in 1429, and the English were finally evicted in 1437. For the rest of the 15th century, French kings preferred to live elsewhere, especially in the châteaux of the Loire valley, such as at Amboise. It was not until the reign of Francis I (1515–47) that Paris once again became the focal point of royal attention. Francis expanded and renovated the Louvre and rebuilt the *Hôtel de Ville* (City Hall) in the style of the Italian Renaissance.

Religious War, Royal Absolutism, and Revolution

During the Wars of Religion of the second half of the 16th century, Paris proved its reputation as a zealously Catholic city. It steadfastly opposed any measure of toleration for the Huguenots, and it was the Catholic zeal of the city's inhabitants which prompted the St. Bartholomew's Massacre in 1572. Paris was also the stronghold of the Catholic League, which resisted the attempts of the Huguenot Henry of Navarre to take the throne as King Henry IV.

By this time, the population of Paris had grown to about 500,000. The first part of the 17th century saw a veritable building boom in Paris. Before his assassination in 1610, Henry IV undertook several major urban construction projects including enlarging the Louvre and building the Place Royale (now Place des Vosges). His widow, Marie de Medici, had built for

P

herself the Luxembourg Palace, and Cardinal Richelieu built the Palais-Cardinal (now Palais-Royal) as his residence. It was during this period that the Ile-St. Louis (upstream of the Ile de la Cité) was developed with housing. Anne of Austria, wife of Louis XIII, had built the church of Val-de-Grace as a thanksgiving for the birth of a son (later Louis XIV). After the deaths of Louis XIII and Cardinal Richelieu, Paris was the focal point of the series of revolts known as the Fronde, against the heavy-handed administrative and fiscal measures of the government under Richelieu's successor, Cardinal Mazarin. Several times the government and royal family were forced to flee Paris, leaving an indelible impression on the child-king Louis XIV. It was also during this period (1622) that Paris became an archbishopric in its own right, having been subject to the archbishop of Sens for centuries.

Despite Louis's dislike of Paris (which caused him to build a magnificent new palace at Versailles, away from the disorderly and rebellious city), he did leave his mark on the city. He established a new official, the *lieutenant-général de police,* to ensure order in the city. Previously the city had been subject to a number of rival and conflicting jurisdictions, which made law enforcement cumbersome at best. He enlarged the Louvre, adding the Cour Carrée in a dignified classical style. He demolished the old outmoded walls of the city, replacing them with grand boulevards

and triumphal arches at the Portes (gates) St. Denis and St. Martin. He built the Hôtel des Invalides to care for the veterans of his many wars and constructed the Place Louis-le-Grand (now Place Vendôme).

Construction continued on a grand scale throughout the 18th century, with the Place Louis XV (now Place de la Concorde), the Palais Bourbon (now home to the National Assembly), the Panthéon, and innumerable aristocratic town houses.

More than any place else in France, Paris was the home of the French Revolution. On July 14, 1789, revolutionaries stormed the royal fortress and prison of the Bastille in order to forestall armed repression of their movement. France's national holiday is still celebrated on Bastille Day, July 14. In October, an angry mob of Parisian women marched to Versailles and forcibly removed the royal family and government back to Paris. With this, the ordinary citizens of Paris, the *sans-culottes* (literally, "those without breeches," i.e., those who wore trousers rather than the knee-breeches of the middle and upper classes) gained a decisive voice in the Revolution, eventually resulting in the overthrow of the monarchy, the establishment of the Republic, and the Reign of Terror in 1793–94. In the Place Louis XV, now renamed the Place de la Revolution (now Place de la Concorde), Dr. Guillotin's macabre invention, the "razor of the nation," carried out its bloody work, beheading more than 1,300 people. In January 1793, Louis XVI (known simply as "Louis Capet") was beheaded, followed in October by his wife Marie Antoinette.

After his seizure of power in 1799, Napoleon Bonaparte continued to embellish the city, notably through constructing the Arc de Triomphe, filling the Louvre (a museum since 1795) with treasures plundered from the rest of Europe, and constructing the arcaded and architecturally uniform rue de Rivoli.

The 19th Century

With the coming of the Industrial Revolution to France, Paris's population began to swell with industrial workers, housed in crowded and unsanitary slums. By 1870 the capital's population had swollen to two million. In 1830, a cholera epidemic claimed 20,000 lives. These conditions, combined with the political tensions which were the legacy of the Revolution, made 19th-century Paris a volatile place. There were significant revolts in 1830, 1832, 1834, 1848, and most seriously of all, the Paris Commune of 1871.

This was, nevertheless, a time of significant urban development for the city. Gradually, the worst of the slums, which had aided the spread of cholera, were replaced by more sanitary housing. Much of this development took place under Emperor Napoleon III (1852–71), and especially under his prefect of the Department of the Seine (of which

Paris was the major part), Baron Georges Haussman. Haussman, more than any other single individual, is responsible for the look and feel of Paris today. He demolished whole sections of the city, replacing the cramped quarters and narrow, crooked streets of the medieval city with straight and wide tree-lined boulevards, such as the Champs Elysées. He dictated the style of new buildings, which lives on to this day: six or seven stories high, with mansard roofs and facades of gray stone. His reconstruction also had the intended side effect of rendering nearly impossible the barricades which had blocked streets in the various revolts, hindering their suppression by the police and the army. It was also under Haussman that work was begun on supplying the populace with running water, sewers, public transport, and large green spaces such as the Bois de Vincennes and the Bois de Boulogne. But all was not to be sweetness and light.

Just a few days after the armistice was signed with the Germans following the French defeat in the Franco-Prussian War in 1871, France was faced with a civil war of its own: the Paris Commune. Complex enough in itself, the event has been made more difficult to understand by the fact that Karl Marx promptly hailed the Commune as the first great uprising of the proletariat against its bourgeois oppressors, and since then, a Marxist mythology has grown up around the event. Though

P

there was an element of class struggle in the event, it was certainly not a workers' uprising: It was more to do with Paris feeling abandoned by the rest of rural France. The Parisians were tired and irritable after the long siege of Paris and were outraged that rural France had elected a monarchist-dominated assembly that had signed what the Parisians regarded as a dishonorable peace. They were further angered when the assembly ended the wartime moratorium on debts and cut off payments to the National Guard which had been resuscitated in Paris after the Empire fell. Aware of the ugly mood in Paris, Adolphe Thiers and the assembly decided to disarm the National Guard, which was no doubt the very worst course of action. On March 18, he sent troops to confiscate the National Guard cannon on the butte of Montmartre. A crowd gathered, a struggle ensued, and two generals were caught and lynched. Violence quickly spread through the city, and Thiers took the government troops and retreated to Versailles. The Parisians then elected a council that adopted the name The Commune of Paris, and tried to promote a policy of decentralized governing communes throughout France (several appeared, in Marseille and Lyon, but were quickly suppressed). Then, on May 21, the government troops in Versailles struck Paris, and what is known as the "Bloody Week" ensued. The Communards resisted street by street but were pushed back to the center of Paris. In their desperation, they executed several hostages, including the archbishop of Paris, and in the last days set fire to many public buildings including the Tuileries Palace, adjoining the Louvre, and the city hall (*Hôtel de Ville*). The government repression was terrible: 20,000 Communards were killed or executed on the spot, and thousands of survivors were deported to the penal islands.

Following this inglorious defeat and civil war, Paris entered on what may have been the most glorious phase of its history, the "Belle-Epoque." When many think of Paris, many of the images which come to mind are from this period: the Eiffel Tower, Sacré Cœur, the posters of Toulouse-Lautrec, the Can-Can, sidewalk cafés, the subway system (Métro), etc.

The World Wars and Post-War Paris

When World War I broke out in August 1914, Paris was the immediate object of German attacks. The city, from which artillery could clearly be heard, was saved as a result of the First Battle of the Marne, in which 11,000 men were rushed to the front in Parisian taxis.

Following the war, in the 1920s, Paris once again became a center of artistic and literary life, home to many of the most influential writers and artists of the period: Ernest Hemingway, Gertrude Stein, Pablo Picasso, and many others.

With the French defeat and surrender of June 1940, Paris was forced to submit to German occupation until its liberation in August 1944. Hitler had given the military commander of Paris, General Dietrich von Choltitz, orders to destroy the city rather than allow it to fall into Allied hands. Fortunately, von Choltitz ignored these orders, preserving one of the world's great cities. These events are thrillingly recounted in the book *Is Paris Burning?* by Larry Collins and Dominique Lapierre. As the Allied and Free French forces under Charles de Gaulle neared Paris, outright rebellion against the occupiers broke out in the city. One can still see scattered around the city plaques which commemorate the spots where various resisters died fighting the Germans. Fighting was especially hard on the Ile de la Cité, where the police, who had joined the rebellion, held out against German forces for three days in their headquarters. Paris was liberated August 25, 1944. On August 26, a solemn ceremony of thanksgiving was held in Notre-Dame Cathedral.

The years since the war have been characterized by periodic political instability combined with overall prosperity and continued urban development. Political instability was evident in the late fifties as the French colony of Algeria moved towards independence in a vicious civil war. The French withdrawal from Indo-China provoked a crisis of confidence in the entire governmental system. This resulted in the end of the Fourth Republic, which had been set up

after the war, and in General de Gaulle's return to power as president of the Fifth Republic in 1958.

More serious perhaps were the disturbances of May 1968. On May 3, 1968, what started as a rally of student radicals at the Sorbonne nearly turned into a national revolution. When police broke up the rally which was getting violent, students fought back and street barricades went up in the Latin quarter. Other students and factory workers then joined the protestors, and by the end of May, various radical groups openly stated their intent to carry out a true revolution, by violence if necessary. However, when Communist and trade union leaders opposed further upheavals, de Gaulle sensed the opportune moment and in a dramatic four-minute radio address, he appealed to the partisans of law and order and presented himself as the only barrier to anarchy or Communist rule. Nervous citizens rallied around him, and the protestors were isolated when the Communists refused to resort to force. The confrontation moved to the polls. De Gaulle dissolved the national assembly, and on June 23 the Gaullists won a landslide victory. Nonetheless, in the aftermath of the demonstrations, both students and workers gained some of the reforms they had been asking for.

Paris has also continued to develop and expand as a city. While the population of the city proper has declined somewhat since its peak in the 19th

P

century, the population of the region has continued to expand as workers and commuters are increasingly housed in satellite towns connected to the city by an extensive commuter rail network, the RER. Architecturally, the grip of Haussman's vision has been broken. The skyscrapers of the business district of La Défense were begun in the mid-1950s. In 1969 under de Gaulle's successor President Georges Pompidou, Paris's vast markets at Les Halles were torn down and replaced by what was then a futuristic shopping mall. More successful was the nearby Centre Georges Pompidou, which houses the Centre National d'Art et de Culture, which opened in 1977. Other significant landmarks include the Tour Montparnasse (1973), the renovated Louvre featuring I. M. Pei's glass pyramid entrance (1993), the Opéra de la Bastille (1989), and the new Bibliothèque de France (National Library), opened in 1998.

Paris Today

Over the last few decades, the agglomeration of Paris has sprawled out into suburbs dotted with unsightly high-rise residences. If one takes the train into Paris from Charles de Gaulle airport, out on the far edge of the northeast suburbs, one is well aware of this, and if it's the first trip to Paris, the visitor might find himself wondering, "Is this the beautiful Paris that I've heard so much about?" However, as soon as one steps out into Paris itself, whether it be in Montmartre, the Cité, Les Invalides, Le Luxembourg, or Montparnasse, one is struck by the grandeur and remarkable beauty that loses nothing through the many different aspects that this beauty takes. New York may be intimidating in its attitude, London captivating in its diversity and energy, but Paris remains the grandest and most beautiful city in the world. You can appreciate this beauty and grandeur just by walking around, and you discover more of Paris's charm and personality each time you visit. Where you might need two or three viewings to catch all the details of a great film, you need a lifetime and certainly more to see all there is to see in Paris; and when you've seen Notre-Dame de Paris once, you'll only want more leisure to appreciate it the next time!

Paris has been the center of life— political, religious, and social—in France for many centuries, and this certainly hasn't changed in the 19th and 20th centuries, and it most likely won't change in the 21st! Much as people in England in the 19th century referred to London as "Town," in France even today, you either live in Paris or in Province (everything outside Paris). Marseille, Lyon, and Lille are good-sized cities, but small in comparison. Then there is the simple fact that "everything" seems to happen in Paris. France became an extremely centralized state starting with the monarchy of Louis XIV, continued this trend through the

Revolution and the Empires, and consolidated it yet more under the Republics. Though regional politics has gained some ground over the last few decades, France is probably more thoroughly and efficiently centralized today than it was under Louis XIV or Napoleon. Many civil service jobs, including all teachers, are still recruited directly through Paris and then sent back out to the provinces. Social security benefits like health and unemployment are completely controlled by Paris.

PLACES TO VISIT

Ile de la Cité

The ILE DE LA CITÉ is the historic heart of Paris, the home of the original Celtic fishermen, and the site of Roman Lutetia. Throughout the Middle Ages, it was the focal point of both royal and ecclesiastical administration. The Cité remained virtually unchanged from the Middle Ages through the 19th century when Baron Haussman demolished large parts of it, displacing 25,000 people and renovating its cramped and crooked streets and dangerously old buildings. At the downstream tip of the island is the SQUARE DU VERT-GALANT, a lovely tree-shaded respite with an equestrian statue of King Henry IV (1589–1610), the former Huguenot who converted to Catholicism to gain a kingdom. "Vert-Galant" is a term that is difficult to translate, but which means "lusty," "swashbuckling," or "dashing," and refers to Henry's womanizing ways.

The PALAIS DE JUSTICE (The Law Courts): Continuing from the Vert-Galant across the lovely Place Dauphine, one comes to the Palais de Justice, site of the original royal palace. After Etienne Marcel led the citizens of Paris in revolt against the king (1356), the royal residence shifted across the river to the LOUVRE, and the old royal palace became the seat of the *parlement* of Paris, the supreme law court of the kingdom until the Revolution. Most of the current complex dates from the 19th century, but contained within it are fragments of earlier times, most notably the CONCIERGERIE and the SAINTE-CHAPELLE. The CONCIERGERIE is notable for its superb Gothic halls (the SALLE DES GENS D'ARMES and the SALLE DES GARDES), and for its use as a prison during the Revolution. One can see the cell where Marie Antoinette was kept before her execution. In September 1792, a revolutionary mob broke into the prison, murdering about 1,200 prisoners held there who were suspected of counter-revolutionary activities. In all, more than 2,600 prisoners were led from the Conciergerie to their deaths. The SAINTE-CHAPELLE is a miniature jewel of high Gothic architecture at its purest. The chapel was built for St. Louis (King Louis IX, 1226–70) in just 33 months beginning in 1248. It was built to house a series of holy relics acquired by the saintly king, including what was purported to be Christ's crown of thorns. Indeed, St. Louis spent on acquiring the relics three times what it cost to build the chapel.

P

Originally in the courtyard of the royal palace, in the 18th century, a wing of the law courts was built abutting it. It was seriously damaged by fire in 1630, and skillfully restored in the 19th century. At the Revolution, many of the relics were spared, and are now in Notre-Dame, but the reliquary which housed them was melted down. The most striking feature of this unusual two-storied church is its apparent lack of solid walls. The weight of the structure is borne by slender pillars and buttresses between the 15-meter (50-feet) high windows. The lower story was intended for worship by servants and has been disfigured by a ham-fisted 19th-century restoration. The windows are 19th century. The floor is made up of tombstones of priests who were buried in the chapel. The real attraction is the upper chapel, where the king and court worshiped. Its most notable feature is the vast expanse of stained glass, about two-thirds of it original, the rest a faithful restoration. A veritable Bible in glass, the windows contain numerous scenes from the Old and New Testaments. On the south side is a small chapel where the king could observe the service without being seen. The reliquary containing the relics were displayed in the center of the apse under a wooden canopy or baldachin. Only the king had the key to the reliquary, and the contents were displayed to the court on Good Friday. The Sainte-Chapelle is rarely used for worship today; it is more often used for candle-lit concerts.

CATHÉDRALE NOTRE-DAME DE PARIS. One of the most familiar landmarks in the world, Notre-Dame Cathedral is a universally recognized symbol of Paris. The present structure stands on the site of a Gallo-Roman temple to Jupiter, a Merovingian basilica, and a Romanesque church dedicated to St. Stephen. Construction was inspired by the bishop of Paris, Maurice de Sully (d. 1196). His goal was to provide Paris with a new church worthy of the city's importance, to rival the church then just begun at St. Denis, just outside Paris. Construction was begun in 1163, the main altar was consecrated in 1182, and construction was completed by 1345. To rival St. Denis, Notre-Dame was built in the early Gothic style, then being pioneered at St. Denis. Although the original integrity of the plan was largely preserved, the church does incorporate elements of high Gothic style, including the west facade (c. 1200), the tracery above the great rose window, the transepts (1250–60), the choir, and the unfinished square towers (1225–50). The cathedral remained largely unaltered until the French Revolution, gradually falling into disrepair. In the 18th century the rood screen (*jubé*) and choir stalls were destroyed. At the Revolution, Notre-Dame—as the primary symbol of the power of the Church and its alliance with the monarchy—was heavily damaged. The statues of the kings of France were ripped from the west front. Interestingly, some were preserved by a royalist and stowed away in his mansion, where they were rediscovered in 1977. These fragments are now on display at the Musée de Cluny. The church was converted into a Temple of Reason and of the Supreme Being. All but the Great Bell were melted down, and the church was used for a time to store forage and food. The church was saved by the romantic movement of the early 19th century and its fascination with the Middle Ages. This was especially true after the publication of Victor Hugo's *Notre-Dame de Paris* in 1841, a dramatic evocation of life in medieval Paris centered on the cathedral and Quasimodo, its hunchbacked bell-ringer and his doomed love for the beautiful gypsy girl Esmerelda. Between 1841 and 1863, Notre-Dame was restored by the master restorer, Viollet-le-Duc. It was at this time as well that the medieval buildings which crowded up against the cathedral were leveled, creating the Parvis Notre-Dame (Notre Dame Square), which provides spectacular views of the facade. The cathedral managed to escape unscathed from the violence and destruction of the Commune and both World Wars. Further restoration was begun in 1992 and is scheduled to be completed in 2005. Over the centuries, Notre-Dame has been the site of many historic events. In 1430, in the midst of the Hundred Years' War, young King Henry VI of England was crowned king of France here. In 1572, in the days preceding the Massacre of St.

Bartholomew, the young Huguenot Henry of Navarre waited outside the door while he was married by proxy in a Catholic ceremony to the king's sister. In 1804, Pope Pius VII was about to crown Napoleon Bonaparte emperor of the French, when the impetuous and arrogant dictator grabbed the crown and crowned himself and then his wife, Josephine, a scene depicted in Jacques-Louis David's enormous painting now in the Louvre. On August 26, 1944, a service of thanksgiving for liberation was held. In 1970, Requiem Mass was held for General de Gaulle, and in 1980 Mass was celebrated by Pope John Paul II.

THE EXTERIOR: The west facade is striking in its harmony and balance, with vertical and horizontal elements in perfect juxtaposition, with its three tiers corresponding to the three levels of the interior. The central doorway features the Last Judgment, but little remains of the original statuary—most of what you see is a restoration. The tympanum was destroyed in the 18th century to allow a ceremonial canopy to pass through and was restored by Viollet-le-Duc. It shows Christ separating the saved and the damned, while on the lintel below is the Resurrection. The archivolts depict the celestial court. On the right is St. Anne's portal, which dates mostly from the 12th century and shows scenes from the life of Mary. On the tympanum are Mary and the Christ child in regal splendor, with Bishop Sully standing to her left and King Louis VII kneeling on

P

her right. On the left is the Virgin's portal. The tympanum depicts Mary's coronation by her Son, while the upper lintel shows her dormition in the presence of Christ and the apostles. In the lower lintel are the seated figures of three prophets and three kings of Judah. Flanking and in between the doorways, in buttress niches, are St. Stephen, the Church, the Synagogue (blindfolded), and St. Denis, with his head in his hands. Above the doors is the gallery of kings with statues of 28 kings of Israel and France, restored by Viollet-le-Duc. Above this is the great rose window, ten meters (30 feet) in diameter, forming a halo for the statue of Mary and Christ in front of it. The two square towers, 70 meters (230 feet) in height, were built between 1225 and 1250 and were intended to be topped by spires, which were never built. The south tower may be ascended and offers tremendous views of the roof, the Ile de la Cité, and the city beyond. The side walls and transept doorways illustrate the transition to the more highly decorated high Gothic style, as do the flying buttresses around the sides and apse, which have been compared to the rigging of a ship. The spire, reaching heavenward, was added by Viollet-le-Duc in the 19th century.

THE INTERIOR: Inside, there is a striking contrast between the dark solemnity of the nave and the lightness of the unusually short transepts, lit by rose windows. There is little original stained glass left in Notre-Dame; most of what you see dates from the 18th century and later. The great exception is the rose window in the north transept which shows Old Testament figures surrounding the Virgin. The interior is completely lined with chapels. In the crossing, at the entrance of the choir, stand statues of St. Denis (18th century), and a 14th-century statue of the Virgin, known as the Notre-Dame de Paris (Our Lady of Paris). The choir was extensively altered as a result of a vow made by King Louis XIII (1610–43) in 1638. Still childless after 23 years of marriage, he made a vow to dedicate France to the Virgin if his wife gave birth to a son. The work was carried out under that son, Louis XIV (1643–1715), and features statues of Louis XIII and Louis XIV, and a baroque Pieta. The treasury features various ecclesiastical paraphernalia, including some of the relics formerly housed at the Sainte-Chapelle.

In front of the cathedral is PARVIS NOTRE-DAME (Notre-Dame Square), created during Viollet-le-Duc's restoration of the cathedral. This features a 19th-century statue of Charlemagne, and across the square, the HÔTEL-DIEU, the main hospital for central Paris. There has been a hospital on this site since the 7th century. A new hospital was built at the same time as the cathedral and was pulled down in the course of Haussman's renovations. The current buildings date from 1868–78. At the far end of the square is the entrance to the CRYPTE ARCHÉOLOGIQUE (Archaeological Crypt). In the course of building an underground parking lot in the 1960s, these ruins were discovered and are now on display. Here you can see remains of houses dating from the 16th through 18th centuries, as well as the foundations of the Merovingian church and remains of various Gallo-Roman buildings.

At the very eastern (upstream) end of the island, behind the cathedral and through the treed SQUARE JEAN XXIII, stands the MÉMORIAL DE LA DÉPORTATION (Deportation Memorial), dedicated to the 200,000 French men, women, and children deported to Nazi concentration camps. Above the exit are engraved the words, "Forgive. Do not forget."

Rive Droite (Right Bank)

THE LOUVRE AND SURROUNDINGS

THE LOUVRE: The first building to stand on this site was a fortress built by Philip Augustus in 1200 to protect the weakest point in the new walls he had built for the growing city. This was enlarged and converted into a palace by Charles V (1364–80), who preferred its more secure confines after the rebellion of Etienne Marcel. The foundations of this medieval fortress have been excavated and can be viewed below the Cour Carrée. In the 15th century, kings preferred to reside elsewhere, principally in the Loire valley. Francis I (1515–47), however, embarked on an ambitious building program, which was carried on after his death by Catherine de Medici. This resulted primarily in the construction of the Tuileries Palace, at the far end of the Jardin des Tuileries. Louis XIV, though he detested Paris and preferred Versailles, completed construction of the Cour Carrée in a severely neoclassical style. During his reign, and throughout the 18th century while the court resided in Versailles, the Louvre was occupied by a ragtag army of artists and squatters. It was to the Tuileries Palace that Louis XVI and Marie Antoinette were brought back by the crowd of Parisian women in October 1790. In 1792, a mob broke into the palace, causing the king and queen to seek refuge with the revolutionary government, resulting ultimately in the abolition of monarchy and France being declared a republic. It was during the Revolution, in 1793, that the Louvre was converted into a museum to display the artworks of the royal collections. Both Napoleon I and Napoleon III added extensively to the Louvre, connecting it with the Tuileries to form a giant enclosed space. During the Commune, the Tuileries was burned to the ground. In the 1980s, under President François Mitterand, the Grand Projet du Louvre was undertaken. This was to provide the museum with a much-needed main entrance—the famous glass pyramid designed by the Chinese-American architect I. M. Pei. It also renovated and expanded the exhibition space. In order

P

to achieve this, the offices of the Ministry of Finance were relocated from the north wing. The renovated museum, the largest in the world, was opened by President Mitterand in 1993, 200 years after the museum was first opened to the public.

THE MUSEUM: Louis XVI first envisioned the idea of turning the Louvre into a museum, but it was the Convention in 1793 that actually opened the Grand Gallery to the public. Napoleon made the museum the richest in the world, and though the Allies regained much of what Napoleon had taken, purchases and gifts have since made the Louvre one of the greatest art and ancient civilization museums (Egypt, Greece, Rome) in the world.

MUSÉE D'ORSAY: For the devotee of French 19th-century painting, the Musée d'Orsay holds no doubt the most impressive collection in the world. From the neoclassical contours of Ingres, the stark realism of Courbet, the intensely individual Impressionist styles of Monet, Renoir, Degas, and van Gogh, all the way through the pinpoint composition of the neo-Impressionist Serat, the museum covers the history and evolution of this remarkable century in painting. Among the works displayed are Courbet's *Funeral at Ornans*, Monet's *Rouen Cathedral* and van Gogh's *Bedroom at Arles*.

The museum itself has an interesting history in that it was originally a train station. The proximity of the Louvre and the elegant surroundings meant that the builders were required to cover the industrial metal and glass structure with the splendid exterior modeled on the Louvre. For over 40 years, over 200 trains a day went through the station, but when trains became electric, enabling them to have more cars, the platforms at the Orsay station were too short and it quickly fell into disuse. After serving, among other things, as a safe house for prisoners of war after the Liberation, a theater, and a hotel, it was finally to be demolished in 1973, but happily was saved by a proposal to turn it into a museum dedicated to the 19th century. Today's museum was inaugurated in 1986 by President François Mitterrand.

ORATOIRE DU LOUVRE (Oratory of the Louvre): Across the rue de Rivoli from the Cour Carrée stand the Oratoire du Louvre. Built in the early 17th century by the Carmelite Oratorian Congregation, it was a royal chapel in the reigns of Louis XIII, Louis XIV, and Louis XV. The order was suppressed at the Revolution and the church was used as an arms depot and an opera storehouse. Since 1811, it has been the main Reformed Church in Paris. At the back of the church, facing the rue de Rivoli, is a 19th-century statue of Gaspard de Coligny, admiral of France. Leader of the Huguenot forces during the Wars of Religion, he perished in the St. Bartholomew's Massacre in 1572.

EGLISE DE ST. GERMAIN-L'AUXER-ROIS (Church of St. Germain-l'Auxerrois): Facing the Cour Carrée of the Louvre is the Church of St. Germainl'Auxerrois, which was until the Revolution the parish church of the royal family and court when they were in Paris. Named after St. Germain, a 5th-century bishop of Auxerre, the current church is the third to occupy the site. Built between the 13th and 16th centuries, it combines a Romanesque tower, a Gothic choir, and a flamboyant nave and porch with Renaissance and classical touches to the interior, notably the doorway and the columns around the choir. Note the richly carved 17th-century royal pew in the north aisle. It was the bells of St. Germain which rang as the signal to begin the St. Bartholomew's Massacre in 1572.

ST. ROCH: On the rue St. Honoré is St. Roch church, one of the few Baroque churches in France (most are in Paris). Begun in 1653, but not completed until the 1730s due to a lack of funds, it is only slightly shorter than Notre-Dame. It was home to an impressive collection of paintings and sculptures. These were plundered during the Revolution. In the 19th century, the church was refurbished with decorations from other churches. It is the burial place of the playwright Pierre Corneille (1606–84).

THE VOIE TRIOMPHALE (TRIUMPHAL WAY): West of the Louvre stretch some of the most famous avenues in the world, including but not limited to the Champs Elysées. Beginning at the Place de la Concorde, the Champs Elysées runs uphill to the Arc de Triomphe. Beyond this, the Avenue de la Grande Armée and the Avenue Charles de Gaulle run in a straight line to the new high-rise office district of La Défense.

PLACE DE LA CONCORDE: Site of executions under the Terror, the Obelisk is the oldest monument in Paris. Thirty-three centuries old and covered with hieroglyphics, the obelisk was offered to Charles X in 1829 by Méhémet Ali, viceroy of Egypt, in order to try and gain Charles's favor. The best place to admire both directions of the "Triumphal Way," up towards the Arc de Triomphe and down to the Louvre, is at the base of the Obelisk, but be careful with the traffic!

LA MADELEINE: Officially, L'Eglise Ste-Marie-Madeleine (St. Mary Magdalene Church), but known by Parisians simply as La Madeleine, this church, with its somewhat startling Greek Temple style and stunning view down to the Concorde, is one of the most famous monuments in Paris. Indeed, the surprising aspect of the church reflects a no less surprising history. The original plans, drawn up in 1764, were inspired by the St.-Louis des Invalides church. However, when construction started, the plans were changed to model the Panthéon and the edifice was destined to become, among other possibilities, a bank, a commercial tribunal, or a

P

library. Construction was halted during the revolution, and when Napoleon took it up again in 1806, he insisted the existing structure be leveled and a Greek temple be erected in honor of the army. In 1814, under the Restoration, Louis XVIII decided it should become a church once more, but then in 1837, the administration almost decided to make it the central train station for the first rail service in France. It was only in 1842 that it was finally consecrated, and even then its turbulent history was not finished: during the Commune, the church priest, Abbé Deguerry, was taken hostage and then shot by the Communards.

Les Halles/Beaubourg

North and east of the Louvre is the district of Les Halles/Beaubourg. Les Halles was the primary merchandise market for central Paris, torn down in 1969 and replaced by a nondescript shopping mall.

ST. EUSTACHE: The church of St. Eustache was built between 1532 and 1637 in Gothic style, as the parish church of Les Halles. Though Gothic in conception, it contains Renaissance and neoclassical flourishes—the columns of the nave, the rounded arches, and simple window tracery. In 1793 it was the scene of a Festival of Reason, and in 1795 it was converted into a temple of agriculture. It was the home church of a number of famous and powerful people including many artists and musicians.

Behind the choir, note the tomb of Jean-Baptiste Colbert (1619–83), Louis XIV's great finance minister. There are also memorials to the musicians Rameau and Franz Liszt, as well as to Mozart's mother.

CENTRE GEORGES POMPIDOU/CENTRE NATIONAL D'ART ET DE CULTURE (BEAUBOURG): For those interested in modern art, this museum is a must. All the important movements of the 20th century—cubism, fauvism, surrealism, and abstract—are figured. There is a whole section dedicated to Matisse and many works of Miro, Klee, Picasso, and Kandinsky, just to mention a few. The museum contains over 30,000 pieces in all.

The architecture of the Centre is different to say the least. Devoid of any decorative harmony, bold (some might say garish) in its color scheme, and displaying on the exterior such elements as escalators, ventilation shafts, heating units, and gas and water pipes, the building, like much of modern art, is a testimony to the loss of any scheme of reference in esthetic propriety and reflects on a deeper level the rejection of an absolute value system.

The Marais

East of the Louvre and Beaubourg lies the district of **LE MARAIS** (The Marsh), developed in the early 17th century as an aristocratic district. It contains many lovely aristocratic mansions or hôtels, including the **HÔTEL DE SENS,** which now houses the **ARCHIVES NATIONALES DE FRANCE** (French National Archives). The district is centered on the lovely and elegant **PLACE DES VOSGES** (formerly Place Royale).

MUSÉE CARNAVALET: The Carnavalet Museum is housed in the 16th-century Hôtel Carnavalet and is the museum of the history of Paris. It is especially notable for its exhibits dealing with the French Revolution in Paris. Its many artifacts display the enthusiasm of ordinary people, and the sense of liberation they felt, which unfortunately degenerated into violence and terror.

ST. PAUL–ST. LOUIS: The church of St. Paul–St. Louis is one of Paris's outstanding Baroque churches. It was named St. Louis, as the land was donated by Louis XIII. Built by the Jesuits from 1627 to 1641 as their main Paris chapel, it boasts one of the city's earliest domes. In large part, it was modeled after the Jesuits' mother church in Rome, Il Gesu. The Jesuits were expelled from France in 1763, and the church was converted to a parish church and renamed St. Paul–St. Louis in honor of the nearby demolished church of St. Paul.

East of the Marais stands the **PLACE DE LA BASTILLE**, site of the infamous prison, stormed by the crowd on July 14, 1789. It was subsequently demolished as a symbol of tyranny. The monument in the center of the traffic circle is the **COLONNE DE JUILLET** (July Column) dedicated to those who lost their lives in the revolutions of 1830 and 1848. In recent years the area has undergone something of a renaissance, due in large part to the construction of a new opera house, the **OPÉRA DE LA BASTILLE**.

Montmartre

The highest point in the city of Paris, Montmartre, was until the 19th century home to wheat fields and windmills. It later became the bohemian artist district *par excellence.* Little remains of this fabled past; it is now home to tourist traps and seedy nightclubs, but the district still exudes a certain charm within its narrow and steep cobblestone streets.

ST. JEAN L'EVANGÉLISTE EGLISE (Church of Saint John the Evangelist): Completed in 1904 by the architect Baudot, this is the first church in France constructed in reinforced concrete. Its slender pillars and cross beams are an architectural wonder.

SACRÉ CŒUR BASILICA: After the disasters of the Franco-Prussian War and the Commune, French Catholics wanted to erect a symbol of their faith in the future of the Catholic Church and of France as a nation. They chose to build a church consecrated to the heart of Christ (Sacré Cœur). Begun in 1876, and built in the then-popular neo-Byzantine style, the church was completed in 1914 thanks to over $7 million raised by a national fund drive. For over a hundred years, believers have been relaying day and night to maintain a "perpetual prayer" to Christ the Savior.

P

Rive Gauche (Left Bank)—Quartier Latin (Latin Quarter)

When the original settlement on the Ile de la Cité outgrew the island in Roman times, the population spilled over onto the south or left (facing downstream) bank of the Seine. Of Roman times, little physical presence remains, notably the Arènes de Lutèce and the *thermes* (baths) beneath the Musée de Cluny. In the 12th and 13th centuries, the hillside known as the Montagne Ste-Geneviève became home to scholars and eventually to the University of Paris, the leading academic institution in medieval Europe. Instruction was carried out in Latin, giving the district its name, right up until the Revolution, when the university was abolished as a privileged corporation of the old order. To this day, the area around the boulevards St. Michel and St. Germain are home to universities, colleges, students, and their related activities: bookstores, pubs, bars, cheap restaurants, and shops. Thus, the Latin Quarter has a very different feel than the commercial and aristocratic right bank: more bohemian, radical, and intellectual.

THE SORBONNE: The Sorbonne (corner of rue St. Jacques and rue des Ecoles) was founded in the 13th century as one of the residential colleges which made up the University of Paris. It eventually became the most prestigious, specializing in the study of theology, which was the most demanding and most prestigious course of study. The Faculty of Theology became the most important theological school in medieval Europe, drawing students from all over. By the Renaissance, decline had set in; the University lost its international stature, but continued to play an important role in French religious and intellectual life. In general, it was a stronghold of zealous Catholicism, combating Protestantism and protecting the privileges of the Church against the ambitions of the king. Cardinal Richelieu, as the University's rector, undertook renovation of the Sorbonne's buildings, building the current church which houses his tomb. The University was abolished during the Revolution, then reestablished by Napoleon. The current buildings date from the end of the 19th century. It was at the Sorbonne that the student unrest of May 1968 began. Today, as the Université de Paris (IV), it is one of a number of branches of the University scattered around the greater Paris area.

Across the rue des Ecoles from the Sorbonne is the COLLÈGE DE FRANCE. This was founded by Francis I in 1530 as a humanist alternative to the scholastic and hidebound university. Studies were undertaken in classical Latin, Greek, and Hebrew, hence its other name: Le Collège des Trois Langues (the Trilingual College). It is now an independent, state-supported institution.

ST. ETIENNE-DU-MONT: Built between 1492 and 1586 in a combination of Gothic, Renaissance, and Baroque styles, the church of St. Etienne-du-Mont is (despite its name) dedicated to St. Geneviève, the patron saint of Paris. Among its unusual features are its elaborately carved jubé, or rood screen, the only one left in Paris, and one of the few in France.

PANTHÉON: Adjacent to St. Etienne-du-Mont is the Panthéon. In 1744, Louis XV fell deathly ill while in Metz. In gratitude for his recovery, he made a vow to build a church in honor of St. Geneviève on the site of the ruined Abbey of St. Geneviève atop the hill which bears her name (the Montagne Ste-Geneviève). Hence the Panthéon's original incarnation as the church of Ste-Geneviève-du-Mont. In a dramatic break with past styles, the church was the first neoclassical building in Paris, meant to emulate the harmony and grandeur of ancient Greece and Rome. Begun in 1756, it was not complete until the eve of the Revolution in 1789. Closed as a result of the Revolution, in 1791, the revolutionary government turned it into a shrine to "receive the bodies of great men who died in the age of liberty." Under Napoleon, it was converted back into a church. Under Louis-Philippe (1830–48) it served as a necropolis, and again as a church under Napoleon III (1852–70). Under the Third Republic it served once again as a secular temple, which it has remained since. In the interior are a series of 19th-century murals depicting the life and works of St. Geneviève. The crypt beneath is the same size of the building above and contains the tombs of numerous important French men and women. Memorialized here are the Enlightenment thinkers Voltaire (1684–1778) and Rousseau (1712–78); the writers Victor Hugo (1802–85) and Emile Zola (1840–1902); the statesmen Jean Jaurès (1854–1914) and Léon Gambetta; Louis Braille, inventor of the writing system for the blind (1809–52); the scientists Pierre and Marie Curie; Jean Monnet, one of the founders of the European Union (1888–1979); and most recently (1995), the writer and philosopher André Malraux.

ST. JULIEN-LE-PAUVRE: Just across the Pont au Double from Notre-Dame in a square offering superb views of the cathedral stands the tiny church of St. Julien-le-Pauvre. Built at about the same time as Notre-Dame, it is dedicated to St. Julien, a medieval bishop of Le Mans who was known as "Le Pauvre" (the poor) because of his extensive charitable giving. From the 13th through 16th centuries, it was used by the University of Paris for official functions, such as the election of the rector. In 1524, however, rioting students caused such damage that the church was taken away from the University and given as a chapel to the HÔTEL-DIEU on the Ile de la Cité. Since 1889 it has been a Greek Catholic chapel; hence the iconostasis or icon screen, which separates the sanctuary

P

from the rest of the church. The church itself is extremely simple, reminding one of a simple country church.

ST. SÉVERIN: Just across rue St. Jacques from St. Julien-le-Pauvre is the church of St. Séverin, named for a hermit who persuaded a grandson of Clovis to become a monk, the future St. Cloud. Unusually wide in proportion to its length, construction of the present church began in the 13th century and continued until 1530. The first three bays of the church are in a high Gothic style, while the remainder is flamboyant. Note especially the unusual double ambulatory with its intricate flamboyant vaulting. In the 17th century, Mademoiselle de Montpensier, a cousin of Louis XIV and known as the "Grande Mademoiselle," having grown unsatisfied with her own parish church of St. Sulpice, "adopted" St. Séverin and sponsored its "updating." This involved removing the *jubé* or rood screen, surfacing the pillars with marble, and transforming the pointed Gothic arches into round classical ones. Connected to the church is a small ossuary or charnel house, where the bones removed from cemeteries to make room for newcomers were kept.

MUSÉE DE CLUNY (MUSÉE NATIONAL DU MOYEN AGE—NATIONAL MEDIEVAL MUSEUM): At the corner of boulevards St. Michel and St. Germain stands the Hôtel de Cluny, home to a museum dedicated to medieval art. The *hôtel* (mansion) was built in the 15th

century as the Paris residence of the abbot of the immensely wealthy and powerful abbey of Cluny. It now houses France's most important collection of medieval art. Among its highlights are remnants of the original statues torn from Notre-Dame during the Revolution, and an exquisite series of 15th-century tapestries known as *La Dame à la Licorne* (The Lady and the Unicorn). Anyone interested in medieval art and culture should not miss this museum. For that matter, anyone who thinks that the Middle Ages were a barren time, devoid of art and culture, should not miss this museum. The *hôtel* was built above the Roman baths (THERMES DE CLUNY), which have been excavated and are visible from within the museum and also from boulevard St. Michel.

ARÈNES DE LUTÈCE: For anyone interested in Paris's Roman origins, the only other sight of note is the Roman amphitheater, the Arènes de Lutèce, a short distance away, entered through a passage in the rue Monge. Built in the 2nd century A.D., it could accommodate 17,000 people, nearly the whole population of the city. Discovered only in 1869, excavations began in 1883.

ST. MÉDARD: At the beginning of the medieval rue Mouffetard (now lined by cheap restaurants and souvenir shops) stands the small church of St. Médard, named after a counselor of Merovingian kings. The nave and west facade date from the late 15th century, while the 16th-century choir was "updated" in the

18th century in the fashionable classical style. St. Médard is notable for several reasons. It contains a painting of Joseph with the Christ child by the noted Spanish master Zurbaran. It was also here in 1561 that Parisian Catholics and Huguenots met in a violent clash which foreshadowed the bloody St. Bartholomew's Massacre in 1572. In 1727, a Jansenist renowned for his piety was buried in the churchyard. Devout but sick Jansenists came here to pray for healing, and the site gained a reputation for miraculous cures. King Louis XV demanded an end to demonstrations, the cemetery was closed, and a poster was erected which declared: "By order of the King, let God perform no miracle in this place."

VAL-DE-GRÂCE: In the Catholic religious revival which gripped Paris in the early 17th century, a number of religious communities were established in this district just south of the Latin Quarter. One of these communities was the Benedictine women's convent of Val-de-Grâce, patronized by Queen Anne, wife of Louis XIII and mother of Louis XIV. Still childless after more than two decades of marriage, Queen Anne made a vow to build a magnificent church if her prayers for a son were answered. The child who was to become Louis XIV was born in 1638, and in 1645 he laid the cornerstone for the church, which was completed in 1667. Of all the Baroque churches in France, Val-de-Grâce is the most indebted to the Italian Baroque

and the influence of the Jesuits, its dome clearly modeled on that of St. Peter's in Rome. Across the street at 123 boulevard de Port-Royal lies the CHAPEL of the former abbey of Port-Royal-de-Paris. This was the Paris branch of the Jansenist abbey of Port-Royal-des-Champs near Versailles, the headquarters and stronghold of Jansenism. Though Port-Royal-des-Champs was razed in 1709, the chapel of Port-Royal-de-Paris was spared, and now forms part of a maternity hospital. The chapel contains the tomb of Mère Angélique, the abbess of Port-Royal-des-Champs.

ST. GERMAIN: To the west of the Latin Quarter lies the district of St. Germain, named after the great monastery of St. Germain-des-Prés.

ST. GERMAIN-DES-PRÉS: The church of St. Germain-des-Prés is Paris's oldest church, and virtually all that remains of the once-mighty Benedictine abbey of the same name. (There is also a 16th-century abbot's residence behind the church.) In 542, King Childebert, the son of Clovis, established a monastery here, then outside Paris, to house relics of the True Cross which he had obtained. He and his successors of the Merovingian dynasty were buried here until King Dagobert (d. 639) began the practice of royal burial in St. Denis. The monastery was named after St. Germain, a bishop of Paris (who was also buried here), and since it was located in the fields outside the city, it became known as St. Germain-des-Prés (St. Germain in

P

the Fields). Eventually, the abbey accumulated landholdings of some 42,000 acres, and since it was subject only to the pope, it constituted a sovereign domain within France, and the abbot became enormously powerful. The monastery was sacked four times by the Vikings; parts of the present church date back to the rebuilding, which began in 990. When Charles V (1364–80) provided Paris with a new wall, the abbey (still outside the city) surrounded itself with its own walls, connected to the Seine by a moat. It was not until the end of the 17th century that these walls were pulled down and the St. Germain district (Faubourg St. Germain) was brought within the city of Paris. Over the centuries, the abbey fell away from the high ideals of the Benedictine Rule. In the 17th century, it attached itself to the austere Congregation of St. Maur, and the monks devoted themselves to holiness and learning. The monks of St. Germain became experts in epigraphy (the study of ancient inscriptions), paleography (the study of ancient handwriting), history, and archaeology. At the time of the Revolution, the abbey was suppressed, its rich library confiscated and sold off, the royal tombs ransacked, and most of the abbey buildings destroyed. The church itself was turned into a saltpeter factory. Of the three original towers, only one survives. The Romanesque nave is the oldest part of the church, and virtually the only example of Romanesque church architecture

in Paris. The choir (1163) is early Gothic. The nave and choir feature 19th-century frescoes. The vaulting in the nave and choir is Gothic in style, but dates from the 17th century, when the wooden roof burned in a fire. On your right when you enter is the St. Symphorien Chapel, which housed the remains of St. Germain. In the apse is a chapel containing the tombs of the scientist and mathematician René Descartes (1596–1650) and the learned monk and historian of St. Germain, Jean Mabillon (1632–1707). The small square to the south of the church was once the site of the monks' cemetery, and in September 1792, some 318 monks were massacred here.

ST. JOSEPH-DES-CARMES: A short ways southwest of St. Germain on rue Vaugirard lies the domed 17th-century church of St. Joseph-des-Carmes, once the chapel of a Carmelite convent. During the Revolution, at the height of anti-Christian violence in September of 1792, some 120 monks were slaughtered here. Adjacent is the Institut Catholique, founded in 1875, the leading Catholic institution of higher learning in France.

SOCIÉTÉ DE L'HISTOIRE DU PROTESTANTISME FRANÇAIS (Society for the History of French Protestantism): Just north of St. Germain at 54 rue des Saints-Pères lies the headquarters of the Société de l'Histoire du Protestantisme Français, founded in 1865. The society runs a library and museum dedicated to the history of French Protestantism and publishes a scholarly journal dedicated to the subject. It is also responsible for other key sites in the history of French Protestantism: the memorial at Wassy, the Musée du Désert in Anduze, the Musée Jean Calvin (John Calvin Museum) in Noyon, and the Huguenot Memorial on Ile Ste-Marguerite in the Iles Des Lérins. Fittingly, the motto of the society is "post tenebras, lux" ("After darkness, light").

HÔTEL DES INVALIDES: West of the Faubourg St. Germain lies the most impressive complex of Baroque buildings in all of France—the Hôtel des Invalides. Commissioned by Louis XIV in 1671 as a home for soldiers wounded in the king's service, at one time it housed as many as 6000 retired soldiers. Today it still houses about 80 veterans. Within the complex are two churches. The smaller is St. Louis-des-Invalides, or the soldiers' chapel. The interior is decorated with captured enemy standards, and the crypt (not open to the public) contains the tombs of several important generals including Joffre and Leclerc. Larger and more conspicuous is the EGLISE DU DÔME, built by Hardouin-Mansart (the same architect who completed the palace at Versailles) between 1677 and 1706. On the morning of July 14, 1789, a revolutionary mob broke into the Invalides and stole the weapons stored there, which enabled them to storm the Bastille later that day. During the Revolution, it was converted into a Temple of Mars, the Roman god of war, in keeping with its military connections. It is most notable because it houses Napoleon's tomb, completed in 1861. It was only in 1840, after seven years of negotiation with the British government, that the French were allowed to go to the remote south Atlantic island St. Helena to recover Napoleon's body. After the Hundred Days, Napoleon had been exiled here, one of the remotest spots on earth, where he died in 1821. The church also contains several other notable tombs, including the famed military engineer Vauban (1633–1707), who revolutionized military engineering; two of Napoleon's brothers (Joseph, King of Spain [d. 1844], and Jerome, King of Westphalia [d. 1860]), and of Marshal Ferdinand Foch (1851–1929), one of the French heroes of World War I. The Invalides also contains three museums. The MUSÉE DE L'ARMÉE (Army Museum) is one of the richest museums of military history in the world. On the second floor are found rooms dedicated to World War I and World War II. The MUSÉE DE L'ORDRE DE LA LIBÉRATION (Museum of the Order of Liberation) commemorates those "companions" who contributed particularly to the final Allied victory. The "order," established by de Gaulle in 1940, includes both French and foreign commanders and troops, both military and civilian figures. The MUSÉE DES PLAN-RELIEFS (Museum of Relief Maps and Plans)

P

contains a series of 1:600 scale models of some of the most important military fortifications in France.

There are over 50 Jewish synagogues in Paris. Of these the TEMPLE VICTOIRE, 44 rue de la Victoire, is generally regarded as one of the most beautiful and certainly the most important. Jews have lived in Paris since 582, but little actually remains from the past. The Temple was built in 1874 in the neo-Romanesque style. Another important Paris synagogue is the TEMPLE DES VOSGES, 14 Place des Vosges, which is a classic Sephadic synagogue built in the last century that also houses an interesting Jewish museum. The JEWISH ART MUSEUM, 42 rue des Saules, contains, however, the most important collection of Jewish art in Paris and has an interesting cultural collection.

MEMORIAL TO THE UNKNOWN MARTYR, 17 rue Geoffroy l'Asier, is a harrowing four-story Holocaust museum that documents the destruction of French Jews during World War II.

In a small park on Boulevard Raspail stands a monument to Captain Alfred Dreyfus who was falsely accused of being a German spy and unjustly sentenced by a military court in 1894. The Dreyfus affair stirred intellectuals throughout Europe, leading to the publication of open letters in his defense by such notables as the French author Emile Zola (1840–1902). Later, Dreyfus was acquitted and reintegrated into the French Army, in which he served with honor during World War I. Probably the most important outcome of the Dreyfus affair was the effect it had on a young Austrian Jewish reporter who was covering events in Paris for an Austrian newspaper. The man, Theodor Herzl, was so shocked by the treatment of Dreyfus that he immediately wrote his famous tract *The Jewish State* in his hotel room in Hotel de Castille in Paris. This pamphlet led to the founding of the Zionist movement and, ultimately, the State of Israel.

VICINITY

THE MEMORIAL IN LE DRANCY, Jean-Jaures avenue, Le Drancy, three miles outside of Paris, contains a grim monument to the Jewish transit center that was established there in 1940. Jews were held here before being deported east to Nazi death camps. Despite this, Drancy prides itself as one of the centers of the French Resistance during World War II. In fact, some historians claim that around 25 percent of Resistance fighters and many of its leaders were Jewish. Around 75,000 Jews were deported from France during the war.

ST. DENIS: Ten kilometers north of central Paris lies the community of St. Denis, now a heavily industrialized suburb and traditional stronghold of the Communist party. The only reason to visit St. Denis is its magnificent basilica (cathedral since 1966). According to legend, in the mid-3rd century, this is the spot where St. Dionysius (French: St.

Denis) fell after carrying his head from Montmartre. He was buried where he fell, and a chapel was eventually erected at the spot, which has been a place of pilgrimage since the early 4th century. The first large church was built here in about 475, traditionally at the instigation of St. Geneviève. This church was pillaged in 570, and was rebuilt under King Dagobert I, who also established a Benedictine monastery. In 639 Dagobert was buried here, and for over a millenium, all but a few French kings were buried here. St. Denis had become the patron saint of France, and the monks of St. Denis the keepers of the shrine of monarchy. Though the king was crowned at Reims, the regalia of the monarchy were kept at St. Denis: the robes and crowns, the Sainte Ampoule, and the *oriflamme* (battle-flag of the king). The abbot of St. Denis became an important and powerful figure, not a few of them acting as regents when the king was at war or out of the country. Dagobert's church was rebuilt in the 750s by Pepin the Short, the father of Charlemagne. In the 12th century, Abbot Suger (1081–1151), one of these powerful abbots and boyhood friend of King Louis VII (1137–80), decided to build a new church for the abbey. Suger was one of the most learned men in France, and he acted as regent when Louis was away on the Second Crusade. Suger wanted a new kind of church, one which would reflect his belief in God as light, one that would leave behind the darkness and solidity of the Romanesque churches of the day. St. Denis was, therefore, the first church built in the style later to become known as Gothic. Under Suger were built the west facade and the first two bays of the nave (1136–40) and the choir, apse, and crypt (1140–44). The rest of the nave was completed by 1281. In 1793, the revolutionary government decreed the destruction of the royal mausoleum; the remains were exhumed, tossed into a common pit, and covered with lime. Fortunately the archaeologist Alexandre Lenoir managed to save the best of the royal tombs, which were returned to the church in the early 19th century, along with what could be salvaged of the royal remains. In 1806, Napoleon restored Catholic worship to the church. The church was extensively renovated in the 19th century, by Viollet-le-Duc among others. The exterior displays for the first time some of the features characteristic of the Gothic style:

SAINTE AMPOULE is the vial which contained the holy oil used in the coronation of Clovis and subsequent French kings. According to legend, it was brought from heaven by a dove (or angel) at the coronation of Clovis in Reims. The oil allegedly never diminished or was miraculously replenished for each coronation. It was destroyed during the anti-Christian violence of the French Revolution.

the pointed arches, the symmetrical towers (the north tower was pulled down in 1837 after being struck by lightning), the triple doorway (symbolic of the Trinity), and the rose window in the facade. All these features were to be emulated in Notre-Dame de Paris, Chartres, Amiens, and elsewhere. Yet with massive buttresses and crenellations, St. Denis also maintains elements of Romanesque solidity and massiveness. In the interior we see for the first time the sense of soaring light which we associate with the Gothic.

Pointed arches and ribbed vaults allowed much load to be taken off the walls, which meant that there could be more and bigger windows. The glass dates from the 19th century. The crypt, entered from either side of the choir, was built by Suger around the Carolingian church of the 750s. Scattered throughout the church are the royal tombs. Especially notable are the tombs of Louis XII (1498–1515) and his wife, Anne of Brittany, and of Francis I (1515–47) and his wife, Claude of France.

PAU

P

An elegant and relaxed town at the foot of the Pyrenees mountains, Pau has won France's "Ville fleurie" (Garden City) title so many times that it is now forbidden to enter the contest. Pau holds an important place in the history of French Protestantism. It began as a hunting lodge, built in the 11th century by the counts of Foix on a hill above the river, the Gave de Pau. A town soon grew up around the castle, and in the 13th century, the castle was enlarged by Gaston Phoebus, the most famous of the counts. Through marriage and inheritance, the area came into the possession of the viscounts of Béarn in the 15th century, and in 1512, it became part of the tiny kingdom of Navarre, which straddled the Pyrenees, partly in what is now France

and partly in what is now Spain. Henri II d'Albret, king of Navarre, married the sister of King Francis I of France, Marguerite de Navarre. A scholar, humanist, writer, and musician of real talent, Marguerite was very interested in issues of Church reform. She gathered around her in Pau a community of scholars, artists, and religious reformers. Their daughter, Jeanne d'Albret, queen of Navarre (1528–72), married Antoine de Bourbon, first prince of the blood (the closest relative of the ruling Valois dynasty). Jeanne was a convinced Protestant, establishing Protestant worship throughout her lands, and outlawing Catholic worship. Their son, Henri de Navarre (1553–1610), was born in the château at Pau and was brought up in the Huguenot faith. During the Wars of Religion, Henri de Navarre became the leader of the Huguenot forces. In 1589, upon the death of the childless Henry III, the last of the Valois dynasty, Henri de Navarre became King Henry IV of France, the first king of the Bourbon dynasty, thus uniting France and Navarre (including Béarn). Henry quipped at the time that rather than giving Béarn to France, he had brought France to Béarn. For political reasons, he converted to Catholicism in 1593. In 1610, Henry was assassinated by a fanatical Catholic. His son, Louis XIII (1610–43), would annex Navarre to France and reestablish Catholic worship in Navarre in 1620. In the 19th century, Pau became a popular holiday spot for the English nobility, who brought with them their pastimes: polo, cricket, fox hunting, and golf (Pau is the site of the oldest golf course on the continent, established in 1856).

PLACES TO VISIT

There are few real sights in Pau. Be sure to take in the view of the Pyrenees from the BOULEVARD DES PYRENEES.

Pau's most important attraction, however, is the château. Only the brick keep at the southeast corner remains of Gaston Phoebus's 13th-century structure. The château was massively renovated in the Renaissance style in the 16th century, and contains a wonderful collection of Gobelins tapestries. Note also the tortoiseshell cradle of the infant Henri de Navarre. It was believed that this would grant him the long life of the tortoise. Obviously, this did not work, since Henri was felled at the age of 57 by an assassin's knife. The MUSÉE DES BEAUX-ARTS (Fine Arts Museum) houses a worthwhile collection, with paintings by El Greco, Zurbaran, Rubens, Degas, and Corot. In one of the great curiosities of European history, Pau was the birthplace of a king of Sweden. Jean-Baptiste Bernadotte (1763–1844) was one of Napoleon's marshals who became King Charles XIV of Sweden in 1818. The MUSÉE BERNADOTTE is housed in his birthplace. Every summer, the Festival de Pau offers performances almost every evening, most of them free.

POITIERS

Poitiers, though often overlooked by travelers, is of great historical and Christian significance, and contains a wealth of ecclesiastical and architectural riches. Situated on a hill- top surrounded by a loop in the river Clain, Poitiers was important already in Roman times. One of its natives, and its first bishop, St. Hilary of Poitiers (d. 368) was instrumental in forming the

Trinitarian theology of the early church. In 361, he met St. Martin in nearby Ligugé, encouraging him in his promotion of monasticism in Gaul. In 507, Clovis, king of the Franks, defeated the Arian Visigothic king Alaric, establishing Frankish rule over western and southwestern France, and putting an end to the Visigothic kingdom. The battle took place at Vouillé, 17 kilometers north of Poitiers. According to some, the battle actually took place at Voulon, three kilometers south of Poitiers. However that may be, the memorial to the battle is actually in Vouillé. More than two centuries later, Poitiers was also the site of another crucial battle in the history of France, Europe, and Christianity. In 732, Charles Martel (or Charles the Hammer), grandfather of Charlemagne, defeated a Muslim Moorish army which had invaded from Spain (then largely ruled by Arab Muslims, or Moors). The battle was actually fought at Moussais-la-Bataille, between Poitiers and Tours (26 kilometers north of Poitiers on the N10). This represented the furthest extent of Muslim expansion in Europe. From then on, the Muslims were on the defensive throughout the rest of the Middle Ages, finally being expelled from Spain with the reconquest of Granada in 1492. In the 12th century, Poitiers and its surrounding province of Poitou came under English rule, as it was part of the dowry which Eleanor of Aquitaine brought to her husband,

King Henry II of England (1154–89). During the Hundred Years' War, Poitiers was also the site of another crucial battle, this time between the English and the French. In 1356, the English under the Black Prince, the son of King Edward III, defeated a numerically superior French force under King John II (the Good, 1350–64), capturing not only the area, but also the king himself, who would spend the rest of his life in a comfortable exile in England. Poitiers itself was reconquered by 1368. In the 15th century, Poitiers experienced the climax of its history. From 1368 to 1416 it was ruled by John, duke of Berry, and the city prospered under his enlightened rule. Under Charles VII, the city functioned as the effective capital of France during the last stages of the Hundred Years' War. In 1431, Charles VII established a university in the town, which soon became one of France's most prestigious. Among those who studied here were the religious reformer John Calvin, the humanist and writer François Rabelais, and the mathematician and philosopher René Descartes. The city suffered significant damage during the Wars of Religion of the 16th century.

PLACES TO VISIT

Foremost among Poitiers' attractions are its wealth of churches and other ecclesiastical buildings. The BAPTISTÈRE ST. JEAN (St. John's Baptistery) is the oldest extant Christian building in France. It was originally built in the 4th century, and continued to served as the city's only baptistery until the 17th century. The church of **NOTRE-DAME-LA-GRANDE** was built in the 11th and 12th centuries. It is a classic of the Romanesque style, despite its two unusual towers topped by pinecone shaped domes. The unusual west front is covered with interesting sculptures. At the top, there is a now headless Christ triumphant, along with the symbols of the four gospel writers. The sculptures in lower stories depict various biblical scenes. Adorning the arches are sculptures of St. Hilary and St. Martin and the apostles. The interior is richly decorated with 19th-century imitation Gothic frescoes. The church of **ST. HILAIRE-LE-GRAND** was once an important stopping place on the pilgrimage route to Santiago de Compostela in northwestern Spain. It was built in the 11th century in Romanesque style. When a fire destroyed its wooden roof shortly afterwards, it was decided to replace it with a stone roof, which gives St. Hilaire its unique interior. Because the new stone roof was so much heavier than the old wooden one, greater support was needed. This was accomplished by narrowing the nave and flanking it with a double row of columns on each side. The nave thus has three aisles on each side. The new roof was formed by a unique series of eight domes. St. Hilary himself is buried in the crypt under the choir. The **CATHÉDRALE ST. PIERRE** (St.

Peter's Cathedral) is a 13th-century Gothic structure, which has some original stained glass, most notably one depicting the Crucifixion in the apse, dating from 1212, in which the features of Henry II of England and his wife Eleanor of Aquitaine are (barely) discernable. Note as well the wooden 13th-century choir stalls, thought to be the oldest in France. The cathedral is also notable for its magnificent 18th-century Clicquot organ. The church of **STE-RADÉGONDE** dates to the 6th century. Radégonde was a Thuringian princess whose family was slaughtered by the Franks. Taken captive, she was forced to marry Clothaire, the Frankish king. Fleeing her captivity, she begged a priest to allow her to become a nun. When the priest hesitated for fear of offending the king, Radégonde reproved him, saying, "You would fear this man more than you fear God?" The priest relented and she became a nun. At her request, Clothaire built her an abbey in Poitiers. Upon her death in 587, she was buried in the church which bears her name, and her remains became objects of veneration and pilgrimage. The church was rebuilt in the 11th century and has been extensively renovated since. The crypt contains the 8th–9th-century tomb of the saint, with a black marble sarcophagus, empty since 1562 when the Huguenots destroyed the saint's relics. The statue was donated in the 17th century by Anne of Austria, mother of Louis XIV in gratitude for

P

the king's recovery from an illness. The HYPOGÉE MARTYRIUM is an early Christian cemetery, with an underground chapel. Discovered in 1878, it contains early Latin inscriptions which state that it is the resting place of 72 martyrs, though few actual remains have been found. It also contains what is believed to be one of the earliest depictions of the Crucifixion. Near the Hypogée Martyrium is the dolmen (or Stone-Age tomb) known as PIERRE-LEVÉE, mentioned by Rabelais as a popular spot for outings among 16th-century students. Hidden behind a bland 19th-century facade is the much older PALAIS DE JUSTICE (Law Courts). The GRANDE SALLE (Great Hall) dates to the 12th century, and it was here that the duke of Berry held court in the late 14th and early 15th centuries. The keep, or TOUR MAUBEGEON, dates from the 12th century as well, although extensively altered in the 14th century. It was here, in 1429, that Joan of Arc underwent an extensive and humiliating examination by a team of theologians to be sure that she was not possessed or a heretic.

Near Poitiers are several other sights worth taking in. One is Futuroscope, a futuristic, high-tech cinematic theme park. The other is located in the village of ST. SAVIN, 42 kilometers east of Poitiers on the N151. Here in the church of a formerly great Benedictine abbey are stunning 12th-century Romanesque fresco murals. Painted over in the 15th century, they were rediscovered in the 19th, and have been declared a UNESCO world heritage site. Painted around 1100 by a single team of artists in a period of three or four years, the murals depict scenes from Genesis and Exodus and other biblical scenes, culminating in the Apocalypse and Christ in majesty.

PONTIGNY

Once site of one of the most famous Benedictine abbeys in all of Christendom (it was here that the exiled Thomas à Becket came), today, the Abbey of Pontigny houses the seminary of the Mission of France, which trains priests for ministry in dechristianized zones in France. In 1941, an Episcopal commission found that in industrial areas, less than one percent of workers were practicing believers, and that even in the countryside, entire regions had turned away from Christianity. In some villages, the baptismal register had not been opened for twenty years. Christian demographics in France is, sadly, much the same today, though there are some missions, especially in industrial areas, which have had great impact.

PONTMAIN

O f the twenty-five apparitions in France of the Virgin Mary that are officially recognized by the Catholic Church, the one which happened at Pontmain on January 17, 1871, is perhaps the strangest. A huge vision of the Virgin appeared to two schoolboys and two young girls for over three hours. Though none of the other villagers present could see the vision, there was the inexplicable presence of three stars in the sky which all the onlookers saw and which are in complete contradiction with the astronomical observations of the day. After many inquiries by the bishop of Laval, the apparition was proclaimed and a cult to Notre Dame de l'Esperance (Holy Mother of Hope) was authorized. In 1872, the construction of a vast and original basilica was undertaken. The site receives over 100,000 visitors a year.

LE PUY-EN-VELAY

L e Puy is situated in one of the most unusual geographic settings to be found anywhere. High in the mountains of the Massif Central, there is a fertile bowl which was once the bed of a large lake. Volcanic eruptions emptied the lake and thrust up spires and cones of volcanic basalt stone. The name of the town derives from the Latin name for the hill on which the cathedral is situated, *Podium Aniciense.* Indeed, in Roman times, there was a temple to Jupiter here. A Christian bishop was established here in the 5th century, and at about the same time, a church was built to honor the Virgin. In the Middle Ages, Le Puy was one of the important stops for pilgrims along the road to Santiago de Compostela. In fact, according to legend, it was Bishop Godeschalk of Le Puy who first made the pilgrimage in the 10th century. From the 17th to the 19th centuries, Le Puy was important in the manufacture of lace (French: *dentelle*).

PLACES TO VISIT

The first thing that strikes one in Le Puy are the spires of volcanic basalt. The highest of these is the 130 meter (425 feet) high ROCHER CORNEILLE. It is topped by a 16 meter (52 feet) high statue of the Virgin and Child, cast in 1860 from 213 cannons captured by the French at the Battle of Sebastopol during the Crimean War. Accessible by stairs, the terrace at the foot of the statues offers the finest views of the town and the other rock spires. Atop the

P

narrowest of these spires, the 80 meter (263 feet) high ROCHER D'AIGUILHE, is the Romanesque chapel of ST. MICHEL-DE L'AIGUILHE. Built by Bishop Gode-schalk and consecrated in 962, its facade is almost completely covered with decorative stonework which reflects the Moorish influence presumably brought back from Spain by the bishop. The original bell tower was destroyed by lightning in 1245 and was restored in the 19th century. In the interior, the apse is vaulted ingeniously to follow the contours of the rock, and is covered with 12th-century murals. Note also the Romanesque wooden crucifix.

The CATHÉDRALE NOTRE-DAME stands on the site of the Roman temple to Jupiter. This was followed by a sanctuary dedicated to the Virgin in 430. Construction of the present cathedral was begun in the 10th century and continued through the 12th, with major restoration taking place in the 19th century. In style, it reflects a number of influences. Basically Romanesque, the facade with its black and white stripes and geometric designs reflects the Moorish influence from Spain. The nave is covered by a series of domes, reflecting the Byzantine influence brought to France from the Middle East as a result of the Crusades. At the altar is a copy of the original VIÈRGE NOIRE (Black Virgin), which was destroyed during the French Revolution. The original was brought to France from the Middle East by St. Louis, and may in fact not have been a statue of Mary at all, but rather of the Egyptian goddess Isis. The reproduction is still paraded through the town every August, on the eve of the Assumption. Adjoining the south transept is the SACRISTY, which contains the cathedral treasure, notably the 9th-century THEODULPH BIBLE. Adjoining the cathedral is the remarkable 12th-century CLOISTER, which shows both Romanesque and Moorish influences. It offers spectacular views of the cathedral and the Rocher Corneille. Within the cloister is the CHAPELLE DES RELIQUES, which contains an unfinished Renaissance mural of the seven liberal arts, possibly done by Ghirlandaio, Michelangelo's teacher.

REIMS

As Durcotorum, the chief settlement of the Gallic tribe of the Remi, Reims (pronounced "rans," often anglicized as Rheims) was a bustling settlement when Paris was still a small village. Under the Romans, it achieved a population of 80,000 and was the capital of the province of Belgica. Situated on a chalky plain, now known as the region of Champagne, Reims was an important transportation and economic center, as well as a political and administrative one. The chalk on which the city is built also provided handy building material, prompting the Roman Emperor Hadrian to describe it as the "Athens of the north." Christians were present in Reims by the end of the 3rd century, and the first Christian buildings were built in the early 4th century, including the first of three cathedrals. In 406, the city was attacked and destroyed by the invading Vandals. The bishop, St. Nicaise, was martyred in the courtyard of his recently completed cathedral. Reims began to assume its central symbolic significance in French history in 496, when Clovis, king of the Franks, was baptized in its cathedral by the bishop of Reims, St. Rémi (English: St. Remigius). In 816, Louis the Pious, Charlemagne's son, was crowned here, and from the coronation of Louis VIII in 1223 until that of Charles X in 1825 all but three of France's kings were crowned here. The most notable exception was Henry IV, who was crowned in Chartres because Reims was in the hands of the Catholic League. Without doubt, the most moving was that of Charles VII in 1429. Having roused him from his indolence, Joan of Arc led an army to Reims (then deep in Burgundian territory) where the erstwhile "dauphin" was crowned on July 17, 1429. More than anything else, this represented the turning point in the Hundred Years' War, as the French now felt they were fighting for a divinely anointed king, as witnessed by the divine favor apparently granted Joan. During the Wars of Religion, Reims was held in a tight grip by

the ultra-Catholic Guise family. Indeed, the archbishop at the time was Charles, cardinal of Lorraine, brother of the duke of Guise, who also founded a university here in 1547. Reims was the birthplace of Jean-Baptiste Colbert (1619–83), Louis XIV's great minister of finance and the economy. The city was badly damaged during World War I, with the cathedral sustaining heavy damage, now restored. It was in Reims on May 7, 1945, that General Dwight D. Eisenhower received Germany's unconditional surrender. Situated in the midst of the vine-growing district of Champagne (indeed, only sparkling wine made in the region may legally be called "Champagne"), Reims is, along with Epernay, one of the headquarters of the industry. Many of the great Champagne houses are headquartered here, such as Mumm's and Veuve Clicquot. Their cellars consist of miles of tunnels carved out of the soft chalk beneath the city, and many are open to the public. Toward the end of 1914, the Germans abandoned the city but continued to hold the surrounding hills from which they bombed the town for the next four years. Twelve thousand out of 14,000 homes were destroyed as well as many public buildings. The magnificent cathedral was hit by nearly 300 shells and was severely damaged. Restoration of the cathedral was aided by a large gift by John D. Rockefeller and was finished in 1938. The ST. REMI BASILICA, also terribly damaged in World War I, was not restored to its former splendor until 1958.

PLACES TO VISIT

Reims's crowning glory is the CATHÉDRALE NOTRE-DAME, site of royal coronations and a masterpiece of Gothic architecture at its height. The original 5th-century cathedral built by St. Nicaise (see above) was replaced by a larger structure in the 9th century. This in turn was destroyed by fire in 1210. The archbishop at the time decided to construct a vast new edifice in the Gothic style then being employed in the cathedrals under construction in Paris and Chartres. Construction began in 1211 and was largely completed within 100 years, under the supervision of five successive architects. The architects remained true to the original plans, which accounts for the cathedral's unity of style. The two towers of the west facade were completed by 1428. It was intended to be the largest church in Christendom. The nave is 138 meters (453 feet) long, 30 meters (98 feet) wide, and 37 meters (121 feet) high—longer and higher, but narrower than Notre-Dame de Paris—which accounts for its soaring feeling.

The exterior of the cathedral is notable for its statuary and carved stone. More than 2,300 statues have been counted, though some have been extensively damaged and replaced by reproductions. Some of the originals are on display at the PALAIS DU TAU, next to the cathedral. Note especially the west front, best viewed in the afternoon light. The three doors correspond to the nave and aisles, and are richly adorned with statues and topped by elaborately carved gables. The center door is devoted to the Virgin and includes scenes depicting the Annunciation, Visitation, and Purification, while the gable above shows her coronation. The right-hand door depicts Christ's precursors: Simeon, Abraham, Isaiah, and Moses, while the gable is devoted to the Last Judgment. The left-hand door is devoted to the saints of Reims, including St. Nicaise. Notice here as well, the *Ange au sourire* (Smiling Angel), the most famous of the cathedral sculptures, which has become a symbol of Reims. On the gable above is Christ's Passion. Immediately above the central door is the great rose window, and above that is a carving of David and Goliath. Above this is the gallery of kings, with statues of 56 kings of France; in the center is the baptism of Clovis. Also notable is the north face, with its triple portal leading into the north transept. The central door contains sculptures of archbishops of Reims, while the tympanum illustrates the histories of St. Nicaise and St. Rémi. The statues in the right-hand door come from the earlier Romanesque cathedral. The tympanum is devoted to the Virgin in glory. On the left, the Porte de l'Enfer (Door of Hell) shows the Last Judgment on the tympanum; underneath are statues of six apostles surrounding an unfortunately decapitated "Beau Dieu."

The interior strikes one with its unity, sobriety, clarity, and soaring height. The great rose window of the west facade is exceptional; while most of the original glass has suffered the ravages of time and war, most has been replaced. Most notably, in the chapel immediately behind the choir is a striking blue window designed by Marc Chagall, showing the sacrifice of Abraham, the Crucifixion, the Tree of Jesse, the baptism of Clovis, and the coronation of St. Louis.

Next door to the cathedral is the **PALAIS DU TAU**, the former residence of archbishops of Reims. It is so called because of its T shape ("Tau" is Greek for "T"). It was built in the 17th century, though it incorporates a 13th-century chapel. It now houses some of the cathedral's original statuary, including the Coronation of the Virgin above the central door above the west front. On display as well are tapestries, including two 15th-century Flemish samples showing the baptism of Clovis. There is also the cathedral treasure, which houses an alleged fragment of the True Cross, possessed by Charlemagne, an 11th-century glass reliquary used to house a thorn from Christ's crown of thorns, and the reliquary used to house the Sainte Ampoule which contained the sacred oil used in coronation ceremonies.

In the Place de la République behind the cathedral stands the **MONU-MENT AUX MORTS** designed by Royer and Lefebvre in 1930. In the **PLACE DU PARVIS** in front of the cathedral is a statue of Joan of Arc (1896). Across the street from the Palais du Tau is the **BIBLIOTHÈQUE CARNEGIE** (Carnegie Library, 1930), which contains some superb manuscripts from the Middle Ages.

Also worth visiting is Reims's oldest church, the **BASILIQUE ST. REMI**, begun in 1007. The contrast with the cathedral is obvious and striking. Built in an austere and somber Romanesque style, it is immensely long (122 meters—400 feet) but narrow (26 meters—85 feet). The facade is adorned with two square Romanesque towers. Behind the early Gothic choir is the tomb of St. Remi. Next door to the church is the **MUSÉE ST. REMI**, in the building of the former St. Remi monastery, which contains medieval art and architecture, including a series of 16th-century tapestries showing the baptism of Clovis.

All that remains of Reims's Roman past is a triumphal arch, the **PORTE MARS**, dating from the 3rd century. It is located at Place de la République.

Jews lived in Reims from Roman times until the 14th century when they were expelled from France. They returned to the city in 1820 and built **REIMS SYNAGOGUE**, 49 rue Clovis, regarded by many as one of the most beautiful in France. It was built in 1879.

LA ROCHELLE

Originally a fishing village on France's Atlantic coast, La Rochelle was first fortified in the 12th century. The city which grew up around the fortifications became an important port for the salt and wine trades, and profited during the Hundred Years' War by trading with both sides and increasing its independence. In the 16th century, the fiercely independent town became one of France's most important Huguenot strongholds. Following the St. Bartholomew's Massacres in 1572, La Rochelle became the focal point of Huguenot resistance, surviving a siege by the royal army. Under the Edict of Nantes, La Rochelle was one of the fortified towns granted to the Huguenots to guarantee their liberty of conscience and worship. During the 1620s, however, Louis XIII and his chief minister Cardinal Richelieu determined to strip the Huguenots of their independent military and political power, their "state within the state." In 1627–28, the city underwent a brutal siege, losing all but 5000 of its 28,000 citizens to fighting, starvation, or disease. In order to prevent the English from resupplying the city by sea, an immense jetty was built to isolate the harbor, a marvel of 17th-century military engineering. Though the town's walls were razed (except for one small section), and it lost its political power of self-govern-

ment (it was put under direct royal control), the Huguenots were allowed to keep their right to worship. In the 17th and 18th centuries, La Rochelle prospered as France's major Atlantic seaport, handling the fur trade from New France (Canada) and the sugar trade from France's Caribbean colonies. Ships from La Rochelle would take cloth to Africa, transport slaves from Africa to the Caribbean, and return to France with colonial products. Interestingly, parts of the town are paved with stones from Newfoundland, used as ballast in ships returning from Canada with cargoes of light furs.

PLACES TO VISIT

La Rochelle is an immensely attractive town with its VIEUX PORT (old harbor), tree-lined boulevards, and gracious Renaissance town houses. Little remains of the fortifications which once guarded the town's independence and protected its Huguenots. Guarding the entrance to the VIEUX PORT are two 14th-century towers: the TOUR ST. NICOLAS and the TOUR DE LA CHAÎNE (Chain Tower). At night and at times of danger, a chain was stretched across the entrance between the two towers to control access to the harbor. The heavily fortified TOUR ST. NICOLAS offers excellent views of the town and the harbor, while the TOUR DE LA CHAÎNE houses an interesting multimedia presentation (in French only) on medieval life in the town. Connected to the TOUR DE LA CHAÎNE by the only surviving section of the town's walls is the Gothic spire of the TOUR DE LA LANTERNE (Lantern Tower), the oldest of the three towers and France's first lighthouse. Here one may see more than 600 samples of graffiti left by Dutch, English, and Spanish pirates who were imprisoned here. Also worth noting in La Rochelle are an important AQUARIUM, and the MUSÉE DU NOUVEAU-MONDE (Museum of the New World), illustrating the city's connections with the Americas.

RONCHAMP

Ronchamp is the site of Le Corbusier's famous chapel, NOTRE DAME DU HAUT, no doubt the most original creation of religious architecture in France in the 20th century. Le Corbusier, byname of Charles-Edouard Jeanneret (1887–1965), born in Switzerland, became the leader of the so-called international school of architecture and, like Picasso, a symbol of modernity. He was the first architect to make a studied use of rough-cast concrete, and his buildings combine the functionalism of the modern movement with a bold sculptural expressionism. The Notre Dame du Haut chapel gave rise to a lot of controversy in the religious and architectural communities, and there is no question that, knowing it to be a church, the structure does shock on first sight. The great concrete sail which constitutes the roof at first gives an impression of cumbersome weight, until one sees its fluidity as it contrasts with the stark verticals of the chapel walls. Inside, the marvelous arrival of light, created by Le Corbusier's knowing placement of the "periscopes" in the walls of the side chapels, is quite amazing. In stark contrast with the interiors of most Catholic churches, Notre Dame du Haut is almost completely bare, except for a wooden cross and the polychrome statue of the Vierge de Ronchamp, traditional protectress of Alsace, Lorraine, and Franche Comté, dating back to at least the 13th century.

R

ROTHAU

In 1767, the Protestant pastor Jean-Frédéric Oberlin arrived in this miserably poor area, known as *Ban-de-la-Roche*. He stayed 50 years and reorganized the agriculture, created hospices, established schools, and even built roads and bridges (the bridge between Rothau and Fouday is his work). And,

187

even more importantly, he evangelized the people and thus brought back a soul to the community. His saintly reputation and the amazing work he did in transforming the area ended up attracting thousands of visitors during his lifetime. People all over Alsace talked of going "oberlining," meaning going to see the pastor. He even inspired two of Balzac's novels, *The Country Doctor* and *The Village Priest*. During the Revolution, Oberlin was enthusiastic about the new ideas but also gave asylum to Catholic priests who had refused to sign the oath of allegiance to the government, and this led to his imprisonment. Nine Thermidor (July 27, 1794), the day of Robespierre's fall from power, saved Oberlin from the guillotine. He is buried in the nearby village of Fouday. Oberlin's sons were all pastors and continued their father's ministry and work.

Eighteen years after the death of Oberlin, Tommy Fallot (1844–1904), one of the most important figures of 19th-century evangelism, was born in the Ban-de-la-Roche area. He desired to devote himself to the poorest people of France and therefore went to minister in the working-class districts in Paris. Working in the Villette and La Chapelle neighborhoods, he became an advocate of social justice and founded the movement which later became known as "Social Christianity." This movement believed that churches had lost the social dimension of Jesus' ministry, and that the regeneration of the church depended on Christianity lived out socially. Towards the end of his life, he retired from public life and founded in the Drôme region (rural area south of Lyon in the Rhône valley) what he called "prayer fraternities," which can be seen as the precursor of the Taizé monks. Here he spoke eloquently for ecumenism, saying he preached "the Church of Jesus Christ" and that "if all churches looked for what was praiseworthy in the others, a great step could be taken towards a union of spirit and truth."

ROUEN

Located near the mouth of the river Seine, at the last point where it is bridgeable, Rouen has been important since Gallic times. Capital of a Roman province, a Christian bishopric was established here by the middle of the 3rd century. In 912, the duchy of Normandy was established by Rollo, a Viking chieftain, who made Rouen his capital. In 1066, his descendant, William the Conqueror, invaded England and became king of that country. For the next two centuries, Rouen was the capital of a vast Anglo-Norman empire, which stretched from the Pyrenees to Scotland. In 1204, Philip Augustus of France captured Rouen from King John of England (of Robin Hood infamy). During the

Hundred Years' War, Rouen was again captured by the English, this time by Henry V in 1419 after a long siege. It remained in English hands until 1449. It was during this period that in 1431 Joan of Arc was burned at the stake, having been captured by the Burgundians and turned over to their English allies. During the 16th century, it had a large Huguenot community, and for a time in the 1560s was controlled by the Protestants. It was recaptured by the Catholics after yet another siege. Rouen sustained extremely heavy damage during World War II, having been bombarded by both sides. Its churches and old town have been extensively restored since. It is now France's fifth-largest port, though recently in decline.

Rouen is the birthplace of two of France's most celebrated 19th-century artists, the painter Théodore Géricault and the writer Gustave Flaubert.

PLACES TO VISIT

Rouen is famous for its churches. The writer, playwright, and poet Victor Hugo called it "the city of a hundred spires." The **CATHÉDRALE NOTRE-DAME**, the third church to stand on the site, is a vivid illustration of the development of Gothic architecture from the

THÉODORE GÉRICAULT (1791–1824) was one of the most influential painters in the development of Romantic art in France. Moving away from the somewhat artificial heroism and stoicism of neoclassicism, Géricault's paintings are at the same time more alive and more somber and disturbing. His most famous piece is *The Raft of the Medusa,* an amazing work of macabre realism. Like Goya, he was fascinated by the more disturbing aspects of humanity and did a number of studies of madness. He was also a great equestrian painter, including oil, lithograph, and watercolor. An avid horseman, he died at just 33 from a fall from a horse.

GUSTAVE FLAUBERT (1821–80), most famous for his portrayal of the emptiness of materialist bourgeois life in his novel *Madame Bovary,* is seen as the founder of the French school of realism. Like Proust, perfection in his art was Flaubert's goal, and like Proust, beauty ultimately replaced religion. For Flaubert, attaining perfect beauty meant finding the unique right word to describe something: that word found, he became in his words "like God in the Universe, present everywhere but visible nowhere." How paradoxical, therefore, that his personality should be so clearly discernible in all his work, but what a profound statement about the inescapable truth that we are personal beings, created by a personal God.

R

beginning of construction in 1201 to the completion of the west facade in 1514. As you face the cathedral, all that remains of its Romanesque predecessor is the 12th-century TOUR ST. ROMAIN (St. Romain Tower) on the left. On the right is the TOUR DE BEURRE (Butter Tower), built in the late 15th century in the richly ornamented and intricately carved flamboyant Gothic style. It is so called because its construction was financed by the sale of indulgences to those wishing to eat butter during Lent. Also in flamboyant style is the west facade, which features a Tree of Jesse above the central doorway. This is flanked by earlier and much simpler doorways, honoring St. John and St. Stephen. The iron steeple, at 151 meters (495 feet), dates from 1822 when the earlier steeple was destroyed by lightning, and is the tallest in France. The exterior of the cathedral was immortalized by Claude Monet in a series of paintings now displayed at the Musée d'Orsay in Paris. The interior is striking in simplicity, with the eye drawn upward by soaring columns. The lantern tower in the crossing of nave and transept rises to a height of 50 meters (164 feet). Much of the stained glass is original, having been preserved from destruction during the war. On the north side of the ambulatory, note especially the 13th-century window of St. Julien the Hospitaller, whose construction was financed by members of the Fishmongers' Guild. Here as well are the tombs of many dukes of Normandy, including Rollo and Richard the Lionheart. (Actually, only his heart is entombed here—the rest of his remains are in the Abbey of Fontevrault.)

Behind the cathedral is the 15th-century flamboyant Gothic EGLISE ST. MACLOU (St. Maclou Church). Behind the church is the AÎTRE ST. MACLOU, or medieval plague cemetery. Surrounded by half-timbered houses, it is decorated with skulls, crossbones, grave-diggers' tools, and other macabre items. This is a testimony to both the ever-present threat of sudden death in the Middle Ages, and to people's preoccupation with the macabre. A short walk away is Rouen's largest church, ST. OUEN, the former abbey church of a monastery of the same name. Unlike the stylistic melange of the cathedral, and the flamboyant excesses of St. Maclou, St. Ouen is notable for the unity of its high Gothic style, characterized by flying buttresses and improved arches. This meant that weight was taken off the walls, which could now house more windows. Begun in 1318 and completed in the 15th century, the church is now disused and empty, which ironically serves to display the magnificence of the soaring Gothic nave.

While in Rouen, wander the cobbled streets of the old town, extensively restored after the war, observing the half-timbered houses. In the rue du Gros Horloge, stands the GROS HORLOGE (Great Clock). Built in the 14th century, its tower provides a fine view of the old town. At one end of the rue du Gros Horloge is the PLACE DU VIEUX-MARCHÉ (Old Market Square), where Joan of Arc was burned in 1431. The site is now occupied by a modern shopping complex, though a cross now commemorates the exact spot. There is also an EGLISE STE-JEANNE D'ARC (St. Joan of Arc Church), built in a controversial modern style. There is also a small Joan of Arc museum here (MUSÉE JEANNE D'ARC). One can also visit, in the rue Donjon (near the train station), the TOUR JEANNE D'ARC (Joan of Arc Tower), the last remaining tower of the castle where Joan was imprisoned and tortured. Ironically, during World War II, it was used by the Gestapo for the same purpose.

VICINITY

COLLINE (HILL) AND BASILICA BENSECOURS: three kilometers southeast, the Colline de Bonsecours is crowned with the Basilica Notre Dame (1842) and the monument of Joan of Arc (1892). The hills offer a fantastic panorama of Rouen.

ROYAN

The biggest seaside resort between La Baule and Biarritz, Royan was almost completely destroyed in 1944–45. The German troops dug in here in August 1944 and were not overcome until April 1945, during which time Allied bombing took a terrible toll on the town. However, huge restoration plans developed by the architect Ferret were undertaken almost immediately, turning Royan into one of the most modern resorts on the Atlantic. Indeed, the same qualities that had made it a successful resort before insured its restoration: admirable site at the mouth of the Gironde River, beautiful fine sandy beaches walled in by towering cliffs, lush surrounding forests, and finally, a perfect climate.

PLACES TO VISIT

EGLISE NOTRE DAME DE ROYAN: Modern church designed by the architect Guillaume Gillet. Constructed entirely from reinforced concrete, this original and unique edifice is in the form of an ellipse dominated by a 200-foot steeple. The frame is made of slender, almost veil-like vertical supports which hold up a similarly veil-like vault in the form of a horse saddle. Just near Notre Dame de Royan is the Protestant TEMPLE, another modern structure striking in the purity of its lines.

R

SABLÉ-SUR-SARTHE

S able-sur-Sarthe is a pretty 18th-century town on the Sarthe River dominated by the Château (1720) with its fortified gate. The EGLISE NOTRE DAME was finished in just 1891, but the pilgrimage which necessitated the building of the current church dates back to the 15th century. In 1494, the priest and the whole village witnessed white doves descending from heaven and starlike flames coming from the ground at an old oak tree outside the village. The priest placed a small statue of the Virgin Mary in the tree, and a pilgrimage soon developed and many healings took place. In 1515, the pilgrims were so numerous that a chapel was built to house fragments of the oak and the statue. With the confiscation of all church property under the Revolution, the chapel was sold to a local builder on the condition that he destroy it completely. However, when he went up on the roof to start the demolition, he fell and broke his leg. The chapel was thus preserved. In 1802, after Napoleon put an end to the persecution of the Church, the pilgrimage started up again, and by the end of the 19th century the new basilica was needed.

VICINITY

Three kilometers northeast on the banks of the Sarthe lies the village of SOLESMES. In 1833, the monk Dom Guéranger came to Solesmes and began rebuilding the ABBAYE ST. PIERRE DE SOLESMES. In 1922, the monastery became a permanent Benedictine community. The monastery building, finished in 1896 in 12th-century style, dominates the river. A vast Gothic chancel was added in 1865 to the abbey church, a medieval structure of Roman architecture. The church contains some inestimable sculptures known as the Saints de Solesmes, as well as a tomb of Christ (1496) and a tomb of the Virgin (16th century).

LA SALETTE

O n a small crest in the middle of a wilderness of vast pastures, the imposing and austere BASILICA NOTRE DAME DE LA SALETTE seems almost to have been dropped from the clouds, or to be floating among them. Erected 1852–61, the strangeness of the site reflects the strangeness of its genesis: an apparition, in 1846, of the Virgin Mary to two humble shepherds' children.

The children were questioned for five years before the Church officially recognized the apparition. The following year, 50,000 pilgrims visited the site, and soon after, the basilica appeared. One can get to the basilica by car, but many pilgrims and visitors choose to make the ascension by foot. Notre Dame de la Salette is perhaps the only site of pilgrimage in the world which does not have souvenir shops or restaurants. There are two hotels, one for women and one for men, where visitors can spend the night.

From the basilica, one can, without difficulty, make the one-andone-half hour ascent to Mount Gargas (2,213 meters), which offers an orientation table and splendid panorama of the region.

SÉLÉSTAT

Like Strasbourg, Séléstat was an Imperial Free City of the Holy Roman Empire during the Middle Ages, when it was known as Schlettstadt. In the late 15th and early 16th centuries, it was a center of northern or Christian humanism, which was the attempt to return to the purity of the early church through the study of ancient literature, both pagan and Christian. Foremost among Séléstat humanists was Beatus Rhenanus (1485–1547), friend and correspondent of the greatest of humanists, Erasmus of Rotterdam. Erasmus himself spent time at the academy in Séléstat in 1515. Séléstat was also the birthplace of Martin Bucer (1491–1551), one of the leading Protestant reformers of the age.

PLACES TO VISIT

Séléstat's main treasure is the BIB-LIOTHÈQUE HUMANISTE (Humanist Library). Founded in 1452, it quickly became a magnet for humanists all over Europe, who flocked to the city to consult its works. The famed scholar Beatus Rhenanus bequeathed his collection to the library upon his death. Among the library's prized possessions are a 7th-century lectionary, regulations of

S

HOLY ROMAN EMPIRE. Precursor of modern Germany, the Holy Roman Empire of the Middle Ages was the evolution of the eastern part of the Carolingian Empire, the kingdom of the East Franks. From the 11th–13th centuries, the Holy Roman emperors were involved in a bitter struggle for political supremacy with the papacy. Thereafter, the Empire was a weak federation, in theory headed by the emperor, but in reality ruled by individual princes and cities.

Charlemagne dating from the 9th century, a 12th-century Book of Miracles, the first written reference to "America," and a bone from a wooly mammoth, which according to local legend is the leg-bone of a giant named Sletto, for whom the town was named.

Séléstat also boasts several worthwhile churches. STE-FOY, the church of the Benedictine abbey of the same name, was built in the late 12th century by monks from Conques and has preserved its clean Romanesque lines despite the addition of two symmetrical towers in the 19th century. The much larger Gothic ST. GEORGES, which stands across the square, was built by the townspeople from the 13th to 15th centuries as a kind of protest against the power wielded by the monastery.

The city walls have all but disappeared; only two towers remain: the TOUR DE L'HORLOGE (Clock Tower) and the TOUR DES SORCIÈRES (Witches' Tower). This latter is so called because more than 100 "witches" were imprisoned here between 1629 and 1642, at the height of the great witch hunts of the 17th century.

SENS

C hief fortress of the Gallic tribe of the Senones, who came within a whisker of conquering Rome in 390 B.C., Sens became the capital of the Roman province of Senonia, and was Christianized in the 3rd century. During the Middle Ages, its position at the crossroads of Burgundy, Champagne, and Ile de France gave Sens tremendous administrative importance. The archbishop of Sens was the most important clergyman in northern France. Even the bishop of Paris was subordinate to him until Paris was promoted to an archbishopric in 1627. Sens's decline began with the Hundred Years' War and continued with the Wars of Religion, when the city held steadfastly to the Catholic League.

PLACES TO VISIT

Sens's glorious ecclesiastical past is masked by its present near obscurity, but it is well worth a visit. The old town is surrounded by an oval ring of boulevards which marked the old city walls, of which several sections and one tower survive. A number of half-timbered houses line the narrow streets, many of which are restricted to pedestrians. Sens's chief attraction, however, is the CATHÉDRALE ST. ETIENNE (St. Stephen's Cathedral), which has the distinction of being the earliest Gothic cathedral in France. (St. Denis, though begun five years earlier, was an abbey church rather than a cathedral—the seat of a bishop or archbishop—at least until St. Denis was promoted to a bishopric in 1960.)

Though the foundations were laid between 1128 and 1130, most construction took place between 1140 and 1168. The west facade has three richly sculptured doorways; in 1793, they were heavily damaged during the anticlerical violence of the French Revolution. Only the statue of St. Stephen is original. The south tower collapsed in 1268, following which the church was extensively renovated and altered. The present south tower was completed in the 16th century. The north tower is known as the Tour de plomb (Lead tower) because of its lead sheathing, which was destroyed in 1845. The transepts were built in the 15th and 16th century in flamboyant Gothic style. In the interior, the most notable feature is the wide array of original stained glass. The ambulatory and the north side of the choir feature original 12th-century windows. One of these windows recounts the story of St. Thomas à Becket, archbishop of Canterbury. Following his quarrel with King Henry II of England, Becket took refuge in Sens before returning to England, where he was murdered in Canterbury Cathedral in 1170. The rose window in the north transept, and the Tree of Jesse and St. Nicholas in the south transepts, are Renaissance works from the workshops of the master glaziers in nearby Troyes. Immediately to the south is the 13th-century PALAIS SYNODAL, with its typically Burgundian multicolored tile roof. It contains a museum with an extensive collection of Gallo-Roman artifacts (and, strangely, the hat that Napoleon wore at the Battle of Waterloo), and the cathedral treasury, one of the richest in France. This latter features the vestments worn by the archbishops of Sens, as well as those of Thomas à Becket, and many other items of ecclesiastical paraphernalia.

S

ST-BENOÎT-SUR-LOIRE, ABBAYE DE

The abbey of St. Benoît-sur-Loire was named after St-Benedict (c. 480–543; French: St. Benoît), the founder of Western monasticism and the Benedictine Order. St. Benedict's monastic rule brought order to the chaos of differing and sometimes contradictory monastic rules in the early Middle Ages. He emphasized a simple life of prayer and labor *(ore et labore)*, which spread throughout monastic communities in western Europe. In the 7th century the abbey of Fleury was founded on this site. When word reached the abbot of Fleury in about 672 that invading Lombards had destroyed St. Benedict's original monastery of Monte Cassino in southern Italy and despoiled the tombs of both St. Benedict and of his sister St. Scholastica, he dispatched two of his monks to retrieve the saints' bodies. They were exhumed and brought back to Fleury, which then became known as St. Benoît-sur-Loire. In subsequent centuries, the abbey became extremely powerful and influential. Under Charlemagne, the abbot was the Visigothic nobleman Theodulf of Orléans, Charlemagne's close friend and advisor, and one of the most learned men of the age. It was Theodulf who founded the monastery school, which became one of the great European centers of learning, as copyists reproduced manuscripts and the abbey amassed a great library. The school's most famous student was Gerbert of Aurillac, who became Pope Sylvester II (999–1003). The abbey suffered extensively from the raids of the Vikings or Norsemen in the 9th and 10th centuries. The monks would take refuge in nearby Orléans, bringing with them their prized relics and treasures. Returning home, they would rebuild their ravaged monastery. Throughout the Middle Ages, St. Benoît would remain wealthy and powerful, for the most part remaining true to the vision of the order's founder. Its decline dates from the late 15th century, with the practice of granting the abbacy *in commendam,* which meant that the titular abbot received the revenue and prestige of the position, but had nothing to do with the day-to-day affairs of the monastery. The actual administration of the abbey was left in the hands of poorly paid and often unqualified substitutes. In protest, in the 1520s the monks refused to receive their titular abbot, Cardinal Duprat, one of the chief advisors of King Francis I, and shut themselves up in the belfry. The king had to bring an army and suppress their disobedience by force. During the Wars of Religion, one of these abbots *in commendam,* Odet de Châtillon, was the brother of Gaspard de Coligny, the military and political leader of the Huguenots, and himself a Protestant. He allowed St. Benoît to be looted by Huguenot troops. The monastery's treasure was melted down, including the 39-pound golden urn which held the remains of St. Benedict. The priceless collection of manuscripts was broken up and sold piecemeal. In the 17th century the reformed Benedictine order, the Congregation of St. Maur, was introduced to St. Benoît by Cardinal Richelieu.

By the time of the Revolution, the abbey had nearly ceased to function. The Revolution finished it off, and the magnificent site was deserted. In the early 1900s, one attempt to reinvest the abbey failed because of the restrictive laws prohibiting members of unlawful congregations (almost all religious orders were banned by this law passed in 1880) from holding any educational post, either in a public or a private institution. Finally, in 1944, a group of monks was able to reinstall the regular monastic life. At first just a simple priory, St. Benoît became an abbey once again in 1959. The checkered history of St. Benoît-sur-Loire serves as a microcosm of the history of Christian piety in France, from original purity to corruption, to division and strife, repression, and finally restoration.

Places to Visit

The BASILIQUE ST. BENOÎT (St. Benedict's Basilica) is one of the finest examples of Romanesque church architecture at its height. It was built between 1067, when the crypt, chancel, and transept were begun, and 1218, when the nave was completed. The porch of the belfry or bell tower is notable for its intricately carved capitals, rife with stylized plants and animals intertwined with scenes of the Apocalypse and the lives of Christ and the Virgin Mary. The second column from the left contains the inscription *Umbertus me fecit* ("Umbertus made me"). The aisled narthex was deprived of its spire and reduced in height by order of Francis I in 1527 to punish the monks for their resistance to their titular abbot. The floor of the chancel is paved with a Roman mosaic brought from Italy in 1531 by Cardinal Duprat as a gesture of reconciliation. The chancel also contains the renovated tomb of King Philip I (d. 1108). The transept boasts portions of a carved wood choir screen presented by Cardinal Richelieu when he was abbot *in commendam.* The crypt contains a shrine to St. Benedict. St. Benoît is one of the few places where one can still hear Benedictine monks singing ancient Gregorian chants, open to the public at noon Mondays through Fridays, and at 11:00 A.M. on Sundays.

Five-and-a-half kilometers (3.5 miles) northwest of St. Benoît, on the D60 between St. Benoît and Châteauneuf-sur-Loire, lies the tiny village of GERMIGNY-DES-PRÉS. The attraction here is one of the oldest churches in France, and one of the few examples of Carolingian architecture. It was built in 806 as the chapel for the country villa of Theodulf of Orléans on the plan of a Greek cross (that is, with four arms of equal length), and four apses. A nave was added in the 15th century. The church's greatest attraction lies in the east apse, the only original portion. This is a Byzantine ceiling mosaic brought from Italy by Theodulf. Made of 130,000 pieces of brightly colored glass, its subject is the Ark of the Covenant. It survived only because at some point it was covered with a thick layer of plaster. It was rediscovered in 1840 when an archaeologist noted local children playing with some of the brightly colored tiles. The mosaic gives an idea of what the entire church must have looked like when Theodulf had it built almost 1,200 years ago.

S

ST-GUILHEM-
LE-DÉSERT

Situated in the spectacular gorge of the Hérault River, this remote village is one of the most picturesque in France. Its major attraction is the Benedictine abbey of St. Guilhem-le-Désert, founded in 804 by Duke William of Aquitaine (French: Guillaume, Guilhem in the local dialect). William was one of Charlemagne's comrades in arms, and an indefatigable warrior against the Muslims in Spain, or Saracens. It was during the course of one of these battles that he lost part of his nose, thus earning the nickname "Court-nez," or "short nose." Overlooking the village and the abbey is a ruined castle, once the fortress of Don Juan, a Saracen commander who preyed upon the villagers until defeated by William. William retired here, dying in 812. He was later canonized.

PLACES TO VISIT

Your car must be left in the parking lot outside the village itself, which boasts picturesque streets and narrow old houses. The EGLISE ABBATIALE (Abbey Church) is on the main square. A gem of Romanesque architecture, this building was consecrated in 1076. When William founded the abbey in 804, he donated to it a piece of the True Cross, originally owned by St. Helena, mother of the Emperor Constantine, which had in turn been given to William by Charlemagne. This fragment is now in the south transept. Little remains of the original cloisters; in the 19th century, the cloisters with their richly carved capitals were sold, dismantled, and transported to New York, where they now grace the Cloisters Museum high above the Hudson River. The history of St. Guilhem demonstrates several important features of early medieval Christianity: the hunger for physical relics of the holy, displayed in the reverence for the fragment of the True Cross and other relics; the crusading zeal, as evidenced in William's campaigns against the Muslims; and the conviction that a truly holy life could be lived only in isolation from the world, evidenced in the foundation of this and countless other monasteries in remote locations, and in William's retirement here when his active political and military career was over.

ST-PIERRE-DE-CHARTREUSE

In 1084, St. Hugues, bishop of Grenoble, had a prophetic dream in which he saw seven stars guiding him to a solitary place in the mountains where Christ was building a lodging. A few days later, his old master St. Bruno came with six companions asking him to help them find a site for an extremely isolated monastery. Recalling his dream, the bishop promptly set off with them across forest and mountain to the base of the sheer rock face of *Grand-Som*. Here, the monks built wooden cabins and erected a small stone chapel, and so a tiny Carthusian community was started. Yet, it soon developed to be the head of the Carthusian order: the buildings you see today date from the 14th through 16th centuries. During the Revolution, the monastery was pillaged and the monks were forced to leave. In 1816, they returned, only to be expelled in 1903. The 1901 law on associations gave the government the right to dissolve any association which asked its members to abandon man's natural rights. It was of course the religious orders with their vows of poverty, chastity, and obedience which were targeted by this law. The government sent in a troop of armed forces to expel the monks; they also closed the school where the monks were teaching 100 deaf and mute children. It was only in 1944 that the monks were able to return. Since then, the monastery has become once more the head of the Carthusian order, the most rigorous religious order that exists. The monks spend almost all their time in individual cells in complete solitude and silence, receiving food through a window. They gather twice a day and once in the middle of the night to sing the divine office, but no communication is permitted. Only once a week, on Sunday afternoons, do the monks have some recreation time together.

Due to an overwhelming number of curious tourists, a visit to the monastery is no longer permitted, but the monks set up a museum where the visitor can learn all about the Carthusian order. One can visit the 11th-century chapel and see the remains of the original monastery, destroyed by a rock slide in 1132.

STRASBOURG

A Celtic fishing settlement along the River Rhine, the precursor of modern Strasbourg was fortified by the Romans and known as Argentoratum. In the early Middle Ages, it became known as Stratoburgum (Germanic for "city of roads"), in recognition of its strategic position on the Rhine, and also on the roads leading from Germany to France. (In fact, even now the city's name in German is Strassburg, literally "road city.") In 842, two of Charlemagne's three grandsons met in Strasbourg. They were Charles the Bald, king of West Francia (later France), and Louis or Ludwig the German, king of the East Germans (later Germany). They met to plot strategy against their older brother Lothair, and swore the "Strasbourg Oaths" to seal their alliance. In order that their retinues be able to comprehend the oaths, they were read aloud and sworn in the two languages commonly spoken. These texts have survived as the earliest written examples of the ancestors of modern French and German. This also reflects the growing cultural divide between the western and eastern halves of Charlemagne's empire, between the Gallo-Roman heritage of France and the Teutonic heritage of Germany, and also Strasbourg's important situation at the crossroads of the two spheres. Throughout the Middle Ages, Strasbourg was a German-speaking city, technically within the Holy Roman Empire, but as an Imperial Free City, self-governed by its wealthy inhabitants, or burghers. Because of its German ethnicity and language, Strasbourg was especially receptive to the message of religious reform and liberation proclaimed by Martin Luther, and had by the mid-1520s adapted its own form of Protestantism. Religious reform in Strasbourg was spearheaded by Martin Bucer (German: Butzer), a native of nearby Sélestat (German: Schletstadt). Bucer was one of the more tolerant of Protestant reformers, and Strasbourg remained relatively tolerant (by 16th-century standards at any rate), housing communities of Catholics, Jews, and Anabaptists. It was also renowned as a center of humanist and Protestant scholarship. The reputation of its schools led to the formation of a university in 1566, and a young John Calvin lived here for several years after his first ill-fated sojourn in Geneva. In the 17th century, Strasbourg felt very keenly the threat from the ever-more-powerful kings of France to the west, as they sought to solidify their eastern frontier against their archenemy, the Holy Roman Emperors of the Habsburg dynasty. In 1648, as a result of the Treaty of Westphalia which ended the Thirty Years' War, most of Alsace was ceded to France, but Strasbourg remained independent. This situation changed when the city was annexed by Louis XIV in

1681. This was achieved with the collusion of Catholics living in the city, who struck a medal with the inscription *Clausa Germanis Gallia* ("Gaul closed to the Germans"). The city managed, however, to hold on to some of its precious privileges, gaining the title "Royal free city." These privileges were suppressed at the time of the Revolution. It was in Strasbourg in 1793 that the French national anthem was first heard, as "The Marching Song of the Army of the Rhine," subsequently known as the *Marseillaise.* When Germany was finally united as a nation in 1870 under the king of Prussia and his "Iron Chancellor," Otto von Bismarck, "recovery" of the "lost provinces" of Alsace and Lorraine was seen as a matter of national honor. After a seven-week siege, Strasbourg surrendered to German forces on September 27, 1870. The city, as well as the provinces of Alsace and Lorraine, remained part of Germany until the end of World War I and German defeat. But three centuries of French rule had left their mark. During the German occupation, Alsatians remained fiercely French in outlook and loyalty, despite their Germanic dialect, culture, and cuisine. Strasbourg was once again occupied by the Germans from 1940 to 1944. Since World War II, Strasbourg has assumed an important place in the "New Europe," reflecting its cosmopolitan history and location at the intersection of French and Germanic worlds. It is now the seat of the Council of Europe, the European Parliament, and the Europe Human Rights Commission. Strasbourg was the birthplace of a number of famous figures in recent French history, one of the most interesting of whom is Charles de Foucauld.

PLACES TO VISIT

The old town is neatly contained by the branches of the River Ill, and displays Strasbourg's German past, with its half-timbered houses and overhanging eaves. Its most picturesque section is LA PETITE FRANCE (Little France), on an island at the western end of the old town. The name is derived from an old French hospital in the area. This was the old tanners and fishermen's quarter.

CHARLES DE FOUCAULD (1858–1916). As a young man, Foucauld was a lieutenant in the army, but at 32, he felt the call to devote his life to Christ. In 1890, he entered the Trappist Monastery in Labastide (Ardèche) and took his vows just ten days later. His studies completed, he went to a monastery in Armenia, but desiring yet greater solitude and severity of conditions, asked permission to go as a solitary missionary to Algeria. In his efforts to reach out to the Islamic people, he put together a fascinating study of Morocco and also wrote the first French-Tamahag dictionary. Faithful to the last to his work of evangelization, he was killed by assassins in 1916.

Locks and canals allowed water access to virtually all the shops on the island. Note the *ponts couverts,* a series of 14th-century covered bridges.

Strasbourg's major treasure is the CATHÉDRALE NOTRE-DAME. Clovis had first built a church on this site in 496. This was rebuilt by Charlemagne, and was largely destroyed by lightning in 1007. The present structure was begun in 1167, and though the basic conception is Romanesque, it became an essentially Gothic structure through the extensive statuary, and especially through the addition of a Gothic spire, completed in 1439. The intricately carved tower rises to a height of 142 meters (466 feet), and was for more than 500 years the tallest church spire in the world. The west facade is remarkable for the stone tracery and the number of statues. Note above the south door the portrayal of Jesus' parable of the wise and foolish virgins. The vast interior is a fine example of high Gothic. Note especially in the south transept, the PILIER DES ANGES (Angels' Pillar) depicts the Last Judgment and its heavenly jury. Beside the Angels' Pillar is HORLOGE ASTRONOMIQUE (astronomical clock), which at 12:30 reenacts Peter's denial of Christ. To the south of the cathedral, across the Place du château, lies the MUSÉE DE L'OEUVRE NOTRE-DAME, which houses many of the cathedral's original statues. It also displays the architects' drawings, and the oldest stained glass in existence, from the 10th century, as well as the Wissembourg Christ (from Wissembourg in northern Alsace), believed to be the oldest representation of the human figure in stained glass.

Between La Petite France and the cathedral, in the ancienne cité, lies the EGLISE ST. THOMAS (St. Thomas's Church), (1270–1330), which has been Strasbourg's principle Protestant church since 1549. With its Romanesque facade and Gothic towers, it houses the tomb of Martin Bucer, and also the ornate 18th-century tomb of the Marshal de Saxe, a French general. It also contains a 9th-century sarcophagus. In 1908, Albert Schweitzer performed a concert of Bach's organ works on the church's organ, beginning a tradition of honoring the composer on the anniversary of his death (July 28, 1750).

For centuries Strasbourg was dubbed the Jerusalem of Europe because so many Jews made the city their home. The city's historic Consistoriale du Quai Kleber Synagogue was destroyed during World War II by the Nazis. The present building, which stands on the site of the earlier synagogue, was dedicated in 1958. In the nearby ALSATIAN MUSEUM, 23 quai St. Nicolas, there is also a rich collection depicting the history of the Jews in Alsace-Lorraine.

STRUTHOF CONCENTRATION CAMP is found on route D130 some 50 kilometers west of Strasbourg. It is the only Nazi concentration camp in France and was used for medical experiments, among other things. The camp was liberated on November 23, 1944.

ST-THÉGONNEC

I n many ways Brittany (French: Bretagne) is the most anomalous part of France. Ethnically, linguistically, and culturally distinct from the rest of the country, it was originally settled by Celtic refugees from Britain in the wake of the Anglo-Saxon conquest of that country in the 5th century. Strongly devoted to their Celtic language and culture, their unique social structure and version of Christianity derived in large part from medieval Irish traditions, Brittany remained an independent duchy throughout the Middle Ages, with varying degrees of cooperation with and hostility towards the French to the east. By the end of the 15th century, Duchess Anne of Brittany had been married to two French kings (Charles VIII and Louis XII), and Brittany was joined to France in a purely personal union. In 1532, Francis I formally annexed the duchy to the kingdom of France (despite a solemn promise never to do this), but the Bretons continued their independent ways, despite persecution and repressive measures which sought to suppress their distinctive language and culture. Religiously too, Brittany is unique within France. For centuries throughout the Middle Ages, Bretons, though nominally Roman Catholic, practiced a unique form of Christianity, in part derived from medieval Irish Christianity, and in

part a hybrid of ancient Celtic practices and local lore. To the reformers of the Counter-Reformation, this was unacceptable, and the Bretons were hardly better than pagan savages. Brittany was thus the focus of intense missionary effort, the same missionary impulse which brought Jesuit missionaries to New France (now Canada). As often happens, the objects of this missionary activity took to the new religious forms with great fervor. One of the results of this religious zeal was the construction of *enclos paroissiaux* (parish closes), such as those at St. Thégonnec and Guimiliau discussed below. During the French Revolution, the extremely Catholic peasants of Brittany proved resistant to the secular and anticlerical nature of the revolutionary governments, and were the backbone of the revolt of the Vendée.

PLACES TO VISIT

ENCLOS PAROISSIAUX (parish closes), of which the one at ST. THÉGONNEC is the most famous, began to spring up in the Breton countryside in the second half of the 16th century. They typically consist of a church, a calvary (representation of the Crucifixion), and a charnel house. (A charnel house, or ossuary, was intended to house the bones of bodies exhumed from the cemetery to make room for new arrivals. Though it may seem morbid to us, to contemporaries such practices served as reminders of the potential of sudden and unexpected death, and also of illustrating the indivisible community of living and dead Christians.) St. Thégonnec is named for Tigernach, bishop of Clogher and Clones in Ireland (d. ca. 550). The close is entered through a lavishly decorated *porte triomphale* (triumphal arch), built in 1587 in Renaissance style. The Calvary dates from 1610 and shows angels collecting Christ's blood, while the base has scenes from the Passion and Resurrection. There is also a statue of Tigernach which shows his cart being towed by the wolf which had eaten his donkey, which he then tamed and harnessed. The ossuary (1676) has been transformed into a funerary chapel *(chapelle funéraire),* which features an elaborately carved and painted wooden portrayal of the Entombment. In the church *(église),*

the entire east wall is an elaborately carved and painted retable. The pulpit as well is an acknowledged masterpiece of Breton woodcarving.

Eight kilometers (5 miles) southwest of St. Thégonnec is the parish close of **GUIMILIAU**, which contains the most exuberant and elaborate Calvary of any Breton close, with more than 200 carved figures. Carved between 1581 and 1588, besides recounting the Crucifixion, it also tells the Breton legend of *Catel Gollet* (Breton for "Lost Kate"). According to the legend, she was a flirtatious serving girl who failed to reveal all at confession, whereupon she discovered that her lover was the Devil, who then carried her off to hell. This illustrates nicely two important features of the Breton parish closes: their didactic function— to teach moral lessons—and their incorporation of Breton lore and legends in order to reinforce the message of the Counter-Reformation Catholic Church.

ST-VÉRAN

At 2,040 meters, St. Véran is the highest village in Europe. The old chalets with their balconies are lovely, and even today, some are still one-room houses which, in winter, serve as stable, bedroom, and kitchen all together. The church dates from the 17th century, and the fields on the north slopes are irrigated by a canal system which goes back to the 6th century. Six kilometers to the southeast and at 2,390 meters is the picturesque **CHAPELLE DE**

CLAUSIS, place of worship for both French and Italians.

St. Véran was evangelized during the Reveil of the 19th century. The man responsible for the evangelization was the Swiss pastor Félix Neff (1798–1829). Though born in Geneva, he was from a Catholic family, and a soldier by profession, he had the task of protecting Catholic meetings. Indeed, he swore to plant his saber in the stomach of the perpetrators of the Reveil. However, on hearing the message of the Protestant Reveil preachers, he was converted, and after being a pastor in Geneva for a while, was sent into the remote valleys of the Alps. Architect, engineer, doctor, teacher, and devoted servant of the people, Neff died at just 33, having worked himself to death. Having learned he was in his last days, a number of Catholic priests came to thank him for his ministry and offer him a supreme *adieu.*

TOULOUSE

Situated on the plain of Languedoc, and straddling the banks of the Garonne River, Toulouse has been an important city since Roman times, when as Tolosa, it was the third largest city in Gaul. It was evangelized in the 3rd century by St. Sernin (St. Saturninus), who was martyred in 250 by being tied to the tail of a wild bull and dragged to his death. After the fall of the Roman Empire in the West, it was the capital of the Visigothic kingdom before it was conquered by the Franks in the 7th century. From the 9th through 13th centuries, the city and its surrounding territory were ruled by the counts of Toulouse of the Raymond dynasty. Though theoretically subject to the king of France, Toulouse was far removed from Paris and the court, and the counts were virtually independent of outside control. Under the counts, Toulouse was a prosperous and cultured city. The counts were accused of complicity in the Albigensian or Cathar heresy, and resisted several sieges led by Simon de Montfort, who was killed in one of them. Finally, in 1271, the county of Toulouse was absorbed into

the kingdom of France as the province of Languedoc. It was so named after the local language, the *langue d'oc* (language of oc), in which the word for yes was "oc," rather than the northern "oui." The Inquisition, run by friars of the Dominican Order, had been established in the area to suppress the Cathar heresy, and was officially suspended only in 1279, well after the heretics' final defeat at the Château de Montségur in 1244. In 1229, a university was founded in Toulouse to keep the lid on heresy; it is the second oldest university in France, after Paris. After the depredations of the Cathar crusade, the city began to flourish again in the 16th century when it was discovered that the local woad plant produced a highly prized blue-black dye for use in textiles. In the aftermath of the campaign against the Cathars, Toulouse remained a zealously, even fanatically, Catholic city. During the Wars of Religion, it was riven by conflict between Catholics and Huguenots, and hundreds perished in the St. Bartholomew's Massacre.

In the 18th century, Toulouse was the site of one of the great *causes célèbres*

205

of the Enlightenment. In 1762, a young Huguenot named Calas was found hanged in his room, an apparent suicide. His father, Jean Calas, however, was accused by the religious and civil authorities of having murdered his son to prevent his imminent conversion to Catholicism. Under torture, the unfortunate man confessed, was found guilty, and executed. This episode came to the attention of Voltaire, who saw in it the epitome of all he despised: fanaticism, intolerance, bigotry, and superstition; all, in other words, that was expressed in his motto, "Ecrasez l'infâme" ("Crush the infamous thing"—see Historical Introduction). Voltaire mounted a campaign to clear the father, while embarrassing the Church and government. The verdict was eventually overturned, although of course poor Calas remained dead.

In the 20th century, Toulouse has emerged as France's high-tech center. A pioneer in aviation, it is now the headquarters of Airbus and Aerospatiale, the manufacturer of the Concorde and Ariadne rocket used by the European Space Agency. It is now France's fourth largest city (after Paris, Lyon, and Marseille), and with its student population of 40,000, the largest university town outside of Paris. Though it is a modern and vibrant city, its old center is well preserved, and is known as *la ville rose* (the pink city), because of the local reddish brick of which many of the buildings are constructed.

PLACES TO VISIT

Toulouse is home to several notable churches. Of these, probably the most significant is the Dominican church known as L'EGLISE DES JACOBINS (the Jacobin Church). The Dominican Order was founded in 1215 by St. Dominic to aid in the suppression of heresy through preaching. In order to accomplish this, Dominic insisted on a rigorous theological training for all Dominican friars. This explains the dominance of Dominicans within both the Inquisition and the universities of the Middle Ages. This church, begun in 1230, was the first church built explicitly for the order. The name "Jacobins" derives from the fact that in Paris, the Dominican priory was located at the St. Jacques gate. The exterior is quite plain, rather like the cathedral at Albi. The octagonal tower dates from 1298 and became the model for Gothic churches all over southern France. The real attraction here, however, is the interior. An unusual double nave is divided by a row of seven massive columns so tall they appear slender. The last, or easternmost of these pillars, supports 22 brick arches, laid out like palm branches. The glass in the rose windows in the west wall dates from the 14th century. Under the altar, a golden casket contains the ashes of the most learned Dominican of them all, St. Thomas Aquinas. His remains were transferred in 1974 to commemorate the 700th anniversary of his death. Through a door in the northwest corner of the nave, one may enter the cloisters, a reproduction of the original, which offers an excellent view of the church's exterior. At the Revolution, the monastery was confiscated by the government, and the church was used for several decades by the army as a stable for its horses. The army abandoned it in 1865, and restoration was begun about the beginning of the 20th century, being completed only in the 1970s.

Toulouse's other architectural treasure is the **BASILIQUE ST. SERNIN** (St. Sernin Basilica). A church was first built on this site in the 4th century to commemorate the martyr. The current structure was built between 1080 and 1350, as a stop on the pilgrimage route to Santiago de Compostela. It is France's largest Romanesque structure, with a nave 115 meters (377 feet) long and a barrel-vaulted roof 20 meters (66 feet) high. The exterior is dominated by the five-story octagonal tower. The lower three stories are Romanesque with the typical round arches, while the top two stories have typically Gothic pointed arches. Its function as a pilgrimage church explains the unusually broad nave and transepts, as well as the double aisles flanking the nave, designed to hold large crowds of pilgrims. In the north transept are well-preserved Romanesque murals uncovered in the course of restorations in the 1970s. From here, for a small fee, you may enter the ambulatory where there is an 11th-century marble carving of Christ and the Evangelists on the end wall of the choir. Behind the altar is the 8th-century tomb of St. Sernin, resting on bronze bulls. The crypt contains an extensive collection of shrines and relics.

Toulouse's cathedral, the **CATHÉDRALE ST. ETIENNE**, is an unexceptional structure, built with no consistency of style between the 13th and 17th centuries. The nave and transepts are misaligned, resulting in an awkward-looking structure.

The other notable church in Toulouse is the 14th-century **NOTRE-DAME DU TAUR** (Our Lady of the Bull), built on the spot where, according to legend, St. Sernin was dragged to his death. The church is a masterpiece of the ornate brickwork for which Toulouse is famous.

TOURS

Situated at the confluence of the rivers Loire and Cher, Tours was one of the most important religious sites in France throughout the Middle Ages, though you might never guess it today, based on the city's quaint old town and sprawling industrial suburbs. An important settlement in Roman times, it was evangelized by St. Gatien (St. Gratian) in the 3rd century. Its real fame came, however, starting in the 4th century, with its third bishop, St. Martin of Tours. After

T

his conversion, the former Roman soldier tirelessly evangelized Gaul, combating paganism with unflagging zeal and covering Gaul with churches and chapels. The people of Tours begged him to come be their bishop. At Tours, he founded the monastery of Marmoutier. St. Martin died in 397 at Candes, downstream from Tours. His body was claimed by both the monks of Marmoutier in Tours, and by those of St. Ligugé in Poitou (which Martin had also founded). While the monks of St. Ligugé slept, the monks of Tours spirited the body away and rowed hard for home. According to legend, as the saint's body passed, trees and flowers miraculously burst into bloom (it was November). A great basilica was erected over the saint's tomb in 470; Tours became the most important pilgrimage site in early medieval France. People came from all over to seek healing. The church was endowed by kings and nobles, in imitation of the generosity of St. Martin, and grew immensely rich. In the 6th century, the bishop of Tours was Gregory of Tours (d. 594), originally from Clermont-Ferrand, the scion of a wealthy and aristocratic Gallo-Roman family. Gregory is most famous for his work *The History of the Franks,* in which he recounts the history of the Frankish people, including the conversion of Clovis. This work is our most important source of knowledge of the history of early medieval France. Gregory was concerned to display the hand of God in history, that the Franks were now God's instrument. In a naive fashion, he

describes Clovis alternately as a new David and a new Constantine, glossing over his many barbarous acts. After describing in graphic detail his victories and cruelties, he states that Clovis "walked with an upright heart, doing what was right in the eyes of the Lord," in imitation of Old Testament prophets describing the godly kings of Israel. Gregory was also instrumental in popularizing the cult of St. Martin. A hagiographical *Life of St. Martin* was written, copies of which have been found as far away as Egypt and Syria. At the end of the 8th century, the bishop of Tours and abbot of St. Martin was the famous Alcuin of York (c. 730–804), whom Charlemagne had brought to his empire to revive learning and education. From the mid-12th century until 1242, the city and surrounding province of Touraine were possessions of the kings of England. In the 15th century, Tours enjoyed a period of prestige and prosperity, as the kings of France made their home in the châteaux of the Loire valley. Tours was the favorite residence of Louis XI (1461–83), whose efforts established the silk industry here. In the 16th century, it was a Huguenot stronghold, and it was the site of a massacre of Huguenots in 1562. Its prosperity was ruined by the Wars of Religion. It was heavily damaged by both German and Allied bombing in World War II. Tours was the birthplace of two of the great thinkers of 19th- and early 20th-century France, Henri Bergson and Anatole France.

HENRI BERGSON (1859–1941) was a philosopher who accepted evolution and the mechanistic facts about life processes, but, seeing intuitively the reality of creativity, rejected a purely determinist philosophy. This rejection of determinism led him inevitably toward God. In his 1937 will, Bergson wrote, "My reflections had led me closer and closer to Catholicism, in which I see the complete fulfillment of Judaism." However, the rise of anti-Semitism, unchecked and even supported by the Catholic Church, turned Bergson away from Christianity. He wrote: "I would have become a convert, had I not foreseen for years a formidable wave of anti-Semitism about to break upon the world. I wanted to remain among those who tomorrow were to be persecuted." Indeed, the Catholic Church's failure to combat anti-Semitism can be compared with the failure of many American churches to combat slavery.

ANATOLE FRANCE (1844–1924) has been termed a skeptical humanist, though it is difficult to see how the two terms can be compatible. Indeed, he exemplified the admired man of letters of the 19th century, which is to say someone greatly influenced by the Enlightenment philosophy of rational positivism, a philosophy which, if honest in one's observations of humankind, leads inevitably to skepticism and therefore to a complete contradiction of one's original positivist philosophy. Like Diderot or Voltaire, and later, Sartre or Camus, France held onto a passion for social justice which was inconsistent with his professed philosophy, but which reveals so clearly man's fundamental need to live in the image of God.

T

PLACES TO VISIT

Little remains of Tours's glorious ecclesiastical history. A new basilica was built to house St. Martin's tomb in the 11th and 12th centuries, after raiding Norsemen destroyed the original. It was severely damaged by the Huguenots in 1562, and by the revolutionaries in the 1790s. It was pulled down in 1808 to make way for streets and Place Plumereau (Plumereau Square). All that remains are two towers: the TOUR CHARLEMAGNE (Charlemagne Tower), which dominated the north transept; and the TOUR DE L'HORLOGE (Clock Tower), which was the south tower of the west facade. A new basilica was built adjacent to the site between 1887 and 1924 in the neo-Byzantine style then popular. This church now houses the shrine of St. Martin and is still an object of pilgrimages.

Tours's other site of interest for Christian visitors is the CATHÉDRALE ST. GATIEN (St. Gratian's Cathedral), named for Tours's evangelist and first bishop. It was begun in 1125 and not completed until 1547; it serves therefore as an interesting illustration of the evolution of Gothic architecture. The cheviot is typical of early Gothic, while the west facade is in flamboyant style, its two towers topped by Renaissance-style cupolas. The interior is notable for its stained-glass windows. Those of the chancel date from the 13th century, the rose windows of the transepts from the 14th, while the great rose window of the nave dates from the 15th. They are especially remarkable for their deep reds, a quality rarely achieved in stained glass.

TROYES

The chief site of the Gallic tribe of the Tricassi, then a Roman settlement, Troyes was evangelized in the 3rd century. In 451, Troyes was threatened by the Huns under Attila. It was saved from destruction by its bishop, St. Loup, who went to Attila and begged him to spare the town, offering himself as a hostage. Troyes was ruled by its bishops until the 10th century, when it was taken over by the Counts of Champagne, who made Troyes their capital. The counts of Champagne were one of the most powerful feudal nobles of France, on occasion able to challenge the might of the king. Under the succession of able counts, Champagne and Troyes became prosperous in the 12th and 13th century through the establishment of a commercial fair in Troyes. One of a series of fairs established throughout the province and held on a rotating basis throughout the year, they became the prime focus of commercial interchange in medieval Europe. In 1284, when the daughter and sole heir of the last count, Thibaud V, married King Philip IV (the Fair), the county of Champagne was united with the kingdom of France. During the Hundred Years' War, it was in Troyes in 1420 that a treaty was signed between Henry V of England and Isabeau of Bavaria, wife of the mad Charles VI of France, which disinherited her son (the future Charles VII and the object of Joan of Arc's suasion) and granted the English king most of northern France. In the 16th century, Troyes became prominent as a textile center; to this day the city is renowned for its manufacture of hosiery. It gained a significant Huguenot community in the 1550s and 1560s, and was the site of a St. Bartholomew's Massacre in 1572. Thenceforth, Troyes was a stronghold of the Catholic League. In 1590, a royalist army based in nearby Châlons-sur-Marne attacked the city and actually gained entrance. The day was won for the League, however, when royalist soldiers were sidetracked and began to gorge themselves on *andouillette,* the tripe sausage for which Troyes is still famous.

Today, the major reason to visit Troyes is for its well-preserved old town of narrow cobblestone streets and half-timbered houses, and for its wealth of churches.

PLACES TO VISIT

The old town of Troyes is known as the *bouchon de Champagne* (champagne cork), not because it is a center of the champagne industry (it isn't), but because of its shape, which resembles a champagne cork. The most impressive church in Troyes is the CATHÉDRALE ST. PIERRE AND ST. PAUL (Cathedral of St. Peter and St. Paul). Built of the local soft chalk, it was constructed between the 13th and 17th centuries, and thus displays a range of styles. The west facade is flamboyant Gothic, though the statuary was destroyed during the Revolution. Of a projected two towers, only the western one was ever built, not being completed until 1640. At its base a plaque commemorates the presence in Troyes of Charles VII and Joan of Arc, July 10, 1429. The five-aisled nave is exceptionally long (114 meters; 374 feet), but not terribly high (29 meters; 95 feet), probably because of its location on an island in the Seine River. The real attraction of the interior is the wealth of original stained glass, 16,000 square feet in all. The windows in the choir and ambulatory are 13th century and depict great personages such as popes and emperors, and scenes from the life of the Virgin Mary. The great rose window of the nave was completed in 1547 and

depicts Christ and the apostles. In the fourth chapel of the north aisle is the "pressoir mystique" or "mystic wine-press," completed in 1625, in which a vine grows from Christ's breast, while the blood which flows from his side is collected in a chalice. Another of Troyes's notable churches is the BASILIQUE ST. URBAIN (St. Urban's Basilica). It was built at the instigation of Pope Urban IV (r. 1261–64), a native of Troyes. Its interior was built in less than 30 years, from 1262–86, and its unity of Gothic style is striking, despite the west facade which was added only in the 19th century. Like the cathedral it too retains a good deal of original stained glass. STE-MADELEINE is the oldest church in Troyes, dating from the 12th century. It is notable especially for its rood screen or *jubé,* elaborately carved in stone in the 16th century, built to separate the nave from the choir. The rood screen shut the clergy off from the laypeople, graphically demonstrating the late medieval distinction between the clerical and lay worlds, and the clergy's separate and superior status as the custodians of the Sacraments and as intermediaries between God and humanity. Only seven survive in all of France. Other notable churches in Troyes include: ST. JEAN (14th–16th centuries), where in 1420 Henry V of England married Princess Catherine of France to seal the Treaty of Troyes; ST. NIZIER (16th century) with an unusual multicolored tiled roof; and ST. NICOLAS (16th century).

T

VERDUN

Verdun is synonymous with the bloody struggle of the Great War which sent to their death a whole generation of young Frenchmen. At Verdun alone, 700,000 French soldiers died. For 18 months, Verdun was the site of intense combat on which the outcome of the war hung. Indeed, were it not for the remarkable courage of those soldiers, inspired by their respect for Marshal Pétain, the commanding officer of the defense, the war might well have had a very different ending. In early 1916, having failed to break through at the battle of the Marne, the Germans decided to attack at Verdun and thus destroy France's rear line of defense, just 25 miles from the Franco-German border. On February 21, the Germans launched a huge attack which in just a few days took them to the forts of Douamont and de Vaux, on the hills outside Verdun. They succeeded in taking the former and then, with wave after wave of relentless attacks, attempted to conquer the zone that separated them from the town. However, the French defense held strong and two incredible French counteroffensives led by General Mangin, on October 24 and December 15, took most of the lost terrain. The Germans, seeing they could not take the town, concentrated on the surrounding French positions at Argonne, Les Eparges, and Mort-Homme (Dead Man's Hill). In early July 1917, they almost took the Souville fort, the last French defense, but just then, the fighting at the Somme forced them to cease their offensive. The Allies countered, and by August 20, 1917, the hell of Verdun was over.

PLACES TO VISIT

Battlefields

FORT DE VAUX: Heroic defense by the Commandant Raynal, though the fort was taken by the Germans in 1916.

FORT DE SOUVILLE: Last French defense in June–July 1917. The furthest point of the German offensive is marked by a monument commemorating Verdun. Just near is a stela indicating the village of FLEURY, completely destroyed in the fighting. A chapel and monument have also been erected.

FORT DE DOUAMONT: Taken on February 25, it was recaptured on October 24. From the summit, one can see the whole battlefield of Verdun. A memorial tower, lit at night, looks out over 15,000 graves. Underground is an OSSUARY with a long gallery containing 46 sarcophagi, each one corresponding to a different part of the battlefield. A Catholic chapel celebrates Mass daily. Descending from the fort through the *Ravine of Death,* on the right is the monument of the TRANCHÉE DES BAÏONETTES, which covers a trench where a company of soldiers were buried alive.

LE MORT-HOMME (Dead Man's Hill): Occupied by the Germans from March to August 1917. There are monuments to the 40th and 69th Divisions. A few miles from the Mort-Homme is the village of Esnes and the monument of the CALVAIRE D'ESNES, which offers a panoramic view. To the north one sees HILL 304, occupied by the Germans in June–July 1940. The Hill also has a monument commemorating the fighting there.

BUTTE DE MONTFAUCON: Isolated hill on which once stood a village, destroyed during the war and rebuilt lower down. On the hill are the ruins of a Gothic church, next to which stands the MÉMORIAL AMÉRICAIN, a 180-feet tower commemorating the American victories in Argonne in September 1918.

AMERICAN CEMETERY OF ROMAGNE-SOUS-MONTFAUCON: From Montfaucon, going through the village of Nantillois, you come to Romagne-sous-Montfaucon. The cemetery contains 14,000 graves.

VERSAILLES

Louis XIII (r. 1610–43) loved to hunt, and had built for himself a small hunting lodge near the marshy village of Versailles, about ten miles west of Paris. When his son, Louis XIV (b. 1638, r. 1643–1715) took over the reins of government himself in 1661, he determined to build a new palace for himself and his government, away from the disorder and violence of Paris. During the revolts of Fronde (1648–52), Louis as a young child had received several severe frights in Paris. On one occasion, a mob broke into the royal palace and invaded the young king's bedroom, to make sure that he had not been taken out of Paris. For the site of his monument to royal power, Louis chose his father's hunting lodge at Versailles, of which he had fond memories. The palace which was eventually built here was shaped by several factors: Louis's virtually unlimited self-esteem (drummed into him as a child by his tutors), the desire for a fitting residence for the greatest monarch in Europe, and envy. His finance minister Nicolas Fouquet had built for himself at Vaux-le-Vicomte, southeast of Paris, a new type of country residence. Rather than a fortified château, Vaux-le-Vicomte was intended as a luxurious pleasure palace, with sumptuously decorated interiors and extensive gardens integrated into the overall design of the palace. On one occasion, Fouquet entertained the king and his court at Vaux in such grand style that Louis felt that Fouquet was trying to show him up. This envy was a minor, but contributing, cause of Fouquet's fall from power. (The more important cause was that the young king felt intimidated by Fouquet's power and experience, and feared that he would become his finance minister's puppet.) Tried on trumped-up charges of corruption, Fouquet spent the

V

rest of his life (he died in 1680) in a remote prison in the Alps. In any case, in order to surpass Fouquet in the construction of his own palace at Versailles, Louis hired the three men responsible for Vaux-le-Vicomte: the architect Le Vau, the decorator and painter Le Brun, and the gardener (perhaps landscape architect is a better title) Le Nôtre. (After 1676, Le Vau was succeeded as architect by Jules Hardouin-Mansart.) In order to construct the palace, land had to be drained, an artificial hill built (atop which the palace now sits), and the river Bièvre diverted to provide water for the canals and 1,400 fountains which graced the enormous gardens. Construction was begun in 1662 and continued until 1690, though the king, court, and government took up residence there in 1682. At its peak, the palace housed approximately 20,000 people; besides the king and the royal family and their servants, there were the great nobles and their servants, government ministers and their staffs who required proximity to the king, as well as soldiers, sycophants, and fortune-seekers of all descriptions. Outside the royal apartments, life in Versailles was cramped, crowded, and unhygienic. Under Louis XIV, Versailles was the setting for the spectacle of absolute monarchy. Governed by a precise protocol centered on the person of the king, life at court resembled an intricate ballet, with a backdrop of intrigue, gossip, spectacle, and the quest for power, for the king's ear. After Louis

XIV's death in 1715 (when his five-year-old great-grandson became King Louis XV), the royal court moved back to Paris. Upon his majority, Louis XV moved the court back to Versailles, but court life no longer resembled the public spectacle it had been under the previous king. Louis XV lived a more private life and renovated the palace to suit his needs. At the time of the French Revolution, Versailles was still the home of the court and the government. In October 1789, however, a mob of Parisian women marched on the palace seeking cheaper bread. They forcibly brought back to Paris King Louis XVI (1774–92), his wife, Marie Antoinette, and their family. The palace itself was looted. The furniture was auctioned off, the paintings taken to the Louvre, and the building itself allowed to fall into disrepair. The process of renovation began in the 19th century under Louis-Philippe (1830–48), who financed it with his own money, but did not really get underway until the 20th century. In 1871, the Hall of Mirrors was the site of the proclamation of the German Empire, Prussia having defeated France in the Franco-Prussian War, and in 1919 of the signing of the Treaty of Versailles, which ended World War I.

PLACES TO VISIT

It may seem strange to include an entry on a royal palace with no overt significance for the Christian heritage of France in this guide, and indeed, this entry makes no attempt to give an inclusive description of the palace. Nevertheless, it has been included because it does have significance for the Christian visitor to France, in the sense that it helps one understand the context of a very important reign in French history, specifically the religious context of political power, and also the anti-Christian (or at least the anticlerical) tendencies of the French Revolution, and hence the tension and ambiguity between church and state in modern France. The French monarchy and Christianity had been closely tied together since the baptism of Clovis in the 5th century. The ritual of coronation was believed to bestow a special status on the king. Unique among laymen, the king was entitled to receive both the bread and the wine at the sacrament of Mass. The king was believed, by virtue of his anointment with the sacred oil of the Sainte Ampoule, to possess the power to heal the disease of scrofula by the laying on of hands. At his coronation, the king swore an oath to defend the Christian faith and the Catholic Church, and to extirpate heresy. He was awarded the title "Most Christian King," and according to the tenets of Gallicanism, held a great deal of authority over the Catholic Church in France. The kings of France numbered among their ancestors one genuine saint, St. Louis (Louis IX, 1226–70), and two others generally held to be saints, even if not formally recognized by the Church: Clovis and Charlemagne. The kings of France always reckoned that their power and right to rule were of divine origin. Following the violence and disorder of the Wars of Religion and the murder of two kings (Henry III in 1589 and Henry IV in 1610), greater emphasis was placed on the divine right of kings. It was thought that emphasizing the divine origins of kingly power would elevate the king above mere mortals, making resistance and disobedience more difficult to contemplate. The chief theorist of divine-right monarchy was Jacques-Bénigne Bossuet. According to Bossuet, "Princes act as ministers of God, and as his lieutenants on earth. It is by them that he exercises his rule. Thus we have seen that the royal throne is not the throne of a man but the throne of God himself." Louis XIV was a firm believer in his divine right to rule. He was a devout but conventional Catholic; Louis saw himself and God almost as equals in ruling France. In some ways, Versailles is a grandiose testament to this belief. The very construction of the palace and gardens, with their remaking of nature, the imposition upon nature of Louis's grand design, is a kind of parallel to God's power over the universe. Within the palace, note the frequent allusions to and portrayals of the sun. Louis was the Sun King, *le roi soleil*, denoting the source of power and light, and also the center of the universe. (By this time the view that the sun rather than the earth was the center of the universe was nearly

V

universally accepted among educated people.) By the same token, note the frequent allusions to the king as Apollo, the Greek god of the sun. Classical mythology was part of the mental apparatus of educated people of the time, and many allusions that are lost on us were perfectly clear to contemporaries. Thus, the *Salon d'Apollon* (Apollo Room), one of a series of rooms dedicated to the planets and their namesakes (Venus, Mars, etc.), is the former throne room, perhaps the most extravagantly decorated in the palace. On the ceiling is a painting of Apollo in a sun chariot attended by the seasons. Likewise, the Apollo Basin at the head of the Grand Canal features a massive sculpture of Apollo in his chariot rising from the sea to light the world. The chapel, which may be viewed from an upper vestibule, is a striking example of Baroque church decoration. More striking (and revealing) is the fact that when the king attended Mass (which he did daily), he sat in the balcony above, while the other worshipers sat facing the king, that is with their backs to the priest and the altar. In other words, the others were there not to witness the Mass, but to watch the king watching the Mass, which speaks volumes about Louis's view of religion and God. Is it any wonder then, that the French Revolution manifested anticlerical and even anti-Christian tendencies? The institutions of monarchy and Church were so closely interwoven that it was impossible to separate them. Even had they been so inclined, the revolutionaries would have been hard put to dismantle the absolute monarchy without also dismantling the religious apparatus which buttressed and legitimized it. It was impossible to overthrow the monarchy without also attacking the Church.

JEAN RACINE (1639–99) is considered along with Pierre Corneille (1606–84) one of the greatest tragic dramatists in French literature. He received a Jansenist education at Port-Royal, and the intellectual, moralistic, and austere Jansenist approach to life shows up in his plays. He left literature for several years in 1661 to study for the priesthood, but ultimately returned to Paris and his literary career. His tragedies are all based on Greek and Latin literature, and deal with the problems of characters unable to control their own emotions, problems which eventually lead to their downfall. Racine's plays are still performed widely today as part the repertoire of the Comédie Française (the leading classical theater company in France), and the leading roles are considered a standard test for French classical actors, much like Hamlet or Lear in English theater.

VICINITY

ABBAYE DE PORT-ROYAL-DES-CHAMPS:

Just south of Versailles lie the ruins of the abbey of Port-Royal-des-Champs, the 17th-century stronghold of Jansenism. There had been a convent in this peaceful valley since the 13th century, but it only became prominent after 1602 when it received a new Mother Superior, Angélique Arnaud, known as Mère Angélique (Mother Angelica). Under her leadership, the abbey became the leading Jansenist institution. By 1625, the abbey had outgrown its convent, and a branch was established in Paris, Port-Royal-de-Paris. In 1648, having outgrown its new quarters, the nuns returned to Port-Royal-des-Champs, where Mère Angelique was still in residence. The controversy over Jansenism convulsed France in the 17th century, with the Jesuits as their leading opponents. They were defended by Blaise Pascal, the scientist and mathematician. Opposed by Louis XIV, Mère Angélique went into exile in Flanders, the convent was forbidden to take in novices, and in 1709, the convent was razed and the ground plowed over. In 1713, Jansenism was firmly condemned by the pope. Though its headquarters were destroyed, Jansenism remained popular among the elite throughout the 18th century, as evidenced by the episode at the church of St. Médard in Paris in 1727. On the site of the convent, there is now a museum, the MUSÉE NATIONAL DES GRANGES DE PORT-ROYAL.

VÉZELAY

Situated atop a rocky ridge in the northern foothills of the Morvan highlands, Vézelay is known as one of the most picturesque villages in France. The real reason to stop here, however, is the BASILIQUE STE-MADELEINE (St. Mary Magdalene Basilica). A Benedictine abbey was founded here in the 9th century, but remained in obscurity until 1050 when the monks acquired the remains of the saint, and it was dedicated to Mary Magdalene. Vézelay then became one of the great pilgrimage churches in France, situated along one of the routes to Santiago de Compostela in northwestern Spain. It was here in 1146 that St. Bernard of Clairvaux preached the Second Crusade, and in 1190 Richard the Lionheart of England and Philip Augustus of France met here on their way to the Third Crusade. In 1280, however, the monks of St. Maximin in Provence claimed to have discovered the authentic relics of Mary Magdalene, a claim which gained official recognition. Vézelay went into a long period of decline. The monastery was pillaged by Huguenots in the Wars of Religion. At the Revolution, the monastery and its lands were seized

V

by the government and the actual monastery buildings destroyed. The church was neglected and on the point of destruction when restorations were begun in the mid-19th century. The moving spirit was Prosper Mérimée (1803–70), celebrated writer of exotic short stories, who had another only slightly less exotic occupation: in order to pay the bills, he was a state inspector of historical monuments. It was in this capacity that he discovered the imposing and magnificent abbey church of Vézelay. Not without difficulty, Mérimée managed to attain the necessary public funds to have this unique basilica restored. However, one after another of the specialists he solicited refused, afraid of the extreme fragility of the long-abandoned church. Finally, Mérimée asked a then unknown architect, the

young Viollet-le-Duc, who accepted readily. Thus, this unique jewel of a sacred building was saved by a man who was to become one of France's greatest architects. Vézelay was also the birthplace of Thédore de Bèze (Beza) (1519–1605), Calvin's successor in Geneva.

PLACES TO VISIT

The original portions of the BASILIQUE STE-MADELEINE were constructed between 1096 and 1106 in classic Romanesque style, though the flying buttresses were added in the 13th century. The huge narthex was added about 1150 to accommodate the crowds of pilgrims. The main feature is the tympanum above the central doorway leading into the nave, a masterpiece of Romanesque art. It shows Christ sending the apostles into the world. Christ is

THÉODORE DE BÈZE (or Beza in English) was born in Vézélay in 1519. Like his mentor John Calvin, Beza studied law at Orléans, Bourges, and Paris. Following a serious illness in 1548, he converted to Protestantism and joined Calvin in Geneva, where he became renowned as a teacher and scholar. Following Calvin's death in 1564, Beza assumed his position as leader of the Genevan church and, by extension, of international Calvinism. Beza played a large role in the religious wars in France, eventually compiling the *Histoire ecclésiastique des églises réformées au royaume de France* (*Ecclesiastical History of the Reformed Church in the Kingdom of France*), a massive chronicle of the advent and progress of the Reformation in France. He also contributed two Greek editions and one Latin edition of the New Testament. His Greek editions were the foundation of both the Geneva Bible of 1560 and of the King James Version of 1611. His other writings include a biography of Calvin. Under Beza's leadership, the Genevan church united with the Protestant church in Zürich to form a single Swiss Reformed Church. He died in Geneva in 1605.

V

of superhuman size, with exceptionally large hands stretched outwards, passing his power on to the apostles. His long legs elevate him above the mass of humanity, depicted below. These include ordinary people going about their business, as well as fantastic creatures, including giants, pygmies, and dog-headed heathens. In the outer arch, notice the beautifully carved signs of the zodiac and labors of the months. The nave itself was rebuilt following a fire in 1120 in which 1000 pilgrims died. The arches are notable for their alternating use of dark and light stone, creating a striped effect. Also notable in the nave are the richly carved capitals of the columns; there are 99 all together. At the end of the fourth bay on the right is the finest of all, known as the "Mystic Mill." It shows Moses pouring grain (representing the Old Testament Law) through a mill (Christ), with the flour (the New Testament) being collected by St. Paul. The choir (built 1185–1215) is in a pure early Gothic style, a striking contrast to the Romanesque nave. Tours of the church are provided by Christian volunteers in English in July and August, and by appointment the rest of the year. Down the hill, a COMMEMORATIVE CROSS marks the spot where St. Bernard preached the Second Crusade in 1146.

WASSY
(VASSY)

On the morning of Sunday March 1, 1562, François, duke of Guise, found himself in the small town of Wassy (then known as Vassy). He was on his way back to Paris after visiting his mother in the family's ancestral home at nearby Joinville. Wassy already had a strong Huguenot community, led by a particularly fiery preacher named Jean Gravelle, and there had been previous run-ins with members of the Guise family, one of the most prominent noble families in France and renowned for their zealous Catholicism. That morning, while attending Mass, the duke and his entourage were disturbed by the sounds of Protestant worship coming from a nearby barn. What happened next is unclear—different accounts give different versions, according to the faith of the reporter. In any case, a melee ensued in which approximately 60 Huguenots were killed. This "massacre of Vassy" came at the end of a decade of growing religious tension in France, and in a period of political instability and uncertainty. Though it was not unique or unprecedented, more than any other single event it marked the beginning of the

W

religious wars which were to convulse France for more than three decades. Guise arrived in Paris to the triumphant acclamation of the crowd in that very Catholic city. The Huguenots decided that they needed to take up arms to defend themselves. Under their military leaders the prince of Condé and Gaspard de Coligny, admiral of France, Huguenot armies seized a number of towns throughout France, including Rouen and Lyon, the second and third cities of the kingdom. The massacre in Vassy was followed by similar episodes in Sens and elsewhere.

PLACES TO VISIT

The Protestant Church (LE TEMPLE) is situated on the site of the barn where the massacre took place. It houses a Protestant museum with an exhibition on the history of the Protestant church in Wassy in the 16th and 17th centuries, with an audiovisual presentation on the revocation of the Edict of Nantes (open June 15–September 15, 3:00–7:00 P.M.). NOTRE-DAME CHURCH dates from the late 12th century, and features a Romanesque tower and Gothic portal, with Romanesque capitals on the interior pillars.

W

GLOSSARY OF RELIGIOUS TERMS

ARIAN/ARIANISM: Named after Arius (d. 336), a priest in Alexandria. A heresy which downgraded the divinity of Christ, making him a sort of demigod. Arianism attracted many followers, but was condemned at the Council of Nicea in 325. This was the most serious challenge to the doctrinal unity of the early church. Many of the barbarian tribes which settled in the western part of the Roman Empire (e.g., Visigoths, Ostrogoths) had been converted to Arian Christianity, which made for religious tension with the peoples they ruled, who followed the form of Christianity established in Rome.

BENEDICTINE RULE: A monastic rule (Latin: *regula*) established by St. Benedict of Nursia (480–543), an Italian monk. The Benedictine Rule came to dominate monastic life in western Europe. It emphasized that a monk's life was to incorporate both prayer and manual labor *(ore et labore).* The Benedictine Rule was the foundation of many monastic orders established throughout the Middle Ages, such as the Cluniacs and Cistercians.

CATHAR/CATHARISM: A medieval heresy, which incorporated elements of Christianity with non-Christian elements, such as Manicheanism, which preached a duality between a good god and an evil god. Cathars emphasized the corruptness and evil of the material world. The elite, or *perfecti,* denied themselves physical pleasures, often to the point of starving themselves to death. In protest against the wealth and corruption of the medieval Church, Catharism became very popular in southern France before a crusade was declared against them in the early 13th century, when they were forcibly repressed and persecuted. The kings of France used the Cathar crusade to extend their power in southern France.

CISTERCIAN(S): Monastic order founded at Cîteaux in 1098 by reformers who were dissatisfied with the worldliness of the Benedictine and Cluniac orders of the time. They were very austere, emphasizing a life of prayer and labor. They built monasteries only on undeveloped land and thus were important in the economic expansion of the Middle Ages. The order expanded very quickly in the 12th and 13th centuries. The most influential Cistercian was Bernard of Clairvaux (1090–1153).

CLUNIAC(S): Monastic order founded at Cluny in the 10th century by reformers dissatisfied by the lax observance of the Benedictine Rule in most monasteries. It was tremendously important in the religious revival of the high Middle Ages (10th–14th centuries), furnishing several popes, including Gregory VII. Unlike the later Cistercians who emphasized austerity and simplicity, the Cluniacs emphasized the liturgy and richness of worship. By the later Middle Ages, the Cluniac order had become lax, prompting the formation of new orders, such as the Carthusians and the Cistercians.

DOMINICAN(S): A mendicant or begging order, founded in 1207 by the Spaniard St. Dominic (1170–1221). Established to combat the Cathar heresy through preaching, Dominicans came to dominate the Inquisition and were prominent in many medieval universities.

FRANCISCAN(S): A mendicant or begging order founded by the saintly Francis of Assisi (1182–1226). The Franciscan Rule emphasized apostolic poverty in imitation of the early church. The first Franciscans owned nothing but their robe and a bowl for begging. Unlike the Dominicans, who were involved primarily in preaching and education, the Franciscans found their calling in caring for the poor and sick.

JANSENISM/JANSENISTS: A movement within French Catholicism based on the writings of Cornelius Jansen (1585–1638). Jansenists believed that the Church emphasized too strongly the role of human effort in salvation and too little the role of God's grace; thus they are often seen as Catholic Calvinists. They were based in the Abbey of Port-Royal-des-Champs, near Versailles. Opposed by Louis XIV, Jansenism was definitively condemned by the Church and Port-Royal was razed in the early 18th century. Nevertheless, the controversy raged on into the 18th century. The debates over Jansenism fragmented the unity of French Counter-Reformation Catholicism.

REVEIL: Literally, "revival" or awakening; refers to the religious revival among French Protestants in the 19th century.

SACRAMENT(S): Ceremonies performed by the Catholic clergy which were vehicles of God's grace. Medieval worship was largely centered on the performance of the sacraments, especially confession and the Mass, rather than preaching. Because of their custodianship of the power of the sacraments, clergy were held to be the intermediaries between God and humankind, setting them apart from and above laypeople; hence the importance of clerical celibacy.

VULGATE: Latin version of the Bible, translated by St. Jerome (340–420) from Greek and Hebrew. It remained the official Bible of the Catholic Church throughout the Middle Ages and beyond. The Church held that it and it alone was the inspired Word of God. The Vulgate was rejected by Protestants at the Reformation, who believed in translating the Bible into the languages of the people.

The Christian Travelers Guides

'In an era that often overlooks the significance of the past as such, and certainly the Christian past, Professor Hexham's well-crafted guides for heritage tourists truly fill a gap. Don't leave home without one!"

—J. I. Packer, Author of *Knowing God*

By describing and interpreting the religious significance of people, places, and events in various countries, Irving Hexham illustrates the incredible impact Christianity has had on Western Civilization. Each guide is organized alphabetically according to the names of the cities and sites. The Christian Travelers Guides will help you deepen your faith by bringing to life the struggles and triumphs of great Christian leaders and common believers through the living witness of places where the saints once walked.

The Christian Travelers Guide to France

Irving Hexham, General Editor;
Written by Mark Konnert, Peter Barrs, and Carine Barrs

- Relive the experience of the Huguenots and the creators of such masterpieces as Chartes and Notre Dame.

Softcover 0-310-22588-4

The Christian Travelers Guide to Germany

Irving Hexham, General Editor;
Written by Irving Hexham and Lothar Henry Kope

- Experience the church's struggle against Nazi paganism, ponder the sorrow of the Thirty Years' War, and see where the modern missionary movement was born.

Softcover 0-310-22539-6

The Christian Travelers Guide to Great Britain

Irving Hexham, General Editor;
Written by Irving Hexham

- Come into contact with the Venerable Bede, who almost single-handedly preserved European civilization in an age of death and destruction, become a pilgrim with John Bunyan in his beloved Bedford, and see where John Wesley preached against slavery and converted thousands.

Softcover 0-310-22552-3

The Christian Travelers Guide to Italy

Irving Hexham, General Editor;
Written by David Bershad and Carolina Mangone

- Experience a wealth of art and architecture stretching back to the early church and the age of martyrs, travel where Christians died in the arena, and see where great artists such as Michelangelo depicted unforgettable scenes of biblical truth.

Softcover 0-310-22573-6

Pick up a copy today at your favorite bookstore!

We want to hear from you. Please send your comments about this book to us in care of the address below. Thank you.

ZondervanPublishingHouse
Grand Rapids, Michigan 49530
http://www.zondervan.com